HEIDEGGER AND ARISTOTLE

Continuum Studies in Continental Philosophy
Series Editor: James Fieser, University of Tennessee at Martin, USA

Continuum Studies in Continental Philosophy is a major monograph series from Continuum. The series features first-class scholarly research monographs across the field of Continental Philosophy. Each work makes a major contribution to the field of philosophical research.

HEIDEGGER AND ARISTOTLE
Philosophy as Praxis

MICHAEL BOWLER

continuum

Continuum International Publishing Group
The Tower Building, 11 York Road, London SE1 7NX
80 Maiden Lane, Suite 704, New York, NY 10038
www.continuumbooks.com

First published 2008

British Library Cataloguing-in-Publication Data
A catalogue record for this book is available from the British Library.

ISBN–10: HB: 0–8264–9846–9
ISBN–13: HB: 978–0–8264–9846–5

Library of Congress Cataloging-in-Publication Data
Bowler, Michael J.
   Heidegger and Aristotle : philosophy as praxis / Michael Bowler.
      p. cm.
   Includes bibliiographical references.
   ISBN–13: 978–0–8264–9846–5 (HB)
   ISBN–10: 0–8264–9846–9 (HB)
   1. Heidegger, Martin, 1889–1976. 2. Aristotle. 3. Philosophy. I. Title.

B3279.H49B6844 2008
193–dc22   2007036702

Typeset by Aarontype Limited, Easton, Bristol
Printed and bound in Great Britain by Biddles Ltd, King's Lynn, Norfolk

To my loving wife, Monica, for her endless support and patience.

Contents

Introduction

Heidegger is both a man of his time and an anachronism. In many ways, this is just what you would expect from someone who wrote that the 'situation of interpretation, i.e. of the appropriation and understanding of the past, is always the living situation of the present'.[1] That is, when Heidegger began lecturing and writing he was deeply engaged with the significant philosophical currents of his time. For the most part, this consisted of the broadly Kantian philosophies that populated the philosophical landscape of the late nineteenth and early twentieth century, e.g. Neo-Kantianism, Husserl's phenomenology and Dilthey's critique of historical reason and his worldview philosophy. But his work also harked back to the philosophy of the ancient Greeks, particularly Aristotle. He had such sympathy for Aristotle's thought that Gadamer recounts how, in Heidegger's lectures on Aristotle, 'we were often so personally touched that we no longer knew whether he [Heidegger] was speaking of his own concern or that of Aristotle.'[2]

This book concerns the confluence of these two elements in Heidegger's thought. In essence, it is an attempt to elucidate Heidegger's reappropriation of key elements of Aristotle's thought within the hermeneutic situation of the limitations Heidegger sees in the philosophies that were most influential in the first few decades of the twentieth century.

Heidegger's own time, i.e. the period following the First World War, both in terms of philosophy and in general, was permeated by talk of crisis.[3] Philosophically this time was shaped by the collapse of German idealism, the self-assertion of the positive sciences against their philosophical tutelage, the great methodological struggle (*methodenstreit*) between the human sciences (*Geisteswissenschaften*) and natural sciences (*Naturwissenschaften*), and philosophy's in some ways desperate attempt to validate itself within the larger context of increasingly manifold forms of scientific knowledge. In addition, philosophy was increasingly viewed as having lost touch with life. It no longer spoke to people and their concerns – and not just everyday concerns, but to the 'profound' questions of value in culture as well as life. It was felt that philosophy needed to do more than simply address questions

of logic, viz. issues in the theory of knowledge. Rather, philosophy needed to
address the deeply important questions of life.

The result of this crisis was a flourishing of philosophies that, to a significant degree, spurned purely speculative problems and claimed to be more
relevant, more concrete and more in touch with life. In some cases, traditional philosophical questions were simply reduced to an object of study for
one or other of the empirical sciences, e.g. psychologism, positivism and
historicism. Rather than treating philosophical questions through the rari-
fied methodology of Kantian and post-Kantian philosophy, these 'scientific'
philosophies would use the proven empirical strategies of the positive
sciences and thereby achieve 'results'. A different response to the perceived
alienation of philosophy from life was to call on philosophy to produce a
'worldview' (*Weltanschauung*).[4] That is, philosophy's task should be to produce an all-encompassing scheme of human values in which all the important concerns of an age could be unified.

To those contemporaneous philosophers most influential in Heidegger's
own development, i.e. Heinrich Rickert, Edmund Husserl, Paul Natorp
and Wilhelm Dilthey, these various attempts to 'solve' the crisis facing philosophy by making it more relevant to life resulted in the dissolution of
philosophy as an independent and distinctly scientific discipline. Worse yet,
these philosophies led to various forms of relativism, which undermined the
validity of knowledge altogether. For instance, knowledge was reduced to
particular, factual psychological or historical processes.

In response, Rickert, Husserl, Natorp and Dilthey tried to rearticulate
the philosophical enterprise such that it would be relevant to life, yet at the
same time remain scientific. In their minds, philosophy needed to ground
the objective validity of all scientific knowledge. That is, philosophy
needed to return to its Kantian roots while at the same time remaining per-
tinent to issues of life and 'culture'.

Thus, Rickert argued that philosophy's task was to ground knowledge in
the absolute validity of the universal value of truth. That is, all knowledge is normative and represents the human desire for the absolute value of
truth. Husserl believed that a genuine scientific philosophy, namely phenomenology, must securely and absolutely ground the essential and universal meanings present in all aspects of our lives, scientific or otherwise.
This was to be accomplished by examining the way in which meaning is
constituted in pure, absolute consciousness or the 'pure stream of lived-
experience'. Natorp hoped that philosophy could secure the objective validity of knowledge, but he also recognized that the task of philosophy was,
ultimately, to use the objective laws of knowledge to allow us to grasp

our own lived-experiences and life, i.e. the way in which we 'subject-ively' experience the world. Finally, Dilthey, who Heidegger believed had come closer than any of the others to genuinely understanding life, sought the foundation of knowledge and of the sciences in life itself by under-standing the structures of life and the ways in which life expresses itself in worldviews.

To one degree or another, each of these thinkers was concerned to demon-strate that philosophy could *scientifically*, i.e. rigorously, theoretically and objectively, examine life itself.[5] This required that philosophy show that it could achieve theoretical objective knowledge of life and lived-experience itself. It was believed that, if it could do this, then one could secure the valid-ity of objective, scientific knowledge against the onslaught of relativism.

Early in his career, Heidegger criticizes these various philosophical attempts to secure access to life and lived-experience. In his famous lecture course in the 'War Emergency Semester' of 1919,[6] Heidegger argues that attempts to grasp life and lived-experience objectively ultimately distort the very thing they hope to discover. In essence, philosophy as a form of the-oretically objectifying knowledge reveals life and lived-experience in a deformed and 'de-vivified' way.

Many interpretations of Heidegger's early philosophy take as their start-ing point this critique that Heidegger gave of his predecessors. Moreover, many interpreters believe that Heidegger's critique was not designed to show that his predecessors were misguided in their attempt to grasp life and lived-experience, but that they approached it in an inadequate way because they believed that philosophy could achieve objective, theoretical knowledge of life and lived-experience. Consequently, Heidegger's early philosophy is seen to consist of formulating a radically new approach to gaining 'access' to life and lived-experience.

This does not mean that these interpreters believe that Heidegger thought that we could have objective, theoretical knowledge of life and lived-experience. Rather, in their minds, Heidegger recognized the futility of that project. Thus, according to a number of authors, his own philosophy is an attempt to show that life is objectively incomprehensible and, according to some readings, he tries to formulate a new, non-objectifying approach to grasping life. This can take different forms.

One, for example, is the deconstructive approach of van Buren wherein Heidegger's early philosophy is seen as the project of deconstructing the categories by which the tradition has attempted to rationalize life, although van Buren admits that Heidegger himself wavered in this regard.[7] Perhaps more common are the various interpretations that see Heidegger struggling in his early philosophy to find a radically new, pre-objective, pre-theoretical approach to life and lived-experience.[8]

One of the central themes of this book is that these readings of Heidegger's early philosophy, although interesting and illuminating in their own right, miss the true significance of Heidegger's critique. The first four chapters of this book will try to show that Heidegger was not merely dissatisfied with the way in which Rickert, Husserl, Natorp and Dilthey approached life and lived-experience, but that they had failed to see what was really at issue. In other words, what is at stake for Heidegger is not whether philosophy can or cannot give us access to life and lived-experience, but rather to understand how philosophy itself is lived and situated in life.

That is, Heidegger recognizes that the previous attempts to grasp life philosophically failed because philosophy itself had become divorced from life and therefore the attempt to approach life philosophically was an artificial effort to grasp life 'from outside'. Moreover, this signifies that the very questions of whether, how and in what way philosophy can 'access' life are, although important, secondary to the more significant issue of how philosophy is lived, i.e. the question of how it is located in life and what role it plays in the activity and movement of life. Heidegger maintains that if this latter issue is set aside, then any consideration of the former question will be left ungrounded. Moreover, he thinks that, when this happens, the question of our access to life will appear under a critical, epistemological guise. This is precisely what he believes happened in those philosophies he criticizes. That is, each of them reduced the question of grounding knowledge in life to the critical, epistemological problem of formulating an objective, theoretical science of life and lived-experience.

On the contrary, Heidegger approaches the issue of the relation between life and philosophy by considering the 'idea of philosophy as primordial science'. That is, Heidegger examines how philosophy is the living source for all of our knowledge. In other words, Heidegger attempts to situate philosophy in life in such a way that the special sciences are understood as also arising in life and for life. In this way, both philosophy and the derivative sciences are made 'relevant' to life in so far as they are constitutive of life itself, i.e. they fully participate in the activity and movement of life.

Accordingly, we shall see that the thrust of Heidegger's critique is not that previous philosophies had simply failed to grasp life, although that surely happened, but that previous philosophies *presuppose* life and also the living character of philosophy itself. In essence, their failure to grasp life in and for itself is due to the fact that life is always already present in the background of their philosophy. Each of the above-mentioned figures, with the exception of Dilthey who was at least able to glimpse life, were forced to import an 'extra-philosophical' element into their philosophy, namely something that could animate the essentially de-vivified structures of their philosophies. For Rickert, this is the 'metalogical subject'. For Husserl, the living 'pure Ego'. And, for Natorp, the living 'task of knowledge'. Because of this, their very attempt to grasp life always came too late.

Heidegger's own enterprise was to attempt to bore down to the very foundations of these different philosophies in order to elucidate and explicate the origin and source of philosophy in life. Early on, Heidegger realized that this required retracing the way in which philosophy becomes alienated from life. Or, in his earliest writings, how philosophy became divorced from metaphysics as this was understood by Aristotle. Thus, in the conclusion to his *habilitation*, Heidegger says that, 'We cannot at all see logic and its problems in their true light if the context *from* which they are interpreted is not a translogical one. *Philosophy cannot for long do without its authentic optics: metaphysics*' (emphasis added).[9]

As we shall see in the last two chapters of this book, Heidegger believes that Aristotle had glimpsed metaphysics as it existed in and for life. That is, how 'first philosophy' is situated in life and how it is constitutive of life. However, Heidegger was sensitive to the fact that any appropriation and understanding of a past philosophy must always be hermeneutically situated in the present. For example, Heidegger disparages any attempt to appropriate Aristotle's metaphysics so as to simply reject outright the present hermeneutical situation. For instance, he rejects any attempt to resurrect ontology if this signifies 'a rallying motto for the now popular attacks on Kant, and . . . in principle, on all open questioning not frightened in advance by possible consequences – in short, ontology as the alluring call to a slave revolt against philosophy as such.'[10]

In other words, if philosophy is to be resituated in life, it will do no good to simply rummage around in the history of philosophy looking for a different, more 'animated' version of philosophy, any more than if one were to try to understand one's own situation in life by looking to other people who seem to be living life more fully.

Rather, only by tracing back the present activity of philosophizing to its source in life can one then reappropriate and *apply* a past form of philosophizing to the present situation. To this end, we must first examine how Heidegger resituates the philosophizing of his own time in life. That is, we must demonstrate how Heidegger retraces the philosophy of his own time back to its source in life and in this manner reappropriates Aristotle's philosophy.

Heidegger's hermeneutic return to and appropriation of Aristotle's notion of philosophy is the subject of the last chapter, wherein it is argued that Heidegger appropriates from Aristotle the notion of philosophy as the fulfilment of the *praxis* of life, i.e. an activity whose end or purpose is that very activity itself. There we will show how Heidegger appropriates aspects of Aristotle's metaphysics, physics, logic and ethics. In other words, beyond the standard interpretations of Heidegger's reading of Aristotle,[11] which rightly emphasize Heidegger's reappropriation of the notion *phronesis* from the *Nicomachean Ethics*, it will be demonstrated that Heidegger looks equally to other Aristotelian texts, such as the *Metaphysics*, *Physics* and *Posterior Analytics*, for his appropriation of Aristotle's notion of *praxis* and of philosophy as *praxis*. In large part, this is due to the fact that Heidegger is attempting to relocate science and philosophy within the movement of life.

I wish to acknowledge Stephen Watson, Karl Ameriks and Fred Dallmayr for their past and continuing support of this project, the Department of Humanities at Michigan Technological University for a generous summer stipend to finish this book, and my wife Monica for her unfailing support and for her editorial work on the bibliography.

Rickert, Value Philosophy and the Primacy of Practical Reason

In this chapter we will examine the development of Heidegger's thought through his engagement with the philosophy of value, most specifically in relation to the work of his *habilitation* director Heinrich Rickert. Rickert was arguably the most influential and significant proponent of the philosophy of value. In fact, Safranski reports that Rickert played 'the role of a superprofessor'.[1] A thorough account of Rickert's philosophy is beyond the scope of this book, however.[2] Therefore, in this chapter we will focus on his argument for the 'primacy of practical reason' and particularly his claim that theoretical reason is essentially practical, which, according to Heidegger, amounts to 'the founding of theoretical scientific thought in practical belief and will to truth'.[3] We shall then consider Heidegger's critique of the philosophy of value in the context of his notion of philosophy as primordial science. The goal of this chapter is to raise the issue of the idea of philosophy as primordial science.

1. Philosophy of value and the primacy of practical reason

In essence, value-philosophy contends that knowledge is primarily purposeful or goal-directed and must be analysed as such. Any account of the nature of knowledge that leaves this out of consideration is essentially incomplete and misguided. In other words, any account of knowledge that is grounded purely conceptually, sensibly, psychologistically, or any combination of these is, according to the philosophy of value, inadequate. In this respect, value philosophy regards the not uncommon analysis of knowledge in terms of the dual function of spontaneous understanding and passive sensibility as insufficient. It is essential that consideration of the ultimate purpose or goal of knowledge be included.

Although the philosophy of value is typically associated with Neo-Kantianism (and only the so-called Baden or southwestern school of Neo-Kantianism), Heidegger argues that because of its vigorous defence and systematization of the primacy of practical reason 'one could almost characterize it as Neo-Fichteanism'.[4] According to Heidegger, Fichte was the first to recognize teleology as the method of philosophy, leading Rickert to characterize Fichte as the 'greatest of all Kantians'.[5] Thus, in important respects, Rickert's philosophy of value represents an engagement with and extension of Fichte's philosophy.

Fichte's philosophy centres on the 'first, absolutely unconditioned principle' of his *Wissenschaftslehre*, namely that the I posits itself absolutely.[6] By rejecting the thing-in-itself as an illegitimate, dogmatic infringement on the absolute freedom of the absolute Ego, Fichte had maintained that no absolute limitation is imposed on the spontaneous activity of the transcendental Ego in its positing of the world, i.e. in its positing of the finite Ego and its finite object. In essence, Fichte's belief in the primacy of practical reason had made the world into a mere instrument for the Ego's realization of practical goals. Breazeale describes this interpretation of Fichte's philosophy as a 'grotesque narcissism', namely a theory where 'everything beyond the self is merely a reflection or creation' of the absolute self which 'constitutes for itself an external world as a sort of moral gymnasium – a sphere in which it can dutifully "work out" and where it can have something to "struggle against"'.[7] Accordingly, Fichte opened the door to metaphysical or transcendental voluntarism as illustrated by Schopenhauer's interpretation of the Ego as absolute will. In this case, theoretical reason is subject to the absolute, transcendental caprice of the absolute will.[8]

To be sure, Rickert had no intention of resurrecting the idea of the thing-in-itself which could externally affect a passive Ego, rather he sought to articulate absolute, universal values that were external to the subject and its activity and that could independently and 'objectively' legitimize the exercise of reason, e.g. in its activity of knowing. Significantly, however, these values were not something that actively limited the subject's freedom in its exercise of reason. This is an important component of value-philosophy's claim that theoretical reason is practical. Theoretical reason is freed from the constraint of the immediate intuition of an object – a hallmark of the traditional Kantian account of theoretical reason – and so it is free to 'construct' knowledge conceptually, i.e. it can freely form concepts that serve particular theoretical interests without being constrained by the brute, sensible givenness of an object, as will be examined more thoroughly below. However, it is also under the practical-theoretical obligation to realize by means of normative principles the absolute, universally valid value of truth. In terminology common to the philosophy of value, the knowing subject *ought* to strive after truth *as an ideal value*, and this striving is not constrained by what *is* the case, i.e. 'being'.

Although both Fichte and Rickert maintain the primacy of practical reason, Rickert understood his philosophy in opposition to Fichte's absolute idealism. To see why, it is important that we examine the philosophical context of late nineteenth-century thought. First, it was a common conviction among philosophers at this time that speculative or absolute idealism as a viable philosophical project had collapsed under the increasing pressure exerted by the success of the special sciences in conjunction with the belief that they no longer required *philosophical* guidance or grounding. Increasingly, the philosophical systems of idealism seemed to fade into irrelevance as the progress of the special sciences marched confidently on, i.e. philosophy, especially in its idealistic variations but also in general, was increasingly viewed with suspicion and seen as a useless, unscientific exercise in pure speculation. The special sciences could fulfil their task quite well without the help of philosophy. In response, many philosophers felt compelled to make their discipline germane to the special sciences.

Rickert was no exception. To a large extent, Rickert was sympathetic to these criticisms of the systems of absolute idealism. However, the collapse of idealism spawned numerous pseudo-scientific philosophies which were 'scientific' only to the extent that they naively modelled themselves on the special sciences, e.g. positivism, or absolutized what they took to be the subject matter of the sciences, e.g. materialism and historicism, or straightforwardly identified philosophy with one of the special sciences, e.g. psychologism. By the end of the nineteenth and the beginning of the twentieth century many philosophers had begun to realize that all of these philosophical '-isms' threatened to destroy the validity of knowledge, since each appeared to entail another, truly dangerous '-ism', namely relativism. That is, they were incapable of securing the objective validity of knowledge because they grounded knowledge in factual physical, historical or psychological processes. Thus, the criticism was similar to Kant's argument that if human action were entirely determined by factual physical, historical or psychological processes, then truly ethical action could never be realized, but merely hoped for. Value-philosophy argued that if thought was similarly determined then valid, objective knowledge could never be achieved.

Rickert was one of those who sensed an impending crisis for philosophy and he endeavoured to defuse it. Generally, the response was to argue that only a renewed, scientific critique of knowledge could resolve the crisis and that such a critique should be the authentic task of philosophy, i.e. philosophy should formulate a 'science of knowledge'. For value-philosophy in particular, the lesson to be learned from the collapse of German idealism was that philosophy should not attempt to play a constitutive role in the special sciences. In other words, philosophy should not be in the business of providing the sciences with fundamental, *a priori* constitutive categories. It was believed that, in large measure, the attempt to perform such a constitutive role had led to the undoing of absolute idealism.

The special sciences had demonstrated that they were not going to abide by the constraints philosophers attempted to place on *what* they could think – no matter how abstract or general those constraints may have been. Many philosophers were sympathetic to this attitude and consequently argued that philosophy *should* not place such strictures on the special sciences, believing that if it did so it would be illegitimately transgressing its own limits by infringing on another discipline's rightful domain.

According to value-philosophy, however, the fact that philosophy should not be in the business of dictating to the special sciences *what* to think does not preclude philosophy from directing them as to *how* to think. In other words, philosophy can say something about the *practice* and *activity* of scientific thinking because it investigates the proper use of reason. In particular, value-philosophy sought to critically articulate both the *a priori* universally valid values towards which reason in its logical, ethical and aesthetic employment is striving, as well as the normative principles of valid reasoning. For instance, philosophy investigates how one must think in order to acquire valid, objective knowledge. Consequently, philosophy's task is to tell the special sciences how they ought to think, not what they must think. Indeed, according to value-philosophy, philosophy should be nothing other than transcendental philosophy of value.

By emphasizing the absolute distinction between ought and is, i.e. between ideal value and 'being', as this was formulated by Lotze and systematized by Windelband and Rickert, the philosophy of value was able to ensure that it would not repeat the excesses of absolute idealism. In this way, value-philosophy hoped to protect transcendental idealism from overreaching its proper bounds. As Heidegger remarks, philosophy of value presents itself as 'a safeguarding of the continuity and connection with German idealism, but simultaneously a critical deflection of speculative idealism'.[9] For similar reasons, value-philosophy also tried to avoid any ontological claims. It was to remain purely 'logical'. Thus value-philosophy's teleological approach had nothing to do with the traditional, 'metaphysical' notion of teleology in which, for instance, teleological principles exist as component parts of nature and are used in causal explanations. Rather, value-philosophy's domain was the region of ideal values, which is entirely distinct from the 'region of being'. In Rickert's terminology, transcendental philosophy of value deals only with 'rationalistic teleology'.[10]

A second, connected catalyst for value-philosophy's rejection of absolute or speculative idealism was the profound division rending the special sciences in the latter half of the nineteenth century. In other words, it was not only the progression of the natural sciences (*Naturwissenschaften*) that was undermining or at least making irrelevant the systems of absolute idealism. Even more important was the rise of the human sciences (*Geisteswissenschaften*) and the subsequent 'controversy over methods' (*Methodenstreit*), i.e. whether the human sciences could be methodologically assimilated to the natural sciences or needed their own unique methodology. For those philosophers who believed that the methodologies of the two sciences must remain separate, absolute idealism's attempt to constitutively unify all the sciences seemed hopeless. That is, one principle alone could not account for the distinct constitutive categories required by the knowledge of nature (*Natur*), on the one hand, and that of spirit (*Geist*), on the other.

That is, if all knowledge was constitutively the result of one principle then, at some fundamental level, the sciences must share a methodology. For instance, take the case of philosophical naturalism. If all knowledge is ultimately to be reduced to the knowledge of nature then, at a fundamental level, the sciences of spirit must share the methodology of the natural sciences. In the case of Fichte and Hegel's absolute idealism, reality is at bottom dialectical and therefore knowledge too must employ a dialectical method. Consequently, both the natural and human sciences must employ, at a fundamental level, the dialectical method. To many in the latter half of the nineteenth century, it seemed sheer nonsense to suggest that the natural sciences should be governed at any level by the dialectical method, and it looked highly implausible that the human sciences should be either. Since it was a defining characteristic of the southwestern school of Neo-Kantianism that the methodologies of the natural and human sciences must be kept distinct, they believed that no single principle could be found to constitutively ground knowledge in the special sciences.

However, it was believed, or at least hoped, that some principle could unify the sciences since, after all, every science consisted of theoretical knowledge. Philosophy of value hoped to unify the sciences by means of the goal common to all theoretical knowledge, namely truth. In other words, it aspired to unify the special sciences by means of the regulative, i.e. non-constitutive, 'rationalistic' teleological principle of the universally valid value of truth. This seemed to have a distinct advantage over the constitutive approach to unifying the sciences in so far as it seemed obviously true that there could be multiple possible ways of realizing the same end. That is, generating difference out of a constitutive monism is a task that is, at best, tricky and, at worst, spurious. On the other hand, viewing different methodologies as simply different ways in which the sciences realize the same goal seemed eminently credible. This does not mean that the methodologies of the sciences are teleological. On the contrary, they are merely means of achieving the goal of universally valid truth. Therefore, transcendental philosophy of value seemed perfectly situated to realize a transcendental unity among the sciences.

Heidegger points to a third reason for the failure of the system of absolute idealism, namely that its dialectical-teleological method was 'uncreative'. He says, 'Dialectic in the sense of resolving ever newly posited contradictions is *substantively uncreative*.'[11] In other words, Heidegger is suggesting that dialectic alone is incapable of accounting for the very dialectical-teleological movement in which that very dialectic process is realized. This interpretation is borne out when Heidegger later says, 'The dialectic of antithesis and synthesis cannot be activated by itself: it remains condemned to an unproductive standstill, or else it unfolds itself on the implicit and arbitrary basis of something substantively given, or at least presupposed.'[12] This criticism relies on the fact that the systems of absolute idealism worked to give a substantive account of the genesis of knowledge using dialectic alone. On the other hand, value-philosophy represented a much more moderate attempt to give a logical, i.e. critical-epistemological, analysis of the validity of knowledge irrespective of the way in which it is realized.

However, it is not the case that value-philosophy achieves what absolute idealism failed to accomplish, viz. articulating a philosophical method that is 'substantively creative'. Rather, by emphasizing the dichotomy between validity and being, between ought and is, and giving philosophy the sole task of investigating transcendental validity and value, the philosophy of value places the whole issue of the actual realization of knowledge outside of the realm of philosophical investigation – that is, questions of being do not impinge upon questions of value. Therefore, value-philosophy does not need to explain how valid knowledge actually comes about.

This apparently allows value-philosophy to freely presuppose a 'substantive material guideline' (*sachlichen, materialen Leitfadens*) in its investigation of value without fear of circularity. This 'material pregivenness' (*Materialvorgebung*) consists of the psychological processes in which 'the goal of reason might realize itself, and in which the actions of reason are themselves to be discovered in their universal character'.[13] This material pregivenness is not an axiom or principle that grounds ideal values, but rather 'is, so to speak, only an occasion and impetus for finding them [values]'.[14]

That is, this material pregivenness serves two functions: (1) as a material condition for the realization of the value of truth and (2) a methodological function. What supposedly guarantees the material pregivenness of values is sought in the application of the fundamental Kantian thesis that 'ought implies can'. In this case, one cannot have an obligation and duty to realize the value of truth without the real possibility of actually bringing it to fruition.

The methodological function of material pregivenness in the philosophy of value is by far the more important of the two and an analysis of this comprises the bulk of Heidegger's critical analysis of the philosophy of value as primordial science (*Urwissenschaft*). In order to get a handle on the methodological function of material pregiving we must ask: What are the material guidelines that value-philosophy presupposes? Heidegger remarks that, 'The teleological method [of value-philosophy] receives a solid foundation in the domains of psychology and history.'[15] More exactly, the results of the empirical-scientific disciplines of psychology and history are supposed to provide the material foundation upon which value-philosophy's teleological method works. Psychology and history provide 'forms and norms of thought' from which the critical-teleological method will select those that further the aim of truth and discard those that do not.[16] In other words, psychology provides general, explanatory laws that govern psychic thought-processes – that is, it provides a collection of 'forms of thought' – while history, and more specifically the history of 'cultures', supplies a set of 'norms of thought', where what is meant by 'a culture' is a concrete, historical system of values and norms.

The critical-teleological method looks to the ideal aim of thought, i.e. universally valid truth, to select from the pregiven material those concrete forms and norms of thought that further this goal. The selected forms and norms of thought represent *in concreto* the ideal and valid norms and forms of thought. Thus, by a process of formalization, one should be able to acquire the purely ideal and valid norms and forms of thought. We shall consider the critical-teleological method in more detail when we look at Heidegger's criticism of this method. At this point, however, we can see how this differs from the method of absolute idealism. By assiduously trying to avoid any attempt to constitutively analyse knowledge and by focusing solely upon the ideal aspects of transcendental philosophy under the guidance of the primacy of practical reason, value-philosophy believes that it can disregard the thorny issue of how valid knowledge is actually realized. This latter issue, value-philosophy maintains, is the rightful domain of other disciplines, e.g. empirical psychology and history. It is only concerned with the *quaesti juris* and in this regard only with respect to validity.

Moreover, this demonstrates why value-philosophy's assertion of the primacy of practical reason applies directly to philosophy and only indirectly to the special sciences. As we shall see, the special sciences are not exercises in practical reason. Of course, they implicitly strive to realize the ideal value of truth and follow ideal valid norms, i.e. they try to acquire valid knowledge, but they need not be, and usually are not, explicitly aware of these ideal-ities.[17] Put differently, the aim of the special sciences is to produce principles of explanation, e.g. laws of nature, not principles of evaluation, e.g. norms. Of course, researchers in the special sciences wish to produce *true* principles of explanation. But this does not require an explicit knowledge of values or norms, rather these are implicitly embedded in their practices. For example, a physicist does not need an explicit understanding of the nature of truth in order to formulate valid principles of physical explanation. In fact, accord-ing to value-philosophy, having such an explicit understanding would con-tribute little towards actually achieving physical explanations. Indeed, time spent worrying about the nature of truth would be time spent not doing phy-sics. It is philosophy, not physics, which investigates the nature of truth and the norms of valid thinking.

Of course, the special sciences must have an implicit grasp of the nature of truth or else their ability to produce true principles of explanation would be accidental and haphazard. In large measure, this explains the confidence value-philosophy has in its method since the success of the special sciences suggests that valid norms are implicitly embodied in their practices. This is what was referred to in the Neo-Kantian tradition as the 'fact of science'. Moreover, this is why Neo-Kantians believed that threat of scepticism and relativism had little or no real effect upon the special sciences, although it was important that *philosophy* overcome them. The 'fact of science', viz. the very practice, products and progress of the special sciences, 'demonstrates' that scepticism and relativism are wrong. In essence, philosophy's purpose is to explicitly articulate and systematize the universally valid value of truth and the norms of valid thought that are implicitly at work in the special sciences and embodied in the empirical sciences of psychology and history.

I have been emphasizing the non-constitutive quality of the grounding and unification of knowledge that transcendental philosophy of value hoped to fashion, because I believe that this is crucial for understanding its fundamental, philosophical impulses. Indeed, value-philosophy's aversion to constitutive principles is indicative of its acceptance of the Lotzean dichotomy between ought and is and its belief in the primacy of practical reason in philosophy. However, it was also well aware of the way in which absolute idealism had been chastised by the special sciences in the middle of the nineteenth century. This helps to explain its tendency toward formaliz-ing abstraction, which led Heidegger to complain that value-philosophy provided nothing more than an 'empty methodology' in which 'mere schemes of sciences are laid down and taken as basic'.[18]

This propensity toward empty formalization is exceptionally on display in one of Rickert's most distinctive contributions to the philosophy of value, viz. his theory of concept formation (*Begriffsbildung*). This theory is of particular interest because Rickert's account of concept formation inhabits the realm between the region of value and the region of being, the ideal and the real, and the regulative and constitutive. That is, in the theory of concept formation the self-imposed strictures that value-philosophy places on itself are pushed to the limit. In addition, Rickert's theory of concept formation presents a concrete example of the critical-teleological method at work.

2.   Rickert's theory of concept formation

For philosophy of value, nothing better represents the thesis that there are different paths toward realizing the same goal of knowledge than the fact that the natural and human sciences, while having distinct methodologies and utilizing radically different kinds of concept formation, still had the same goal in mind, viz. realizing the universally valid value of truth.

The classic statement of this appears in Wilhelm Windelband's lecture 'History and natural science'.[19] In this lecture, Windelband distinguishes methodologically between the natural and historical sciences. He argues that the natural sciences are 'nomothetic' in that they strive towards principles of explanation that are universal 'laws of occurrences' while history is 'idiographic' and tries to capture the individuality of 'processes and events'. Windelband says, '... we have before us a purely methodological classification of the empirical sciences that is grounded upon sound logical concepts ... One kind of science is an inquiry into general laws. The other kind of science is an inquiry into specific historical facts.'[20] More simply put, the natural sciences aim at natural laws while history aims at individual events, persons or processes. Thus, Windelband continues, 'the objective of the first kind of science [the natural sciences] is the general, apodictic judgment; the objective of the other kind of science [history] is the singular, assertoric proposition.'[21]

The need to *methodologically* distinguish the natural sciences from history is intended to deflect the attempt by some to distinguish them through the (apparently) dogmatic procedure of accepting two distinct regions of being, viz. the 'region of nature' and the 'region of spirit'. This, Windelband asserts, was the mistake made by Dilthey. According to Windelband, and Rickert as well, a genuinely critical theory of knowledge requires that the sciences are distinguished in a purely methodological fashion.

'Rickert,' Heidegger says, 'whose logical and dialectical talent is far superior to that of Windelband, conceives this idea more precisely as the problem of *concept-formation*.'[22] That is, Rickert recognized that the division between the sciences rested on a difference in the way in which they formed their concepts. In essence, the formation of concepts in the natural sciences serves the aim of enunciating general laws of nature, while the concepts of the science of history make possible a grasp of 'historical individuals and events' as well as an understanding of the significance of these individuals and events for larger historical or cultural nexuses. However, it is not the case that a particular mode of concept formation determines how a science achieves its aim. Quite to the contrary, it is the aim of a science that determines what manner of concept formation it will employ. In conformity with the primacy of practical reason, value-philosophy maintains that the goal or purpose of a science determines the style of its conceptualization. This requires that concept formation in the sciences not be constrained by what is given in the sensible manifold of experience. According to Rickert, there is but one manifold of experience, but there are very different ways of conceptualizing it. Just as Windelband before him had spurned the attempt to distinguish the sciences based on a substantive distinction between nature and spirit, Rickert denies that there are fundamentally original regions of experience to which the natural sciences and history refer.

The concepts of the natural sciences abstract from all individuating aspects or differences in things. Rickert argues that, 'when we abstract from the individual configuration of things in natural science, this does not bother us in most cases . . . We have no interest in the fact that every leaf on a tree appears different from the leaves next to it, or that no fragment of a chemical substance in a retort is exactly like any other fragment of the "same" substance and will ever reappear.'[23] Concepts of this sort facilitate the positing of nomological principles of explanation, because they capture the generalities in things.

Correspondingly, concepts in the science of history are suited for comprehending individual, historical persons, events, etc. Namely, 'the problem of concept formation in history, therefore, is whether a scientific analysis and reduction of perceptual reality is possible that does not at the same time – as in the concepts of natural science – forfeit individuality.'[24] Rickert maintains that such individualizing concepts are formed by means of explicit reference to values, i.e. these concepts are 'value-related'. In demonstrating this, Rickert refers to the difference between a particular lump of coal and the Koh-i-noor diamond. Of course, on a basic, non-scientific level the lump of coal and the Koh-i-noor diamond are equally individuals. However, Rickert argues that the Koh-i-noor diamond is an individual in a way that the lump of coal is not, viz. the Koh-i-noor diamond is of value to someone or some culture, whereas the lump of coal, qua this individual lump of coal, is not. Things become individuals in this way, because they are uniquely valuable. He says, 'We *take note* of uniqueness and have occasion to become explicitly aware of it only when they are related to a value and thereby become indivisibly unified in their uniqueness.'[25]

Similarly, the science of history conceptualizes individual persons or events by relating them to values, i.e. by seeing them as uniquely valued. For example, 'If we compare a personality such as Goethe with any average person ... it follows that Goethe is related to such a person in the same way the Koh-i-noor diamond is related to a lump of coal ... the individual Goethe is an individual in the same sense as the individual Koh-i-noor: His distinctive status as an individual is valued by *everyone* for its individuality' (emphasis added).[26] Central to Rickert's theory of concept formation in the science of history is that if history is to be an objective science then the historical researcher must not introduce his or her own historically specific values into their scientific inquiry, i.e. 'history is *not* a *valuing* science but a *value-relevant* science' (emphasis added).[27] In other words, the historical researcher conceptualizes the individuality of Goethe by relating him in a unique way to the values embodied in his historical and cultural nexus, e.g. German romanticism, European history, etc.[28]

More important is Rickert's argument for the independence of concept formation vis-à-vis experience. Namely, how is it that the very same sensible manifold of experience can be validly conceptualized in two entirely different ways? Rickert responds by arguing that concepts do not *represent* experience and therefore need not be constrained by experience. He maintains that there is an unbridgeable gap between finite conceptualization and the infinite sensible manifold of experience that precludes the possibility of a genuine representational relationship between concepts and experience. In other words, following Fichte, Rickert argues that there is a *hiatus irrationalis* between concept and 'reality'. Rickert makes the substantive claim that reality, by which he means 'the immediately experienced or given reality in which we live our sentient existence',[29] is a continuum of irreducible uniqueness, particularity and infinite complexity. That is, reality is both 'extensively' and 'intensively' infinite. As Heidegger remarks, reality for Rickert is a 'heterogeneous continuum'.[30] Because of this, no concept could ever represent either the whole of or any part of reality 'in its totality'.

What this demonstrates, Rickert maintains, is that the 'picture theory' of concepts whereby concepts are conceptual or mental 'pictures' of reality is misguided. In essence, all concepts abstract from experience and such abstraction requires a 'principle of selection'. In other words, abstraction selects from out of the infinite manifold of experience certain features and then articulates these features by means of concepts. Moreover, since all science is conceptual, this shows that '... the perceptual and individual configuration of reality is not encompassed by *any* science'.[31] Indeed, the gap between thought and reality is founded on the disparity between rational conceptualization, on the one hand, and irrational experience, on the other. For this reason, Rickert maintains that knowledge does not consist of the reproduction of empirical reality, but with constructions that further the aims and purposes of knowledge. In sum, Rickert believes that experience simply does not privilege one mode or another of conceptualization and, in fact, can sustain many different varieties of conceptualization. The question arises then as to what is to guide knowledge in its pursuit of the truth. What prevents us from conceptualizing experience according to our whims?

The fact that reality is an irrational and infinite manifold – one that 'scorns *every* conception' and '*resists* every conception'[32] – certainly rules out that it could guide knowledge in the formation of its concepts. That is, Rickert believes that the spontaneity of thought and conceptualization cannot be limited and constrained by passive sensibility. For these reasons, Rickert is not drawn to what many now call the 'Myth of the Given', or as McDowell characterizes it, 'a craving for rational constraint from outside the realm of thought and judgment'.[33]

Not only does Rickert emphatically embrace the notion that the spontaneity of thought and judgement has no external constraint, but he believes that freedom from such an external constraint is a requirement of valid thought. That is, such external constraint prevents thought and judgement from achieving its essential, intrinsic and 'internal' goal of universally valid truth. On the other hand, this requires demonstrating that thought is not merely a 'spinning in a void'. Rickert is well aware of this and counters that even though concepts do not represent reality, it is also true, as he puts it, that 'they cannot in the least be represented as products of caprice'. He is also conscious of the fact that rejections, like his own, of conceptual realism, 'which regards valid concepts as reproductions of reality', have led 'to skeptical assaults on the significance of science, especially natural science'. Therefore, he believes that the objectivity of knowledge must be secured in some other fashion. His response is to suggest that simply because concepts do not represent or 'picture' reality this does not preclude 'that these concepts stand in a most intimate *relationship* to this reality', namely that they hold '*validly for* individual reality'.[34]

Understanding this will help us see more clearly what Rickert (and the philosophy of value) means when he argues for the primacy of practical reason and claims that theoretical reason is practical. Earlier, we had mentioned that for value-philosophy it is essential that in the analysis of knowledge one take into account the ultimate aim or purpose of knowledge, which has truth as its *telos*. We are now in a position to see that Rickert's theory of concept formation in conjunction with his refutation of the 'realist' or 'picture theory' of concepts amounts to a transcendental argument for the primacy of practical reason. In essence, Rickert attempts to give an argument that the condition for the possibility of 'valid' knowledge is that knowledge is a normative process in which the absolute value of truth is realized.

One of the first steps in such an argument is to show that if knowledge is grounded in factual processes, whether natural, historical or psychological, then this will inevitably lead to relativism, i.e. to the dissolution of the validity of knowledge. The intellectual milieu in Germany at the end of the nineteenth century was replete with arguments to this effect. Therefore, what is needed is yet another 'Copernican turn'. Knowledge must no longer be made to conform to factual processes of knowing, but factual processes of knowing must be made to conform to what knowledge ought to strive for. It must be demonstrated that the traditional account of knowledge in which concepts, judgements and thought reproduce reality, and which thereby requires that knowledge be grounded in the sensible manifold, is wrong. Rickert believes that he has given such an argument in his account of concept formation. This in turn makes room for a practical account of knowledge.

According to Rickert, every 'ought' is founded in a value. Since Rickert believes that, from a transcendental perspective, no factually given value can ground the validity of knowledge, this means that what knowledge ought to strive for is an 'absolute', ideal value. The absolute, ideal value towards which knowledge ought to strive is universally valid truth. That is, if knowledge is ever to secure valid truth then it has a transcendental duty and obligation to strive for the absolute, ideal value of universally valid truth. Thus, what is *a priori* for knowledge is not a system of constitutive categories, but the *telos* of the practice of knowledge, viz. the absolute, ideal value of truth.

Since truth is an absolute and universally valid value it makes no essential reference to a cognizing subject. However, Rickert himself says that, 'in all knowledge as judgment – and this is the only sort of knowledge relevant to scientific concept formation – the object of knowledge and the cognitive subject are necessarily correlated'.[35] For Rickert, the object of knowledge is the absolute value of universally valid truth. How is the cognitive subject necessarily correlated to this? Rickert maintains that if value-philosophy is to remain a transcendental account of knowledge, then the relation of the 'valuing cognitive subject' to this absolute value must be taken into consideration *only* in so far as 'the realization of science necessarily includes the concept of a *valuing cognitive subject*'.[36] That is, this is not an issue that concerns the transcendental validity of knowledge, but simply the realization of valid knowledge.

This still means that the valuing cognitive subject must be guided by the absolute value of truth and, therefore, it is necessary that the subject '*encounters* a norm that demands recognition'.[37] However, since the requisite encounter is of the absolute value of truth the demand for recognition cannot be relative or hypothetical, but must also be absolute. Because of this, Rickert concludes that, 'for the cognitive subject, theoretical value appears as a "categorical imperative" . . . [that is] there is under all [real, historical] circumstances . . . an objectively valid "duty" that holds for the person whose only aspiration is the truth'.[38] This raises at least two questions: (1) What does the 'categorical imperative' of knowledge require? and (2) What role does the cognitive subject play in realizing this imperative?

With regard to the first question we must return to Rickert's theory of concept formation. He regards his theory of concept formation in the sciences as a strictly 'logical' account. In other words, his methodological division of the sciences, viz. between those that are nomological and those which are idiographic, relies solely on the logical structure of their modes of concept formation. This is why, for instance, he can assert that,

> If the logical idea of a theory in natural science is attained, we will find that the content of its concepts contains nothing more of *that* sort of perception that experience directly presents. Therefore we can flatly claim that the complete logical articulation of a concept in natural science depends on the extent to which empirical perception or sense perception is eliminated from its content.[39]

Similarly, the purely logical structure of the individualizing, value-related concepts in the science of history would make no reference to those values that are perceptually or experientially given, but only absolute, ideal values. That is, in the logical idea of a science only the mere form of concepts would be represented.

Once we add to this that 'since Socrates, logic has revolved around the opposition of the general to the particular or the individual' and that this amounts to 'really nothing more' than the 'trivial' logical claim that 'the general is not the distinctive and the individual',[40] we essentially get, from apparently pure considerations of logic, Rickert's theory of concept formation. That is, the purely logical thesis that concept formation must either proceed towards generalized concepts that are suitable for articulating nomological laws or the value-related concepts that are suitable for grasping historical individuality. Thus we can conclude that the categorical imperative of knowledge demands the maxim or norm that concept formation, and consequently judgement and thought, satisfy the formal-logical requirement that they be either generalizing or value-related. Judgements formed using concepts that fulfil this formal-logical requirement are deemed 'valid' by Rickert. Clearly the categorical imperative of knowledge leaves open which constitutive categories may be at work in the sciences and indicates nothing about the determinate, particular concepts that the special sciences might factually posit.

With regard to the second question concerning the role that the cognizing subject plays in realizing the absolute value of knowledge, Rickert first stipulates that this question is not part of the pure logical theory of validity. That is, the validity of knowledge and the absolute value of truth it presupposes in no way depend on the cognizing subject. However, if we are going to account for 'the historical realization of value – in other words, the *real genesis of science by real subjects*' – then Rickert argues that we must allow for 'a *metalogical* real "basis" for the realization of logical values in historical development'.[41] Appropriating notions from Kant's practical philosophy into his theoretical context, Rickert maintains that every real cognitive act is preceded by an 'autonomous' will that wills the value of truth as such. Because of this, a real judgement is more than merely an act which unifies our representations, but is a 'a special kind of value-oriented *action*'.[42] And, consequently, 'science can arise only on the basis of a will to truth'.[43] However, by insisting that this arises only by means of 'metalogical' considerations and therefore does not touch the issue of logical validity, Rickert is able to ensure that value-philosophy does not become yet another system of absolute idealism.

3.   Heidegger's criticism and appropriation of the philosophy of value

Others have pointed out that Heidegger castigates Rickert for engaging in 'worldless, ahistorical theorizing' which leads to a 'transhistorical, timeless, and logical subject',[44] or for reifying values by working with 'the theoretically denatured concept of a "given" or "fixed" value',[45] or for identifying meaning with value to the exclusion of being.[46] In each case, these point to the fact that Rickert neglected historicity and life.

However, what has been neglected is Heidegger's more persistent criticism of Rickert's philosophy of value, namely that outside of perhaps solving a few provincial philosophical conundrums, it is extraordinarily *impotent*. It is for this reason that Heidegger says that Rickert's philosophy amounts to a 'trivialized' and 'empty' methodology that lays down 'mere schemes of sciences' which it takes 'as basic'.[47] It represents a philosophy so chastened by absolute idealism's demise and by the progress of the special sciences that it assiduously avoids hazarding any substantive or constitutive claims whatsoever, and does so by retreating wholly into the logic of validity and value.

According to Heidegger, nothing epitomizes more succinctly the failure of Rickert's value-philosophy than its theory of concept-formation, which merely lays down the 'valid' form of concepts that are utilized in the special sciences. Its 'categories', so to speak, are 'unable to avoid the impression of a certain deathly emptiness'.[48] As Heidegger emphasizes, Rickert 'tells us nothing about the "how" of this concept-formation, about the way philosophical concepts get their structure, and about the basic intention of conceptual explication in philosophy'.[49]

Countering this, Heidegger maintains that what is necessary is a notion of 'productive concept formation'.[50] In *Being and Time*, Heidegger says that what is needed is a 'productive logic'. Rickert's logic is 'the kind of "logic" which limps along after, investigating the status of some science as it chances to find it, in order to discover its "method"'. In other words, it refuses to be *onto*logical. A 'productive logic', on the other hand, would have the task of

> laying the foundations [of the special sciences] . . . in the sense that it leaps ahead, as it were, into some area of Being, discloses it for the first time in the constitution of its Being, and, after thus arriving at the structures within it, makes these available to the positive sciences as transparent assignments for their inquiry.[51]

Indeed, it is largely due to its principled avoidance of ever being productive in this way that philosophy of value withdraws into the sanctuary of ahistorical, worldless, timeless and ideal values and norms of validity. On the other hand, both Kant and Fichte accepted a 'transhistorical, timeless, and logical subject', but argued that this subject was the ground for the constitutive categories of all experience and thus the transcendental ground of every science. Neither of these approaches satisfies Heidegger.

In 1919, Heidegger argues that philosophy must be a primordial science (*Urwissenschaft*),[52] by which he means that philosophy must be the source and origin of every other science. To a significant degree he takes this idea from Husserl, but many other philosophers as well, including Rickert, believed that if philosophy was to be secured from sinking into utter irrelevancy, it must represent primordial science. Moreover, if the validity of the sciences were to be protected from relativistic attacks, their foundations must be secured. The idea of philosophy as primordial science is, in Heidegger's mind, the idea of a philosophy that can found the sciences.

Absolute idealism's *theoretical* approach to philosophy as primordial science failed because it ventured to determine *a priori* the structure of both what the special sciences may think and how they do it. Ultimately, this infringed upon the autonomy of the sciences. Philosophy became, following Habermas, the 'master thinker' who is both the 'usher' for the sciences, i.e. it provides an 'epistemological foundationalism' of 'cognition *before* cognition', and stands over the sciences as their 'judge', viz. by limiting the exercise of cognition and being the 'highest court of appeal' for all the sciences.[53]

By means of his turn towards the primacy of practical reason, Rickert's philosophy of value abdicates the role of usher, but maintains the role of judge and in this respect hopes to remain primordial science. However, as Heidegger argues, even in the exercise of its juridical function, it remains powerless to impose its rule upon the sciences. It merely adjudicates upon the validity or invalidity of the knowledge produced by sciences and does this in a purely formal-logical fashion. Since the theoretical approach of absolute idealism to the idea of philosophy as primordial science had failed and Rickert's attempt to found the sciences by means of practical reason was shown to be inadequate, Heidegger says that, 'The primacy of the theoretical must be broken, but not in order to proclaim the primacy of the practical ... but because the theoretical itself and as such refers back to something pre-theoretical.'[54] That is, the foundation of the theoretical sciences must be discovered in what is pre-theoretical. Heidegger's analysis of the idea of philosophy as primordial science is intended as a path towards an understanding of philosophy as a pre-theoretical, primordial science.

As we have seen, Rickert himself was forced to admit a 'metalogical' factor into his philosophy, viz. the cognizing subject, in order to bridge the gap between the absolute values and norms that are the subject matter of philosophy and the realization of these values and norms in the activity of the special sciences. Therefore, the source and origin of the sciences themselves lie outside of the purview of transcendental philosophy of value. That is, rather than being the source of the sciences themselves, it merely explains their logical validity. And it does this by investigating a 'new' and, Heidegger believes, rationalistically 'constructed' region of values and norms of validity that lie outside of the realm of existence. In other words, it merely examines and grounds a realm of values and norms that, by its own admission, lie completely outside of the realm of the sciences. Therefore, there is no way in which it could be primordial science. In many respects, Heidegger's criticism is analogous to the one that Aristotle set against the doctrine of Ideas, i.e. that it needlessly multiplies entities in its attempt to explain them. Aristotle argues that the mode of explanation offered by the doctrine of Ideas is 'as if a man who wanted to count things thought he would not be able to do it while they were few, but tried to count them when he had added to their number'.[55]

When it comes to the metalogical, cognizing subject who actually brings the sciences into existence, value-philosophy has little to offer except to say that it must exercise an 'autonomous will'. Transcendental philosophy of value is no more than a purely logical analysis of the sciences. As early as 1916 Heidegger was making the case that such a purely logical analysis was insufficient even with regard to issues of logic. He says, 'we cannot at all see logic and its problems in their true light if the context *from* which they are interpreted is not a translogical one'.[56] Rickert was certainly not ignorant of this context, but he maintained that, beyond those aspects of it that are necessary for the practical possibility of realizing ideal, absolute values, philosophy had nothing to say about it.

Very early on, Heidegger thought that metaphysics had a fundamental role to play in philosophy's attempt to understand the metalogical factor that Rickert had largely excluded from the purview of philosophy. Because of this, Heidegger asserts that '*Philosophy cannot for long do without its authentic optics: metaphysics*'.[57] To be sure, metaphysics in this instance does not indicate the kind of speculative metaphysics that Kant had argued was dogmatic and uncritical, viz. a discipline that purports to provide theoretical knowledge of a region of supersensible entities that lay beyond what is experienceable as such. Rather, Heidegger is attempting to reappropriate the Aristotelian notion of metaphysics as that which tries to 'state the most certain principles of all things',[58] but in such a way that it can remain foundational for the sciences in the context of the demise of German idealism and the self-assertion of the special sciences over philosophy.

Absolute idealism had hoped to ground philosophy in the dialectical-teleological method. Rickert, on the other hand, tried to return to Kant's practical philosophy and hoped to found philosophy through the critical-teleological method. Contrary to both of these, Heidegger asserts in 1916 that philosophy as metaphysics 'signifies for theory of truth the task of an ultimate metaphysically teleological interpretation of consciousness'.[59] What this means is that philosophy must be 'productive' in the unique sense in which that term applies to human activity. On one hand, if it is to be productive, it must remain situated within human life and cannot concern itself with purely ideal values.[60] But it also entails that philosophy must be explicitly goal-directed and must therefore transcend the brute immediacy of life and experience.[61] Therefore, Heidegger concludes that 'Philosophy as a rationalistic construction detached from life is *powerless* – mysticism as irrational experience is *without a goal*'.[62]

As we have seen, in 1919 Heidegger raises again the issue of the idea of a genuine philosophy, although this time he does not suggest a return to metaphysics, but rather an examination of the idea of philosophy as primordial science. The issue has not fundamentally changed, but it is presented in such a way that it will appear more relevant to Heidegger's philosophical interlocuters, e.g. Neo-Kantians, phenomenologists, etc. For they understand their own projects as attempts to formulate a primordial science and were generally dismissive of anything flying the standard of 'metaphysics'. That the fundamental issue at stake had not changed is clear from the way in which Heidegger characterizes primordial science in 1919. He says,

> In whatever way one initially takes the concept [of primordial science], it means something ultimate or, better, original, primordial, not in a temporal sense but substantively, first in relation to primary grounding and constitution: *principium*. In comparison with primordial science, every particular scientific discipline is not *principium* but *principatum*, the derivative and not the originary, the sprung-from [*Ent-sprungene*] and not the primal spring [*Ur-sprung*], the origin.[63]

On the other hand, a significant change does occur between 1916 and 1919 in what Heidegger regards as the ground of philosophy. In 1916 he says that philosophy will be grounded in 'living spirit', but by 1919 he has begun to focus on lived-experience (*Erlebnis*).

This certainly represents the increasing influence of Husserl's work on Heidegger's thought, which, although strong in 1916, had significantly increased by 1919. More specifically, according to Husserl, it is in the concatenations of the pure stream of lived-experiences (*Erlebnisstrom*), or pure consciousness, that meaning and intentionality are constituted. Moreover, it is in this that regional ontologies, including those of the special sciences, are constituted. The pure stream of lived-experiences represents for phenomenology the analogue of value-philosophy's 'material pregivenness'. That is, Husserl explicitly points out the need for a layer of pre-theoretical givenness, i.e. a layer of fundamental lived-experiences, that become explicit in phenomenological reflection and which Husserl refers to as 'pre-giving intentional lived experiences'. Using phenomenology Husserl felt that he could constitutively account for both the regions of nature and spirit and in fact the whole range of human activity. The question that will be examined in the next chapter is: Does phenomenology fulfil the idea of philosophy as primordial science?

Before we move on to Husserl, however, let us reflect on the contribution that the philosophy of value has made to our problematic. This has, due in large part to Heidegger's own critical stance towards value-philosophy, been largely dismissed. One of Rickert's enduring insights is that he recognized that unity could be brought to knowledge in its many varied forms by recognizing that it has a common goal or purpose. In this regard one can perhaps see Rickert's philosophy as an early influence that shaped Heidegger's later emphasis on the primacy of the 'for-the-sake-of-which' (*das Worumwillen*) in Dasein's understanding of its involvements within the world, and especially the primacy of the for-the-sake-of-which that 'always pertains to the Being of *Dasein*, for which, in its Being, that very Being is essentially an *issue*'.[64] Indeed, that one is 'always already' ahead of oneself, at least regarding knowledge, is implied by transcendental philosophy of value.

Husserl, Phenomenology and Lived-Experience

In an important sense, Husserl conceives of transcendental phenomenology as a scientific examination of what in the last chapter we referred to as the translogical or metalogical aspect of knowledge, viz. the cognizing subject who realizes knowledge through the activity of science. However, this does not do justice to the extent of Husserl's project. Rather, Husserl proposes to examine the translogical aspect in all facets of our comportment towards the world, including but not limited to our scientific comportments. Thus, Husserl intends by transcendental phenomenology an investigation of the nature of intentionality itself of which knowledge is merely one manifestation. Or, as Husserl typically characterizes it, he wants to scientifically examine consciousness in so far as it is 'consciousness of something'.

Husserl believes that the full panoply of human experience and human action consists of 'consciousness of something' or intentionality. For instance, one can intend something by knowing it, by willing it or by valuing it. Since all possible human comportments are intentionally structured, Husserl will argue the scientific inquiry into intentionality, viz. transcendental phenomenology, is truly primordial science.

On the one hand, transcendental phenomenology and transcendental philosophy of value are worlds apart. For example, the former is constitutive while the latter is not. On the other hand, they arise from largely the same problematic.[1] Like Rickert, Husserl was determined to avoid the mistakes made by earlier transcendental idealisms as well as avoid what he saw as the dead-end philosophies of positivism, naturalism, historicism and psychologism, each of which, Husserl famously argued, amounted to nothing more than pernicious and unacceptable forms of relativism.[2] In addition, Husserl agreed with Rickert that one of the tasks facing philosophy was to unify and ground the validity of the special sciences while at the same time allowing them to remain distinct both in methodological approach and subject matter.

Due to the extensive breadth and depth of phenomenology's subject matter it needed a category capable of circumscribing the vast array of phenomena that it hoped to encompass. In his first major work, the *Logical*

Investigations,[3] Husserl argued that meaning is this category. That is, every possible 'consciousness of something' consists of the *meaningful* givenness of something to consciousness. This is, as the body of Husserl's work amply testifies to, no simple phenomenon. However, given that meaning is fundamental to every consciousness of something, Husserl argues that the proper subject of transcendental phenomenology should be that which constitutes meaning. In other words, an account of how meanings are constituted, in all its variety and aspects, is arguably the most important and overarching task of transcendental phenomenology. As Crowell has put it, phenomenology is the investigation of 'the meaning of meaning'.[4]

Finally, Rickert and Husserl both engage closely with Kant's transcendental philosophy. One of the influential nineteenth-century criticisms of Kant's critical philosophy was that the categories of the understanding that he had laid out were inadequately flexible to keep up with advances in the special sciences and, beyond this, were themselves inadequately grounded. Broadly construed, this was referred to as the 'category problem' and shows up, for instance, in Heidegger's *habilitation*. In essence, the category problem is the question of the origin and ground for the categorial structure of all experience. As one might expect, solutions to the category problem varied considerably. Rickert's turn to the primacy of practical reason can be seen, in part, as mitigating the category problem. As we shall see, Husserl proposes to answer the category problem through a radically theoretical and intuitive approach.

1.   Towards a transcendental phenomenology

A common facet of nineteenth-century appropriations of Kant's critical philosophy was a concern with how one is to correctly understand the transcendental analytic, which Kant remarks is the proper task of a transcendental philosophy. This concern, in conjunction with a more or less explicit dissatisfaction with Kant's own treatment of the analytic, spawned many different species of philosophy in the nineteenth century, all of which claimed, at least in spirit, to be the rightful heir of Kant's philosophy. The dissatisfaction felt at the time was largely a result of suspicion that speculative, dogmatic elements remained in Kant's own handling of the transcendental analytic. Emil Lask is representative of this discontent. Kant, Lask argues, ignored '. . . in his theory of knowledge his own critique of reason, his own knowledge of the non-sensible transcendental forms'.[5] For many thinkers this was exemplified in Kant's use of the antiquated idea of 'faculties' and was further exasperated by apparently serious inadequacies in the metaphysical deduction of the categories of the understanding. Most specifically, Kant claimed to have determined *a priori* a systematically complete table of categories. This claim was commonly challenged both in fact as well as in principle.

Due to the growth and popularity of empirical psychology as well as the profound influence of Mill's *System of Logic*, psychologistic reformulations of Kant's theoretical philosophy thrived in the nineteenth century. By and large, pyschologism believed that, far from being an *a priori*, transcendental affair, the project that Kant envisioned in the transcendental analytic was properly an empirical matter. Consequently, an analysis of the understanding was best left to the positive, empirical science of psychology, which was thought to be pre-eminently capable of giving a truly scientific and theoretical account of knowledge. In other words, among psychologistic philosophers it was believed that traditional philosophy should make way for the empirical science of psychology, just as natural philosophy had been replaced centuries earlier by the natural empirical sciences.

Husserl rejected all such attempts to substitute empirical psychology for philosophy. As far as Husserl was concerned, empirical psychology was incapable of performing one of the primary tasks of theoretical philosophy, namely securing the objectivity of knowledge, for the simple reason that, as a factual, empirical science, it itself presupposed that the objectivity of knowledge had already been secured.[6] Although he rejected psychologistic attempts to reduce philosophy to one particular empirical science, Husserl remained convinced that Kant's critical project was unfinished and therefore needed to be carried through to its proper end, and in such a way that it was cleansed once and for all of any hint of dogmatic speculation. Husserl emphasized Kant's crucial insight in the transcendental aesthetic that it was by means of intuition – 'as signifying immediate presentation' to consciousness – that thought acquires its objective content.

Husserl believed that Kant's failure to produce an adequately critical transcendental philosophy rested upon two interrelated and unquestioned presuppositions. Namely, that intuition is entirely the result of our faculty of sensibility and that, therefore, thought is the result of the unintuited synthetic activity of the transcendental Ego. This, Husserl maintained, naturally lent itself to the psychologistic misinterpretation that one way to connect the latter with the former was through the empirical science of psychology. Husserl challenged *both* presuppositions through a critical, transcendental appropriation of Cartesian foundationalism. In this sense, transcendental phenomenology could be called a *critical Cartesianism*.[7]

Husserl's rejection of the first of Kant's presuppositions is embodied in the phenomenological 'principle of principles'. For Husserl *immediate* intuition is 'seeing in the universal sense'. According to Husserl such seeing is the ultimate ground of all rational knowledge. He writes, '*Immediate "seeing"*, not merely sensuous, experiential seeing, but *seeing in the universal sense as an originally presentive consciousness of any kind whatever*, is the ultimate legitimizing source of all rational assertions.'[8] This represents for Husserl the critically and phenomenologically adequate version of Descartes' doctrine that one must only accept what is 'perceived clearly and distinctly'.

Before Kant, intuition had been modelled on sensation, meaning that it was essentially mediated by empirical representations. It wasn't until the publication of Kant's first critique that modern philosophy was introduced to the *a priori* components of sensation, i.e. pure intuition or the *a priori* forms of space and time. For Husserl this still remained inadequate because it allowed no immediate, intuitive access to the activity of the transcendental subject. Lacking such an intuition of the activity of consciousness one was left to give a 'regressive argument'[9] back *from* experience *to* those structures of consciousness that constitute the transcendental conditions for the possibility of experience.

Although such a regressive approach is perhaps viable, it appeared insufficient to many in the nineteenth century for a couple of reasons. One was the perceived inadequacy of Kant's own attempt to carry out such a project, relying as he did on traditional, syllogistic logic and an outmoded system of judgements and categories. More principally, many believed that any attempt to determine *a priori* the necessary structures of experience was doomed to failure. For experience in this context was taken at the time to indicate not just naive, everyday experience, but rather scientific experience. Scientific experience, it was argued, has and will progress and develop, thus nullifying the structures culled from previous scientific experience. In particular, Kant's first critique was commonly understood at the time to have simply worked out the 'transcendental' structures of experience as embodied in Euclidean geometry and Newtonian natural science. Consequently, because of the addition of new scientific disciplines, e.g. the human sciences, as well as progress in mathematics, logic and physics, it was thought that most of the structures that Kant had laid out were in need of revision. At any point in time, however, the same could happen to any system of 'transcendental' structures of experience. In the eyes of critics, this had been amply demonstrated by the fact that Kant's confidence in his own system had proved illusory. Lacking an absolutely stable experiential foundation, it was believed that any transcendental philosophy was in danger of becoming obsolete.

By broadening the principle of intuition beyond mere sensible intuition, Husserl hoped to alleviate such problems and discover an incorrigible, scientific philosophy. In the phenomenological principle of all principles we see Husserl extending intuition beyond mere sensible intuition to include all legitimate forms of intuition, most famously eidetic seeing (*Wesenserschauung*). However, extending the notion of intuition alone is not enough to alleviate the difficulties facing critical philosophy. That is, even with this, it still requires an absolutely stable experiential basis. To secure such a foundation, Husserl's philosophy takes a second, decidedly Cartesian turn. What is needed in his mind is an intuition of the pure activity of consciousness, which is the transcendental condition for the possibility of our meaningful experience of the world and everything encountered therein. More specifically, philosophy needed to be able to grasp the 'pure' Ego and its 'pure' stream of lived-experiences. In other words, transcendental phenomenology is after the unified flow of *absolute* lived-experiences that is the constitutive foundation for the entirety of our 'natural', worldly lived-experience.

For Husserl, the natural attitude is the attitude in which we simply 'busy ourselves' with objects, e.g. perceiving them, judging them, willing them, using them, etc. The unifying context in which we go about our everyday lives and experience the world in a natural way is the environing world (*Umwelt*) or simply the natural world.[10] Of the environing world, Husserl says that, 'It is continually "on hand" [*vorhanden*] for me and I myself am a member of it. Moreover, this world is there for me not only as a world of mere things, but also with the same immediacy as a *world of objects with values, a world of goods, a practical world*.'[11] Thus, in the environing world are included not only 'physical things' (*Dinge*) but objects (*Objekte*) of use, i.e. 'immediately, physical things stand there as Objects of use, the "table" with its "books", the "drinking glass", the "vase", the "piano", etc. These value-characteristics and practical characteristics also belong *constitutively to the Objects "on hand" as Objects* . . .'[12]

In addition, Egos are there for me (including my own) with all their thoughts, their emotions, their will and even their 'social acts'.[13] At any one time, I 'know of' the vast majority of the objects of the environing world only implicitly, i.e. 'a "knowing of" which involves no conceptual thinking and which changes into a clear intuiting only with the advertence of attention, and even then only partially and for the most part very imperfectly'.[14] In other words, the environing world is the horizon for all possible natural lived-experiences. The very depth and nuance with which Husserl describes the environing world should give pause to those who wish to claim that it was Heidegger's great achievement to have discovered the essentially practical and social nature of our everyday existence.[15] The task of the positive sciences is to scientifically articulate our experience of the environing world.[16] So understood, this world is the horizon of every natural objectivity, i.e. the vast collection of actual and possible natural facts, laws, etc.

However, experience is essentially multifaceted. Indeed, in every experience there is *that* which is experienced and then there is the one *who* experiences. As Fichte once purportedly directed his students, 'Gentleman, think the wall.' After which he told them, 'Gentlemen, think him who thought the wall.'[17] In other words, every experience consists of an object that is experienced and a subject who experiences that object. Husserl stressed that in addition to the subject and object of experience there is also the experiencing itself, viz. the lived-experience. Moreover, he maintained that even in our natural experience, i.e. in the 'natural attitude', we distinguish between these different facets of experience, i.e. experienced object, the subject who experiences and the lived-experiences by which they are experienced. This is of course revealed in natural reflection, which reveals lived-experiences as real acts of a real, individual consciousness by which an object is given to that consciousness. In addition, reflection discloses the 'life' of a real, individual Ego, viz. one's own, as one unified stream of lived-experience (*Erlebnisstrom*), or what one typically refers to as 'my experiences'.

However, unlike every other object that is there for us in the natural world, one's lived-experiences, consciousness and Ego have the unique characteristic of being incorrigible. And the incorrigibility of these latter is given to us in our natural reflection. That is, one need not leave the natural attitude to be cognizant of it. What is this incorrigibility? Whereas objects other than one's own Ego and its lived-experiences are always hypothetically posited in so far as such posits are always in principle capable of being overturned by future experience, lived-experiences are not so posited. For instance, we have all had the experience of discovering that the person coming towards us, who we had thought was our friend, in fact turns out to be a complete stranger. In this case our anticipations and expectations for the future can be frustrated by further experience. When our original positing is 'annulled' by future experience we recognize that what we had hypothetically posited was incorrect. In this case, we reinterpret all our present and past experiences to take account of the fact that it was not our friend coming towards us after all. Put differently, what our past experience had led us to believe, in many instances legitimately about this person, turned out upon further experience to be wrong.

On the other hand, the Ego and its lived-experiences, as we experience it in natural reflection, can never be 'annulled' by future experience. Using the previous example, although experience could demonstrate to us that the person we supposed to be our friend was in fact not, no future experience can convince us that at the time we did not *think* or *believe* that it was our friend. According to Husserl, the Ego with its lived-experiences, even in the natural attitude, are posited not hypothetically, but incorrigibly. For Husserl this peculiar *natural* fact about one's own lived-experiences and Ego points beyond the natural attitude and the horizon of the environing world.

On the other hand, natural consciousness is ignorant of this. Remaining in the natural attitude it interprets the Ego and its lived-experiences as simply natural objects among others. In this way, the incorrigibility of one's own Ego with its lived-experiences remains puzzling. For they seem to be in one sense like any other object that we come across in the world, e.g. we can think about them, talk about them, etc., but in another sense they are totally unlike any other object. The enigmatic character of the Ego and its lived-experiences leads to what has become known as 'the problem of the incorrigibility of the mental'. One way to raise the problem is to ask whether natural reflection is the unique ability to reveal things incorrigibly. And, if so, how?

In Husserl's time, the philosophical school of psychologism argued that natural reflection is not incorrigible in any significant sense. That is to say, psychologism claimed that natural reflection does not provide incorrigible *knowledge* of the Ego and the structures of experience. Rather, only the empirical science of psychology gives such knowledge. Natural reflection may or may not play some evidentiary role in this science, but it itself does not furnish knowledge. Husserl argues that this view, along with materialism and historicism, is predicated on the dogmatic assumption that the Ego with its lived-experiences is *merely* one kind of natural object among others and that, for this reason, it is forever in danger of falling into relativism. That is, according to Husserl, the empirical science of psychology, as with every naturally oriented, empirical science, is only able to posit things hypothetically.

It is not difficult to understand why Husserl believed that this led to inescapable problems with relativism. For psychologism was a philosophical theory about knowledge, viz. the theory that the ultimate conditions of knowledge are comprised of the structures of knowledge postulated by empirical psychology. As far as Husserl is concerned, this signifies that these structures are hypothetical posits and are, therefore, in principle capable of being invalidated by future experience. Thus the psychologistic foundation of knowledge may be *relatively* stable, i.e. it may persist at a time and for a period of time, but it is inherently unstable and insecure as was ably demonstrated by examining the history of empirical psychology. Perhaps more problematic from Husserl's perspective is that, according to psychologism, empirical psychology is supposed to account for its own validity since it is both a form of knowledge and the ground of knowledge. In other words, knowledge is forever chasing its own tail. In Husserl's mind, this circle could only be broken if philosophy were to uncover an absolutely valid (i.e. non-relative) foundation through which valid, scientific knowledge could be constituted.

According to Husserl, philosophy had spoiled Descartes' genuine insight into the Ego and its lived-experiences. That is, Husserl maintained that Descartes documented the incorrigibility of the Ego and its lived-experiences when he discovered that he could not doubt that 'I am'. Additionally, Husserl believed that Descartes rightly proposed that scientific knowledge must be built upon this indubitable foundation. On the other hand, Husserl argued that Descartes did not properly understand his own claim since he proceeded to interpret the Ego according to how it is given in the natural attitude, i.e. he construed the Ego with its lived-experiences as analogous to a natural substance. To be sure, he did substantively distinguish Egos from every other kind of substance by dividing the world into the *res extensa* and the *res cogitans*, but, in doing so, Husserl believed that Descartes had obscured the relation between the Ego and everything else.

For Husserl, the peculiar, incorrigible character that the Ego with its lived-experiences has in the natural attitude is only an indication of something deeper, viz. that the environing world and everything posited within it is meaningfully constituted in experience. In other words, the environing world is 'built up' from experience. For instance, behind the experience of seeing someone that one supposes to be a friend is a whole stream of past experiences and a whole horizon of future anticipations. For example, experiences of this friend, experiences of people in general, experience of objects coming towards us, etc. Fundamental to Husserl's phenomenology is the recognition that objects are constituted in experience, rather than the other way around.

It is crucial however that one realize what is meant by 'experience' in the present context. For it certainly does not refer to the constructs of empirical psychology, i.e. the 'psychic' entities and processes postulated of psychic subjects. Moreover, Husserl contends, it does not signify the natural lived-experiences that one encounters in the natural attitude and which are given through natural reflection. However, this claim represents one of the most difficult and, perhaps, contested aspects of transcendental phenomenology precisely because it comprises the boundary between what is transcendent and what is transcendental or, more exactly, between transcendence and immanence.

Lived-experiences, as we come across them in the natural attitude, belong to the environing world. In essence, as natural entities they *must* be situated within the natural environment, which means that they are located within nature. This is accomplished, Husserl argues, by associating them with an individual human organism and human psyche. In essence, they become 'properties' of an individual human organism and psyche. In this case, the Ego with its lived-experiences manifests itself as a '... *sequence* of conscious *states* of an identical *real* Ego-subject which manifests in them its *individual real properties* and who now – *as* this unity of properties becoming manifest in states – is intended to be united with the appearing organism'.[18] Importantly, under this interpretation, the Ego with its lived-experiences is a component part of the environing world and so incapable of being that through which the environing world is constituted. Put differently, naturalistic interpretations confuse the Ego and its lived-experiences as *posited* in the environing world with the Ego that *posits* the environing world.

What philosophy must secure in order to avoid this naturalistic misinterpretation is not a region of lived-experiences different from those described above, but rather a more fundamental interpretation of those same lived-experiences. That is, philosophy must gain access to those lived-experiences in their absoluteness or, as Husserl puts it, in their 'purity'. As naturalistically interpreted, the lived-experiences have been modified because they have become situated within the environing world. This natural positing of lived-experiences 'adds' something to them, namely an association with the natural world, e.g. being located within the world and, more specifically, an association with a particular object within the world, that is, a human organism and psyche.

In essence, according to Husserl, philosophy must shortcut this addition by preserving the lived-experiences in their purity, which consists of attending only to what is inherent or 'immanent' to those lived-experiences. This is precisely what the phenomenological reduction or *epoche* is designed to do. By 'bracketing' lived-experiences, viz. by refusing to posit them as 'really' existing, it opens up their immanent content for investigation. Furthermore, in an exactly parallel fashion, Husserl argues that there is a pure Ego that lives through these pure lived-experiences.

These pure lived-experiences are the absolute, stable region of experience that Husserl thought was required by a rigorously scientific philosophy. Importantly, Husserl believed that the phenomenological reduction discloses a fundamental ontological distinction, namely the difference between being as consciousness and being manifested in consciousness. That is, the *epoche* provides 'the fundamental field of phenomenology', a field from which every transcendent posit and 'the whole natural world' has been excluded. He variously calls this field 'the phenomenological residuum', 'pure consciousness' or the 'pure stream of lived-experience'. As has been mentioned, Husserl argues that this is the field of 'absolute' being in so far as it is *not posited*, but *posits* everything else. Most importantly, it posits the environing world itself. Husserl says,

> The realm of transcendental consciousness as the realm of what is, in a determined sense, 'absolute' being, has been provided us by the phenomenological reduction. It is the primal category of all being (or, in our terminology, the primal region), the one in which all other regions of being are rooted, to which, according to their *essence*, they are relative and on which they are therefore all essentially dependent. The theory of categories must start entirely from this most radical of all ontological distinctions – being *as consciousness* and being as something which becomes *'manifested'* in consciousness . . . [19]

This primal region, Husserl argues, is what modern philosophy, and Kant in particular, had sought for but failed to grasp. Husserl says, '. . . the transcendental deduction in the first edition of the *Kritik der reinen Vernunft* was actually operating inside the realm of phenomenology, but Kant misinterpreted that realm as psychological and therefore he himself abandoned it.'[20] Thus, Husserl hoped that transcendental phenomenology represented the capstone of modern philosophy by finalizing the project instituted by Descartes and narrowly missed by Kant.

Having secured this absolute realm of being, Husserl must explain how we have access to it. In other words, how is one to thematize and investigate this newly revealed region of pure lived-experience? This cannot be accomplished by natural reflection – which the tradition of modern philosophy had typically conceived as a form of 'inner perception' – because, as we have seen, this is directed solely towards the derivative region of the posited, worldly lived-experience of a posited, worldly Ego. That is, natural reflection is mediated through the self-positings that constitute the natural Ego and its natural states. Husserl therefore maintains that the thematization of pure lived-experience is accomplished by means of *phenomenological* reflection.

Unlike natural reflection, phenomenological reflection is itself a pure act of consciousness, a pure lived-experience. It is that pure lived-experience that thematizes the pure stream of lived-experiences to which it itself belongs, i.e. it is an act of pure consciousness that reveals that consciousness' own activity.[21] Because it remains entirely within the sphere of what is immanent, phenomenological reflection can, in Husserl's mind, immediately intuit the lived-experiences that belong to this sphere, thus making pure consciousness into an object of study and making it 'evidentially apprehensible and analyzable'.[22] Of course, Husserl goes on to argue that, in conjunction with the phenomenological and eidetic reductions, phenomenological reflection is also able to reveal the essential structures of pure consciousness itself. As Heidegger emphasizes, this is why Husserl will insist upon phenomenological reflection's '*universal* methodological function: the phenomenological method operates exclusively in acts of reflection'.[23]

Husserl further argues that phenomenological reflection, and thus the phenomenological method, is a possibility that pertains *essentially* to consciousness. He says that reflection 'has the characteristic of being a *modification of a consciousness* and, moreover, a modification essentially *any consciousness* can undergo'.[24] As is well known, Husserl follows Brentano in characterizing consciousness as fundamentally intentional. But in this case, Husserl is claiming that consciousness is equally delineated through its ability to reflect upon itself. That is, consciousness implies the possibility of 'self-consciousness', or extending this thought, it always has the possibility of being philosophical and, in its purest form, phenomenological.

For Husserl, phenomenological reflection is a modification of the life of the pure Ego. In the natural attitude the Ego 'lives in' one of its acts and lives towards something other than it, i.e. an object in its environing world. Reflection is a modification of such living. In reflection, 'Instead of living *in* them [cogitative positings], instead of effecting *them*, we effect acts of *reflection* directed to them; and we seize upon them themselves as the *absolute* being which they are. We are now living completely in such acts of the second degree, acts the datum of which is the infinite field of absolute lived-experiences – the fundamental *field of phenomenology*'.[25] In this way, the pure Ego is able to grasp its own lived-experiences and, consequently, can know the essential structures of every aspect of our lived-experience, including the essential structures of the constituted environing world and everything in it. In this respect, there are affinities between Husserl's notion of reflection and Kant and Fichte's notion of intellectual intuition, which is, according to Kant, a way in which the subject could 'judge of itself if its intuition were self-activity only, that is, were intellectual'.[26]

What sets phenomenological reflection apart from intellectual intuition is that it has a 'datum', i.e. the pure stream of lived-experiences. This is a passivity of a peculiar kind. In other words, what Kant thought prevented human consciousness from being able to acquire intuitions intellectually was that intuition for human consciousness was essentially tied to passive sensibility. This meant that in order for us to intuit anything required that sensibility be passively affected by the thing-in-itself. Fichte, on the other hand, believed that everything originated primordially in an act of consciousness and that, therefore, there was a fundamental sense in which intuition was 'self-activity only'. For Husserl, on the contrary, reflective intuition reveals something that is already there, i.e. reflection is not creative or 'productive', but at the same time the 'something' that it discloses is not fundamentally different from itself.

Rather, a reflective intuitive act of consciousness exposes and makes known the lived-experiences and acts of that very same consciousness *as they already are*. Husserl remarks that

> When the livingly-experienced lived-experience [*erlebte Erlebnis*] which, at any particular time, is actually being lived comes into reflective regard it becomes given *as* actually being lived, as existing 'now'. But not only that: it becomes given as having just now *been* and, in so far as it was unregarded, precisely as having been unregarded, as not having been reflected on.[27]

Furthermore, because every lived-experience has both retentions – 'primary' memory – and protentions – 'primary anticipation or expectations', i.e. because every lived-experience points back towards past lived-experiences and forward toward future lived-experiences, a whole range of lived-experiences open up as possible candidates for reflection. In this way, the entire 'infinite field of absolute lived-experiences' is available for phenomenological investigation. The point is that phenomenological reflection does not create or produce this infinite field of absolute lived-experiences, but it is not something foreign to it either.

2. The phenomenology of constitution and the trans-phenomenological, pure Ego

As we shall shortly see, in his early lecture courses Heidegger argues that phenomenology's reliance on reflection complicates its ability to be primordial science. Before we examine that, however, we need to briefly examine how Husserl understands the field of absolute, pure lived-experiences as revealed by phenomenological reflection. What does phenomenological reflection reveal about this field? Of course, it reveals the eidetic structures of consciousness, e.g. the essential structures of intentionality, its noetic and noematic aspects, etc. All of these are well-worn facets of Husserl's phenomenological enterprise. More important for our purposes is the lesser-known part of Husserl's phenomenological project which he called the 'the phenomenology of constitution'.

In Chapter 1, we saw how Rickert recognized that his own logical approach to epistemology needed to be supplemented by a translogical account of how the logical structures discovered by transcendental philosophy of value were realized in the realm of being, i.e. in 'reality'. In an important sense, Husserl's phenomenology of constitution performs a similar function. However, it must be kept in mind that Husserl *never* postulated an absolute dichotomy between being as consciousness and being as manifested in consciousness like that between the realm of validity and the realm of being in the philosophy of value, and so faced none of the perhaps insurmountable philosophical difficulties that the latter faced. In other words, for Husserl, being as consciousness and being as manifested in consciousness are inextricably and essentially related in so far as the former is absolute and constituting, while the latter is derivative and constituted.

For Husserl, the environing world and everything in it is 'entirely referred to consciousness and, more particularly, not to some logically conceived consciousness but to actual consciousness'.[28] In essence, it is an 'intentional being' or a 'being *for* a consciousness'.[29] What this means is that it is constituted as an 'intentional unity motivated in transcendentally pure consciousness by immanental connections'.[30] Indeed, Husserl argues that 'Reality [*Realität*] and world are names here precisely for certain valid *unities of sense*, unities of "sense" related to certain concatenations of absolute, of pure consciousness which, by virtue of their *essence*, bestow sense and demonstrate sense-validity . . .'[31]

That is, the entire environing world is constituted in pure consciousness, but unlike in the systems of absolute idealism, Husserl makes it quite clear that this cannot and should not be understood as if the world is a construction arising out of some primordial act of subjectivity. Rather, the region of pure consciousness consists of varied and diverse acts bearing numerous and complex 'motivational' and 'immanental' relations to one another. The environing world is 'built up' from within this complex array of motivated concatenations of lived-experience. Moreover, the positive sciences, which themselves are equally part of the environing world, are also so constituted – not just with regard to their subject matter, but also with respect to their methods, techniques, etc.

The phenomenological examination of the constitution of the environing world in pure consciousness was taken up by Husserl in lectures, notes and manuscripts dating back at least to 1912, but perhaps as early as 1908, and culminated in a manuscript ready for publication in 1925 that would eventually become the posthumously edited and published second book of his *Ideas*.[32] Heidegger, among others, was well aware of Husserl's work in this area.[33] The bulk of the second book of the *Ideas* is taken up with a discussion of the constitution of the natural and spiritual world.

Husserl treats first of the natural world. According to him this is comprised of the three fundamental attitudes that the pure Ego can take towards something within the world. These three fundamental attitudes are the cognitive, practical and axiological attitudes and correspond to the three fundamental activities of the Ego, viz. thinking, willing and valuing.

Husserl believes that objects are given for cognition in what he calls 'doxic-theoretical' lived-experiences, e.g. representing, judging and thinking acts. Over against this, are valuing and practical lived-experiences. What distinguishes doxic lived-experiences from the others is that in these experiences the object is given through intentional, doxic structures. In valuing and practical lived-experiences, on the other hand, the object is given in accordance with the appropriate valuing or practical intentional structures. Husserl calls each of these kinds of lived-experiences 'pre-giving intentional lived-experiences', because in them an object is *first* given to consciousness. That is, in these forms of lived-experience an object [*Gegenstand*] is constituted either *as* cognized, *as* valued or *as* willed.

Yet, what one would call 'everyday experience' consists not of one or another of these lived-experiences, but rather is typically a highly intricate and complicated complex of many such lived-experiences. Indeed, the commonplace, everyday experience of walking into a room consists of a whole interrelated assembly of heterogeneous doxic, valuative and practical lived-experiences. For instance, the table sitting in the centre of the room is experienced indiscriminately as subject to numerous different predicates, valued as beautiful, ugly, etc. and is an object capable of many different uses. The pure Ego in its everydayness lives in these numerous and varied lived-experiences.

However, in addition to such everyday lived-experiences there are also 'pre-eminent' ways in which the pure Ego can live. These consist of the theoretical, valuing and practical attitudes. In these attitudes, the pure Ego lives in a pre-eminent fashion through one of the doxic, valuing or practical lived-experiences exclusively. That is, in the theoretical attitude the pure Ego enacts pre-eminently a doxic lived-experience by, for instance, judging the object to be such and such. Similarly, in the valuing attitude the pure Ego lives pre-eminently through a valuing lived-experience, e.g. when one sees 'the radiant blue sky [and] lives in the rapture of it'.[34] Finally, the pure Ego can live in the practical attitude and thus lives pre-eminently through a practical lived-experience wherein 'the true and proper performance lies in the willing and the doing'.[35] Through such practical acts 'a man [lives] the practical life, utilizes the things of *his environment*, transforming them according to his purposes, and evaluates them from aesthetic, ethical, and utilitarian points of view'.[36]

However, each of these attitudes is irreducible to the others and he acknowledges, as Heidegger will reiterate, that we live in the theoretical attitude 'only intermittently'.[37] Still, Husserl insists that the theoretical attitude has a uniquely important function. By a 'shift' of attitude *any* of the above-mentioned attitudes can become the object of a theoretical regard. That is, instead of *actually* judging, valuing or using something, one can make the judged as judged, the valued as valued, or the used as used the object of theoretical inspection. With this shift of attitude, 'new' objectivities arise, e.g. objects of cognition, objects of value and objects of use. Husserl maintains that 'it is only by means of a *shift* of the theoretical regard, a change of theoretical interest, that they [these objects] emerge out of the phase of *pre*-theoretical constitution into the theoretical'.[38] The phase of 'pre-theoretical constitution' occurs in the aforementioned pre-eminently *lived* acts of the pure Ego. This shift of attitude corresponds to the pure Ego living in an act of reflection. In addition, by means of such reflection, 'higher' objectivities arise, viz. 'logico-categorial' formations in the case of the theoretical attitude (e.g. states of affairs, collections, etc.) and, in the case of the other attitudes, 'analogues of the categorial objectivities of the logical sphere' such as norms, purposes, etc.[39]

A subset of the possible objects of cognition, viz. natural objects, comprise the subject matter of the natural sciences and these are subject to the laws of causation, etc. This includes everything given to cognition as physical, bodily and psychic nature. Moreover, these objects are intended in what Husserl calls the naturalistic or natural-scientific attitude, which is to be distinguished from the broader natural attitude in which we live in the environing world. Most characteristic of this attitude is that it excludes everything having to do with human interest, goals, etc. and is achieved through a sort of disengaging *epoche*. In essence, the naturalistic world contains 'mere things'.[40] Husserl spends the first two sections of the second book of the *Ideas* detailing how nature and its objects are constituted. The naturalistic world, however, is but part of the environing world.

In addition to the natural world, there is also the world of spirit or the 'personal' world and one comports oneself towards this world in what Husserl calls the 'personalistic attitude'. At its most fundamental level, this is that part of the environing world for which a person is the subject. Husserl says, 'As person, I am what I am (and each other person is what he is) as *subject of an environing world*. The concepts of Ego and environing world are related to one another inseparably. Thereby to each person belongs his

environing world, while at the same time a plurality of persons in commu-
nication with one another has a common environing world.'[41] It is, Husserl
says, the 'everyday world' or simply '*the* world'. The personalistic attitude
circumscribes the multifarious forms of Ego interest, spontaneity, affectivity, activity and receptivity. In this attitude is included the Ego's enact-
ments of the theoretical, axiological and practical attitudes, and in it the
Ego is subject to the 'motivations' and 'tendencies' that produce action and
reaction.[42] Thus, the personal or spiritual world is the horizon of the objects
that can act upon or be acted upon by the Ego. In other words, this world is
the objective horizon of 'personal' activity, motivation and tendency.

Unlike the naturalistic world and its naturalistic realities, which are
determined by the law of causation, Husserl argues that motivation is the
fundamental law of the life of the spirit. Motivation is a notion Husserl utilizes as far back as the *Logical Investigations*. There it represents the relation of
descriptive unity between indicator and indicated, i.e. where belief in the
existence of one state of affairs indicates belief in the existence of another
state of affairs.[43] By the time he writes the *Ideas*, motivation has, for Husserl,
taken on an enlarged and far more significant connotation. Namely, it has
become the personal, spiritual analogue of the concept of causality in the
naturalistic world.

In essence, the subject is motivated when an object stimulates the subject and the subject adverts its attention to that object. That is, 'the Object
"intrudes on the subject" and exercises stimulation on it (theoretical,
aesthetic, practical stimulation). The Object, as it were, wants to be an
Object of advertence, it knocks at the door of consciousness . . . it attracts,
and the subject is summoned until finally the Object is noticed.'[44] In this
way, '*Experienceableness* [*die Erfahrbarkeit*] *never means a mere logical possibility*,
but rather a possibility *motivated* in the context of experience.'[45] Correspondingly, motivations engender tendencies. For example, the subject per-
ceives something, which produces the tendency to know it more fully, or
the subject experiences something beautiful and has the tendency to rejoice
in it, or the subject finds something useful and tends to take it up as a
means to fulfil an end. In essence, the laws of motivation and tendency
govern our lived-experiences, i.e. lived-experiences are motivated by one
another and lived-experiences create tendencies that lead to further lived-
experiences. For example, the lived-experience of considering a vaguely
given state of affairs tends to motivate the lived-experience of doubt, which
in turn leads to acts of examination, inquiry, acquisition of evidence, etc.

The last example is an instance of what Husserl calls the 'motivation
of reason', the first of two fundamental kinds of motivation he considers.
The motivation of reason governs the 'motivations of position-takings by

position-takings' or 'of effective acts by effective acts in the sphere that stands under norms of reason'.[46] Husserl gives as an example of this the act of moving from a judgement concerning premises to a judgement inferring a conclusion. The ultimate goal of the motivation of reason is to be motivated by insight and evidence. This type of motivation applies to a 'higher form of consciousness', namely that form of consciousness which intends 'true being'.

The other kind of motivational structure is motivation as association. This includes associations built up and habits formed that relate earlier portions of consciousness to later ones, although not necessarily according to any rule of reason. Thus, this accounts more for personal sets of beliefs as well as personal character, e.g. a person's habitual way of encountering the world or the straightforward associations derived from past experience. Clearly, the former type of motivation is of fundamental significance for the sciences, but the latter should not be discounted either, especially when it comes to the subject matter of the human sciences which study, in part, personal worldviews and personality types.

More significantly, it is through contexts of motivation and tendency, viz. through complex unities of lived-experiences, that the environing world and everything in it is constituted. In other words, what is presently being experienced is motivated in past experiences and traces out tendencies for future possible experience. What distinguishes motivation and tendency from natural causality is that the latter governs *necessity*, whereas the former comprise the Ego's field of *freedom*. That is, motivated contexts of lived-experience open a domain of possibilities for the Ego, i.e. a domain of what 'I can'. When the Ego exercises its freedom, then 'an "I do" succeeds the "*I can*" according to the reigning stimuli and tendencies. Correlatively, the end of the process has the character of a goal'.[47] Thus, 'in a very broad sense, we can also denote the personal or motivational attitude as the *practical* attitude: that is, what we have here always is the active or passive Ego and indeed in the proper intrinsic sense'.[48]

Importantly, what Husserl has done is to open up a much more fundamental realm of what could be considered practical than the *theoretically* construed version of practical reason present in Rickert's value philosophy. Indeed, the philosophy of value was conceived by Rickert as a science of values, viz. a theoretical grasp of ideal, absolute values. Excluded from this was precisely the translogical subject who realized these values through autonomous action. In his analysis of the personalistic attitude, Husserl gives a phenomenological account of the Ego as it engages with the environing world. That is, he gives a phenomenological analysis of the Ego in its practical life. Indeed, Husserl situates the personal Ego, the environing

world, and intentionality within the movement of lived-experience and life.
In many ways, Husserl was a much more subtle and nuanced interpreter of
human life than he is usually given credit for. Far from the theoretically
detached version of Husserl one typically gets, in the second book of the
Ideas we see a Husserl who is deeply concerned with the practical nature of
life and lived-experience. Moreover, it seems clear that Heidegger's own
analysis of Dasein's being-the-world owes much to Husserl's phenomenological studies in constitution.

Husserl argues that even the natural and human sciences are essentially
motivated in and follow out tendencies grounded in our lived-experience
of the environing world, e.g. the natural sciences work within the horizon of
the motivated tendencies of our lived-experience of nature. To this extent,
the special sciences are carried out in the practical attitude understood
in the very broad sense mentioned above. However, the sciences still
approach their subject matter entirely from within the theoretical attitude.
That is, a science begins by raising what is given pre-theoretically into theoretical givenness and investigate it as an object of cognition according to
its proper nature. Put differently, one does not engage in science by living
in value-intentions or use-intentions, but through cognitive-intentions.
Because of this, Husserl maintains that every science works within a disen-
gaged form of 'reduction'. He even goes so far as to say that they perform
their own kind of *epoche* analogous to the phenomenological *epoche*.[49] Even
the human sciences study the motivations and tendencies that govern
life from a theoretical perspective, and thus do not live in the relations of
motivation and tendency that is the object of their study. On the other
hand, this does not mean that value or use is entirely excluded from scientific
investigation. Even the objects of value or use can, by a shift to the theoretical attitude, be studied scientifically.

Husserl is also quite conscious of the fact that, even though they operate
within the theoretical attitude, the natural and human sciences are subject
to valuative and practical considerations as well. For instance, he mentions that although the object of natural science is a mere thing without
value or use, natural science, as well as the individual natural scientist, is
concerned with the value of the natural-scientific enterprise which requires
the use of many things, e.g. instruments, experiments, etc. in order to carry
out its task. That is, Husserl claims that the natural-scientist is certainly
not a purely 'objectivating Ego-subject . . . that in no way strives, wills, or
evaluates'.[50]

All of this is modified with the shift to the phenomenological attitude
after the phenomenological *epoche*. For now we have the region of pure consciousness, viz. the pure stream of lived-experiences and the subject of this,

viz. the pure Ego. As rigorous science, phenomenology is also carried out from within the theoretical attitude. That is, the phenomenologist directs acts of phenomenological reflection – themselves pre-eminently theoretical acts – towards pure consciousness, thereby making it into an object of theoretical inspection and analysis. In this way, *all* possible lived-experiences of the Ego, whether theoretical, axiological or practical, become objects for a higher, theoretical regard.

There is a reason for the ubiquitousness of the theoretical attitude in Husserl's conception of science and, in particular, in phenomenology. That is, even after his penetrating analysis of the practical life of the Ego, Husserl still privileges the theoretical attitude, since he asserts that it is the *only* attitude in which there is a positing of *being*, that is, in which 'what is objective *becomes a theoretical object*, an object, that is, of an *actively performed positing of being* in which the Ego lives and grasps what is objective, seizes and posits it as a being'.[51] In other words, Husserl argues that only within the theoretical attitude is being or a being posited because only this attitude reveals *what* something is or *what* essentially characterizes a region of being. In essence, the being of something consists of its *objective meaning* which can only be given through the theoretical attitude.

Most importantly, only phenomenological reflection, as a unique mode of theoretical reflection, reveals *what* pure consciousness is, i.e. posits it as the absolute being that it is. And only by means of *what* it is are the eidetic structures of pure consciousness revealed. Put differently, pure consciousness must be objectified before it can be phenomenologically analysed. It is because of this that Heidegger can claim that Husserl has restricted the sense of being, including the sense of our own being, to what is 'present-at-hand in the broadest sense'.[52] For Husserl, the being of something cannot be disclosed through the valuative or practical attitude. Although, of course, the being of an object *as* valued or *as* useful can certainly be obtained by theoretical reflection upon our valuative and practical comportments.

Before moving on to examine Heidegger's criticism of transcendental phenomenology, it is important to point out that Husserl himself realized that even phenomenological reflection cannot reach the *pure* Ego. The pure Ego is the 'pure subject' of the acts and lived-experiences of pure consciousness. In fact, the pure Ego is what unifies a stream of lived-experiences and makes it 'mine'. But the pure Ego also accounts for how we live through our lived-experiences, i.e. it animates our lived experiences. Husserl says that '... the "pure" subject of the act: "being directed to", the "being busied with", the "taking a position toward", the "undergoing", the "suffering from", *necessarily* includes in its essence this: that it is precisely ⟨a ray⟩ "emanating from the Ego" or, in a reverse direction of the ray, "toward the Ego" – and this Ego is the *pure* Ego …'[53] Moreover, all acts and lived-experiences, even those not lived-through, 'belong' to the pure Ego as 'its own' and are its 'consciousness-background', its 'field of freedom'.

At the same time, Husserl argues that this pure Ego cannot be made the object of an investigation and is 'completely empty of essence-components, has no explicable content, is undescribeable in and for itself'. It can be known only through its 'modes of relation' and 'modes of comportment'.[54] It is, he says, 'a transcendency of a peculiar kind – one which is not consti-tuted – a *transcendency within immanency*' that cannot be excluded by the phe-nomenological *epoche*.[55]

In essence, there remains a trans-phenomenological element in Husserl's philosophy, i.e. the living pure Ego that unifies and animates our lived-experiences. In other words, without the pure Ego, the unity of the pure stream of lived-experience would not be possible and we could not livingly comport ourselves towards something. For this reason, Husserl was rightly uncomfortable positing the pure Ego. In one of the marginal notes he wrote in the autumn of 1929 next to the paragraph in *Ideas I* about the indescrib-ability of the pure Ego, Husserl simply and tellingly writes '?!'[56] As we shall see, given Heidegger's critique we can perhaps understand why Husserl wrote this.

3.   Heidegger's criticism of Husserl's phenomenology as primordial science

Husserl's transcendental phenomenology has often been criticized for being overly theoretical and rationalistic, i.e. it is not in tune with the practical, lived nature of human existence. On the other hand, our examination of Husserl's philosophy, especially as it is developed in *Ideas II*, has compli-cated this account. For Husserl certainly had a deep sense of the practical aspects of our comportment towards the world. Heidegger was well aware of this and, consequently, his criticism of Husserl works at a more fundamen-tal level. That is, as our explication of Heidegger's critique of Husserl will show, there is a much more fundamental disagreement at work than is some-times recognized.

The true nature of Heidegger's criticism of Husserl's phenomenology con-cerns the question of the nature of philosophy itself. That this is what is at stake Heidegger makes clear in a letter he wrote to Karl Löwith in the early 1920s, where he rather scathingly remarks that 'I am now convinced that Husserl was never a philosopher, not even for one second in his life'.[57] And with equal scorn, Heidegger states in a 1923 lecture course that whereas phenomenology was 'perhaps called once to be the conscience of philosophy, it has wound up as a pimp for the public whoring of the spirit'.[58] Although rather bombastic and uncharitable, these quotations demonstrate that Heidegger did not simply disagree with Husserl about the nature of human existence. Rather, he is at odds with Husserl about the very essence of philosophy.

At the same time, we have already seen indications that Husserl afforded Heidegger important insights about the environing world, lived-experience, intentionality, etc. And though we were only able to scratch the surface of what is contained in the second book of Husserl's *Ideas*,[59] it was enough to see the profound influence it had upon Heidegger. That is, although Heidegger is highly critical of Husserl we should not allow that to conceal the profound impact that Husserl's investigations had on the young Heidegger. For instance, Heidegger makes reference to Husserl's notion of the motivational structure of life when he says that phenomenological critique 'is not refutation or counter-demonstration', but the 'positive sounding out of genuine motivations'.[60] Husserl may not have accepted this characterization of phenomenological critique, but it remains within the sphere of his own constitutional investigations. In this regard, Heidegger's notion of phenomenological critique demonstrates quite well what he is concerned with, namely, that philosophy be situated within life. Thus, when in 1919 Heidegger comes to criticize Husserl's phenomenology, he examines the motivations implicit in Husserl's approach to see if they are genuine. Namely, whether Husserl's philosophy is genuinely motivated by the idea of philosophy as primordial science or whether some alternative motive has taken hold.

To be sure, Husserl avoided Rickert's mistake of relegating philosophy to the impotent realm of ideal values. Indeed, Husserl makes the pure stream of lived-experience the 'material guideline' for phenomenological analysis. Moreover, this is a region of pre-scientific, pre-theoretical givenness, i.e. a region of 'pre-giving intentional lived-experiences'. That is, Husserl attempts to ground meaning in life, not some ideal region of being. What this demonstrates is that Husserl is *in part* formulating a science of the pre-theoretical, namely a science of what is pre-theoretically given in life and lived-experience. Phenomenology claims to be able to theoretically thematize this region of lived-experience as well as the very process in which the pre-theoretical is raised to theoretical givenness. It can achieve this, Husserl believes, because of the possibility of phenomenological reflection and its power of disclosure, i.e. the possibility and power of genuine, pure self-consciousness.

In his influential interpretation, Kisiel argues that it is at this stage that Heidegger discovers a lacuna in Husserl's thought.[61] Namely, he criticizes phenomenology's claim to be able to accurately thematize and describe lived-experience by means of phenomenological reflection. Following Natorp, Heidegger argues that reflection necessarily distorts lived-experience. In this respect, he relies on 'Natorp's double objection' to transcendental phenomenology.[62] The first objection is that, because theoretical reflection is necessarily objectifying, it is incapable of revealing lived-experience or the 'facticity of life' in its immediacy. As Natorp says, in reflection we 'till the stream' of lived-experience and therefore reflection has a necessarily 'dissective or chemically destructive' effect upon the stream of lived-experience.[63] Secondly, since description is only possible using general concepts then concrete, pre-theoretical lived-experience can never be described in its immediacy.[64] In sum, Heidegger argues that both theoretical reflection and description are 'de-vivifying' (*entleben*); that is, they distort lived-experience *as lived* by objectifying it. Consequently, Husserl's science of pre-theoretical lived-experience is doomed to fail.

Thus, in 1919 Heidegger began to try to find a philosophical approach to accessing pre-theoretical life that would not distort life by objectifying and de-vivifying it. At the same time, Heidegger hoped that this philosophical approach would remain scientific, i.e. could still claim to be 'rigorous thinking'. In other words, according to Kisiel, Heidegger thought that philosophy must grasp the primal, non-objectifiable something of pre-theoretical lived-experience. Kisiel argues that this pre-theoretical something is expressed by Heidegger through his use of the German impersonal *es*, e.g. *es wertet*, *es weltet*, etc. Since Natorp had demonstrated that Husserl's *theoretical* approach to this had failed, Heidegger sought a pre-theoretical science of immediate lived-experience and believed that key to formulating such a science was the notion of 'formal indications', viz. a way of accessing the immediacy of life that is neither objectifying or intrusive, but rather open-ended and revisable.[65] Moreover, these formal indications are not extrinsic to life, but are factically situated in life itself. In this respect, Kisiel believes that Heidegger's notion of phenomenology represents a radical departure from Husserl's transcendental phenomenology.

On the other hand, Crowell argues that, if Heidegger's philosophy is guided by the question of our *access* to the pre-theoretical immediacy of life, then it is not accurate to say that Heidegger's philosophy departed radically from Husserl's as Kisiel maintains.[66] Crowell believes that, although Heidegger may have avoided Husserl's *objectifying* interpretation of phenomenological intuition and reflection, he still relies on non-objectifying versions of these, and in fact must do so if any sense is to be made of the claim that philosophy achieves access to the immediacy of life. In other words, philosophy must somehow be able to step back from life if it is to be able to provide access to life. And this means that it must rely on some kind of non-objectifying reflective access to life that provides intuitive evidence of life. In other words, philosophy cannot simply be identical with life, but must be a kind of *thinking about* life. In the end then, Heidegger's philosophy is, according to Crowell, merely an extension of Husserl's phenomenology.

This debate represents a nice springboard for our own re-examination of Heidegger's early criticism of transcendental phenomenology. Crowell has a strong point, but only if we follow Kisiel in believing that Husserl and Heidegger more or less share the same philosophical project of gaining *access* to pre-theoretical life, namely that philosophy is essentially a *reflection upon life*. If this is the case then, to a large extent, Husserl succeeded as a philosopher. Although he did not achieve what he hoped for, viz. immediate access to what is pre-theoretical, he certainly accomplished a kind of mediated access to pre-theoretical lived-experience. Can Heidegger, understood according to Kisiel's interpretation, claim any more? For, on this account, philosophy's access to pre-theoretical lived-experience is mediated by the situatedness of factical life. That is, both Husserl and Heidegger, in their different ways, achieved mediated access to life. This seems ultimately to be Crowell's point. Namely, that Heidegger factically situated intuition and reflection, whereas Husserl did not. And if we are to judge that one approach is better than the other then we must have some evidential criteria for doing so. Thus, Husserl and Heidegger appear to be engaged in the same task, but simply coming from different perspectives.

On the other hand, to describe philosophy as 'providing access' to pre-theoretical life is a misleading way, from Heidegger's perspective, to view the relation between philosophy and life, for it has the connotation that philosophy has some pre-existing subject matter, viz. life as a primordial, pre-theoretical something, that philosophy could thematize and attempt to gain access to.[67] This itself is, even from Husserl's perspective, a theoretical enterprise. Husserl himself remarks that the theoretical attitude consists of 'seeing in a pre-eminent way' such that one is 'directed to the object in *a grasping [erfassend] way*'.[68] That is, under the current interpretation, Heidegger appears to be trying to gain a non-objectifying, although still theoretical, access to the what and how of life. However, since life for Heidegger is radically primordial, viz. an utterly incomprehensible, pre-objective and pre-theoretical something, gaining access to it seems an 'almost contradictory' attempt at 'grasping and expressing the ineffable'.[69]

Under this reading, Heidegger's philosophy as primordial science remains, in an important sense, a theoretical science. That is, it is still the attempt to stand back from life and grasp it in its what and how. To be sure, one cannot grasp life objectively, and thus, it is not a theoretical science in this sense of the word. In essence, philosophy as primordial science becomes according to this interpretation the theoretical science which attempts to grasp what is pre-theoretical, viz. the non-objectifiable, primordial something of life. Moreover, the fact that this science is situated in factical life does not fundamentally alter its theoretical character, for Husserl readily admits that natural science is situated in this sense and yet remains theoretical.

In other words, when Kisiel and Crowell characterize philosophy as a *pre-theoretical* science they take this to mean that it is the science whose subject matter is something pre-theoretical in the sense of something that is non-objectifiable. As we have argued, even this remains a theoretical science in the sense that it attempts to gain access to something. Under this interpretation of Heidegger's early philosophical project, one would tend to understand his criticism of Husserl as merely the demonstration that the pre-theoretical something cannot be objectified without deforming its 'true' character. In other words, the real disagreement between Husserl and Heidegger consists of whether the subject matter of philosophy can be objectively grasped or not.

But there is another way to understand philosophy as pre-theoretical science. Namely, that philosophy is a science that 'precedes' each and every theoretical science, viz. that philosophy is the *primordial* science. This would not simply be a science that reaches into the pre-theoretical immediacy of life in order to access to something already latently there and present it to the other sciences for examination and analysis. That is, it is not a science of a primordial subject-matter from which the other theoretical sciences derive their own peculiar subject matter. Rather it is a primordial science in the sense that it is the original act of inquiry for which the derivative theoretical sciences are but sub-inquiries, i.e. it brings the derivative theoretical sciences into existence by giving them their tasks and thus setting them in motion.

Perhaps sensing the ambiguity in the designation pre-theoretical science, Heidegger begins to describe philosophy simply as a pre-science (*Vorwissenschaft*).[70] The difference between the two senses of philosophy as pre-theoretical science involves differentiating whether the adjective 'pre-theoretical' modifies science or its subject matter. That is, the primordial nature of philosophy consists of the primordial character of its activity, rather than the primordial nature of its subject matter.

The pull of the notion that science – and especially primordial science – must be some form of access to something is so strong that one may ask in what sense the aforementioned primordial science is scientific at all? For an answer, one can start by looking at Kant's formulation of the Copernican turn in science and philosophy. In Kant's view, one misconstrues science if one conceives of it simply as an exceptional mode of inspecting something. Rather, a science is distinguished by the fact that it has a secure path to follow and so will not become a mere random groping. In other words, it must have a clear goal in mind and a secure path for achieving that goal. This is why Kant believed that Galileo was the first to set natural inquiry upon the sure path of science. In other words, Galilean science was not more scientific because it was able to achieve a better insight into nature than its predecessors had, but rather because it had a secure methodology, in relation to which the preceding attempts to inquire into nature appeared to be mere random groping. Thus, 'a new light flashed upon the mind' when it was recognized that natural science must merely explicate and elucidate what it itself had already projected into nature.

It is in this sense that philosophy is primordial science. Namely, it secures the path for every other science in a pre-eminent fashion by specifying their goals and indicating the means for achieving those goals, viz. it determines for them their task. However, neither Husserl nor Rickert understood this. For both, philosophy was merely the science of a primordial region. For example, Rickert believed that philosophy simply studies the region of absolute, ideal values. Similarly, Husserl believed that phenomenology must be the science that discloses that region of being that is absolute, namely pure consciousness. In each case, that is, philosophy is merely a peculiar science, rather than primordial science.

This is why Heidegger criticizes Husserl for making philosophy into the science of (pure) consciousness.[71] That is, Husserlian phenomenology became the theoretical, scientific inspection of a primordial region, rather than primordial science. As before, the difference consists in whether the adjective primordial applies to the science or its region of inquiry. It should be more evident then why it is problematic to suggest that Heidegger understood by philosophy the task of grasping and expressing the non-objectifiable *region* of life.

The implications of this for an authentic understanding of philosophy as primordial science will need to be worked out in the following chapters, but it is important at this stage to make two points. First, we have already indirectly begun to consider an additional aspect of primordial science as Heidegger characterizes it in his early lectures. In addition to being productive, Heidegger maintains that the idea of philosophy as primordial science is circular. In other words, he says that the idea of philosophy as primordial science '. . . must itself be scientifically demonstrated, and, as primordially scientific, only by means of primordial-scientific method'. He somewhat clarifies this in the next sentence when he says that 'The idea of philosophy must in a certain way already be scientifically elaborated in order to define itself.'[72]

As far as Heidegger is concerned, Rickert's philosophy of value and Husserl's phenomenology failed in this regard. How does the philosophy of value secure *its own* validity without presupposing the very values it claims to discover?[73] Furthermore, what is truly at the heart of Natorp's criticism of transcendental phenomenology is that he believes that, while phenomenology claims to achieve *unmediated* access to the realm of pure consciousness, its very method, namely phenomenological reflection, is itself *mediated* by theoretical objectification. That is, Natorp's objection does not presuppose that the theoretical objectification of the stream of lived-experience will necessarily distort or deform it, although at times he certainly suggests as much. Rather, he argues that theoretical reflection is mediated, not immediate, knowledge of that pure stream of lived-experience and that, therefore, Husserl cannot claim to have grasped the pure stream of lived-experiences just as it is.[74] Thus, Heidegger makes clear that the objection, properly understood, demonstrates that Husserl's phenomenology doesn't live up to its own 'primordial', scientific requirement of achieving unmediated access to pure consciousness.

The second point is connected to this last one. That is, it is important that we indicate what Heidegger found problematic about the theoretical attitude in relation to philosophy as primordial science and why the latter must be a pre-theoretical science. Even within the natural attitude the theoretical attitude represents a disengagement from practical and axiological concerns. Therefore, even though Husserl accepts that there are certain practical exigencies associated with the practice of the natural sciences, e.g. experimentation, these are excluded from the goal of the natural sciences, i.e. the theoretical grasping of the object in its 'what' separate from its use or value. The theoretical attitude of the natural attitude, therefore, removes its object from its practical or axiological context in order to examine it just as it is. It is for this reason that Heidegger argues that the theoretical attitude is de-vivifying (*entleben*). Namely, in order for it to be able to grasp its object just as it is, it must set it outside of its life-context.

However, even for Husserl, the natural theoretical attitude does not detach its object from the motivated context of lived-experience in which it is constituted for pure consciousness. It remains caught up in this. On the other hand, Heidegger argues that phenomenological reflection does isolate lived-experiences from their motivated context. For in phenomenological reflection the pure Ego no longer participates in the motivated concatenations of the stream of lived-experience, but merely looks at it. The pure Ego no longer 'goes along' with the flow of the stream of lived-experience but enacts a higher-level reflection upon it. As a theoretical attitude, this reflection merely seizes upon lived-experiences as objects of that pre-eminent form of seeing which discloses 'what' they are. As Heidegger describes it, in phenomenological reflection lived-experiences are 'no longer lived but looked at. We set the experiences *out* before us *out of* immediate experience'.[75] In this sense, phenomenological reflection excludes even the broader context which Husserl calls the 'practical attitude', namely the context in which the motivations and tendencies of life are at work and in which the environing world and everything in it is constituted.

This is why Heidegger maintains that the environing world collapses when it is subjected to theoretical reflection. And this is due to the fact that the environing world is simply the unified horizon of experience that is constituted in the totality of motivated contexts of lived-experience. It is, so to speak, a product of life itself. Thus, Heidegger says that 'environmental experience is no spurious contingency, but lies in the essence of life in and for itself'.[76] Furthermore, since Husserl himself states that a person is always the subject of an environing world, the person collapses with it.

In essence, philosophy as Husserl understands it, viz. as reflective phenomenology, is unable to be productive because it merely gazes at lived-experiences. This is also why phenomenology cannot exclude or directly grasp the pure Ego by which lived-experiences are lived-through. Namely, phenomenological reflection is itself due to a living act of the pure Ego which is not itself a lived-experience or part of the stream of lived-experiences. One is reminded of Heidegger's criticism of the deductive-dialectical method of absolute idealism, i.e. that it is 'substantively uncreative' (*sachlich unschöpferisch*), and therefore must presuppose something hidden and obscure if it is not to be condemned to an 'unproductive standstill'. Similarly, without the activity of the trans-phenomenological, living, pure Ego, phenomenology is condemned to an unproductive standstill.

Thus, in emphasizing the idea of philosophy as primordial science, Heidegger wants to resituate philosophy within life, i.e. he wants to place philosophy back into the motivational structure of life. It is for this reason that philosophy must precede the theoretical attitude. Yet, this is not so that it then can achieve some kind of repetition of life, i.e. an unproductive 'access' to life, but rather so that it can be a full participant in life.

Finally, when Heidegger speaks of the circularity of primordial science, i.e. that the idea of philosophy as primordial science must itself be scientifically discovered and determined, he argues that this means that it must already be scientifically elaborated. On the view that philosophy is a kind of access to a primordial something, the above requirement appears to entail the almost nonsensical demand that philosophy already has access to what it is striving to get access to, i.e. the so-called 'Münchhausen problem of the mind'. Once one recognizes that primordial science is so because it is a primordial activity, then the paradox disappears. For in any active process there is always the possibility, and sometimes the necessity, of moving back through the process to its origin. As Heidegger says, 'since the river flows, I can return to its source'.[77] Therefore, there is 'the possibility of a *methodological return* to primordial science from the particular sciences'.[78]

Heideggerian Reflections on Paul Natorp

Unfortunately, Paul Natorp remains a largely forgotten figure in the history of nineteenth and early twentieth-century philosophy. Indeed, even though Kisiel lists him alongside Husserl as one of Heidegger's two principal mentors, Natorp's influence on Heidegger has been given scant attention beyond his 'double objection' to phenomenology that we saw in Chapter 2.[1] On the other hand, we know indirectly that Natorp, whom Gadamer describes as 'an ice-gray little man ... with a soft and thin voice'[2], certainly had an influence upon Heidegger. For, as Gadamer relates,

> When we young people, with the irreverent glance of youth, saw the little ice-gray man with large wide-open eyes and the monumentally plain cape, he was often in the company of the young Heidegger on a walk up the Rotenberg, the younger man's attention turned respectfully to the honorable old man.[3]

Natorp, a member of the Marburg school of Neo-Kantianism, was deeply influenced by Kant's critical philosophy, but was also one of the most prominent interpreters of ancient philosophy in nineteenth-century German thought. Much of his work consisted of trying to reconcile Ancient thought, especially that of Plato, with critical philosophy – a project not so far from Heidegger's own.

In our examination of Natorp's philosophy we shall see clear affinities on a *methodological* level between it and Heidegger's project of philosophy as primordial science. There are a number of aspects of Natorp's philosophical methodology that have, not coincidentally, mirror analogues in Heidegger's early philosophical project. Perhaps most significant is the weight that Natorp places on the *a priori* task of philosophy and his suggestion that questioning plays a fundamental role in this regard.

1.   The grounding of knowledge in objectivity

In his 1887 essay, 'On the objective and subjective grounding of knowledge',[4] and again in his 1888 study, *Einleitung in die Psychologie*[5] as well as in his 1912 work, *Allgemeine Psychologie*,[6] Natorp seeks to understand knowledge by entering into the debate over whether knowledge must be grounded in objectivity or subjectivity. Unlike many traditional approaches to knowledge, Natorp wants to examine knowledge as it is given on its own and without presupposing any pre-existing conceptions of subjectivity and objectivity. That is, Natorp argues that subjectivity and objectivity are notions wholly derived from knowledge, not the other way around. More fully, objectivity and subjectivity are for Natorp merely two different ways of approaching knowledge. He says that knowledge, 'shows itself from the start as two-sided: as "content" (as what is known or to be known) and as "activity" (*Tätigkeit*) or experience (*Erlebnis*) of the subject (as knowing)'.[7] However, in the end he will argue that both sides of knowledge are grasped through objectification.

As with most Neo-Kantians, but especially those of the Marburg school, Natorp's theory emphasizes the essential connection between lawfulness, objectivity and knowledge. From the outset, Natorp stresses the fundamental import of lawfulness in the analysis of knowledge. Reminiscent of what we have already seen in Rickert's characterization of the natural sciences, Natorp proposes that science by its very nature is assigned the task of unifying discrete appearances by subsuming them under law. However, unlike Rickert he argues that every science is nomological, which was characteristic of the Marburg school. He says, 'Science, theoretical knowledge (*Erkenntnis*) considered as a whole and as a unity, seeks to unfold a unified network of laws, into which all particular laws for given appearances must fit'.[8]

Moreover, critical theory of knowledge or simply 'logic', which alone *is* genuine, scientific philosophy according to Natorp, itself seeks laws. Specifically, it seeks the fundamental lawfulness connecting knowledge with its object. That is, critical theory of knowledge grounds knowledge in the objective connection between knowledge and its object, rather than the subjective connection between the knowing subject and its known object. The question arises as to why Natorp does not think that knowledge must first be grounded in the subject. After all, knowledge is primarily an activity and comportment of the subject, is it not?

Natorp's response to this question previews the entire scope of his philosophy. As Natorp understands it, the question boils down to whether knowledge is to be grounded in given psychological structures, i.e. the view of psychologism, or whether it must be established objectively, i.e. in the objects and laws that constitute what is known. Natorp argues for the latter, because he maintains that the former presupposes the latter. It will be helpful if we first look at Natorp's response to objections against his position.

Natorp considers the objection that his own view, i.e. that knowledge is grounded in objectivity, makes it appear 'as if one were explaining the same by the same' because knowledge begins and ends in the sphere of objectivity, namely it is explaining certain objectivities, e.g. individual objects, by means of other objectivities, i.e. objective laws. Proper explanations, the opposition declares, must assign what is explained and that which explains to different realms. Natorp says that this principle makes psychologism seem more attractive because it appears as if it is *really explaining* the objectivity of knowledge since it refers it to the non-objective sphere of subjectivity. On the other hand, in terms reminiscent of Husserl's critique of psychologism, Natorp points out that in knowledge no explicit reference is made to particular events or occurrences in the psychological subject. For instance, in ascertaining whether it is known that '$2 + 2 = 4$' we are concerned only with the objective validity of the content of this claim. None of the subjective, psychological processes involved in our coming to this knowledge has any bearing on whether it is objectively valid. To interject such processes into our knowledge would end up making knowledge relative to the individual psychological processes within the individual subject, thereby effectively destroying the validity of knowledge. In this respect, any 'appeal to the subject of knowledge and the way in which consciousness participates in knowledge must on the contrary appear to us from the start as a category mistake (*metabasis eis allo genos*)'.[9]

It is interesting to consider Natorp's rejection of psychologism in the context of what first suggested the superiority of the psychologistic approach, namely that it avoids explaining the same by the same. In essence, psychologism seems a plausible explanation of knowledge because of it utilizes *reductive* explanations. Accordingly, explanation involves reducing one kind of phenomenon to another kind. On the contrary, Natorp argues that this is not genuine explanation at all, but is really just a category mistake. Consequently, Natorp gives an account of explanation that is much more akin to phenomenological description. He says,

> It is usually said that the mere reduction to law does not really explain a phenomenon, since after all it simply repeats the given state of affairs in a universal expression. Whoever says this must be understanding something very obscure by explanation. The universal expression leading a particular back to a universal pattern of occurrences contains just what has always been understood by explanation.[10]

In other words, knowledge ultimately seeks objective validity and this requires a validity that is independent of the knowing subject. Therefore,

Natorp believes that any interpretation which attempts to ground objectivity in subjectivity is from the beginning mistaken, since it attempts to ground objective validity in subjective validity.

What Natorp is arguing is that the goal of knowledge is to discover the objective validity inherent in what is to be known. The psychological conditions pertaining to knowledge, which are *ex hypothesis* distinct from what is to be known, are unable to provide the required objective validity. However, Natorp is not arguing that we can simply do away with the subjective side of knowledge. All knowledge includes a subject who knows. What he is precluding is that an analysis of knowledge requires taking into account what is going on inside of the subject. Rather, Natorp maintains that knowledge is a pre-eminent way in which the object is given to the subject who knows.

However, in addition to this argument, Natorp gives a more general argument against grounding knowledge in subjectivity. More specifically, he rejects any attempt to try to found knowledge upon a supposed 'datum' that is immediately given to subjectivity. He argues that any such datum would itself be an objectivity already posited by subjectivity and hence not something immediately given. In the end, he will hold that whatever we can objectively know is *constructed* in the activity of knowledge itself. Thus, the subjective datum is already too late to be a foundation upon which knowledge can be built.

Following the traditional position of the Marburg school of Neo-Kantianism, Natorp believes that knowledge is an infinite *task* the goal of which is to determine through progressively refined objectifications the immediacy of lived-experience.[11] In other words, knowledge of lived-experience is only possible by 'reconstructing' it objectively, i.e. by objectifying subjectivity.

Therefore, Natorp denies any attempt to make immediate lived-experience the basis of knowledge, or the view that he broadly terms 'positivism'. He remarks that

> ... positivism does not fail by seeking the ultimate given, the subjectively original 'phenomenon of ultimate authority' and seeing in it the immediacy of (subjective) consciousness. What is false is the opinion that this sought-after (actually, postulated) immediate and original content of subjective consciousness can be made the basis of *knowledge* as an immediate original *datum*.[12]

His argument for this is very telling and makes evident the influence that transcendental idealism had on his thought. Whereas positivism requires that there be some level of givenness *prior* to thought, Natorp believes that this is nothing more than an 'incomprehensible illusion'. He says of something given to us: 'If it is not determinate *for us*, then it cannot be the origin of knowledge for us, but it is only determinate for us in so far as we have determined it, and this can only happen through universal concepts.'[13] That is, Natorp sees no other way of grasping the immediacy of lived-experience than through universal concepts. Even space, time, position, etc. are for Natorp conceptual determinations and, in fact, the most general of conceptual determinations. Therefore, without the use of universal concepts, lived-experience would be entirely inexpressible and, therefore, incapable of being grasped at all. In other words, our grasp of lived-experience is always *mediated* by concepts. The very notion of pre-conceptual lived-experience as *absolutely indeterminate* is, he thinks, a mere fiction. Thus, 'The level of *pure* subjectivity would be identical with the level of absolute indeterminacy. One may reason back to this, as to the original chaos, but one cannot lay hold of it in itself'.[14] Accordingly, Natorp claims that philosophy cannot be in the business of securing some privileged region of immediate givenness 'as the primary and sole positive factor which includes [*fassen*] everything in advance'[15], as Husserl had attempted to do. For Natorp, if something is given it must be determined and determination can only be the result of a process of conceptualization.

Knowledge makes determination possible in so far as it uses concepts to unify the original, absolutely indeterminate manifold of lived-experience. Thus, a concept for Natorp is 'the Kantian (also Platonic) "unity of the manifold" ', the most proper form of which is a unifying *law*.[16] For example, the concept of space is a highly discrete law of determination. The original, absolutely undifferentiated continuum of that which is immediately there for subjectivity is discretely determined by imposing the unified, lawful structure of space upon it. A similar process takes place with regard to time. In other words, the 'stream of lived-experience' is not immediately given as a discrete series of lived-experiences. Rather, the latter is 'constructed' by imposing the lawful concept of time upon it. A similar kind of conceptualization is required in any possible determination experience. This is why Natorp thinks that pure subjectivity is nothing but an 'original chaos'. So the notion of grounding knowledge in subjectivity prior to any and all objectification is an absurd project. One can see why many, including Heidegger, described Natorp's philosophy as a 'panlogicism'. In essence, he tried to subsume the transcendental aesthetic under the transcendental logic.

In metaphysical terms, Natorp believed that the mistake positivism had made was to think that there is a determinate sense of being prior to objectivity and which is the datum of knowledge. Natorp argues, on the other hand, that being simply is objectivity and nothing more. That is, being can signify nothing more than 'the lasting unity in which the changing manifold of appearances is unified and determined in thought. This significance of the object, of "being" differentiated from "appearing", has been won for philosophy since Plato, or perhaps since the Eleatics'.[17] If pure subjectivity or pure lived-experience *is* at all, it can only be so as an object and this can only be achieved through the activity of knowledge.

Consequently, the fundamental question for Natorp is how can we ground knowledge in objectivity? Or, to put the same question differently, in what does objective *validity* consist?

2.   The task of knowledge

Even Natorp admits that something must be 'given' before the achievements of knowledge, namely 'something subjectively original and immediate'.[18] What is so given is the *task* of knowledge and that upon which it works: its material, so to speak. The latter represents nothing determinate, but the mere possibility of determination. Natorp calls this the 'undetermined determinable' of knowledge or simply 'appearance' as understood in opposition to being. He says that 'the appearance is only "given" in the act as a *determinable X which is now to be determined*, like an Aristotelian potential being'.[19] In an important sense, what is ultimately *a priori* to knowledge is the very task of knowledge itself and the undetermined determinable.

It is important that we understand the way in which Natorp conceives the task of knowledge. He begins by arguing that the notion of objectivity, from the perspective of knowledge, is analogous to the unknown of an equation. That is, the task of knowledge is originally faced with an equation to be solved that contains something unknown. In the present case, this unkown is the object that is to be known or the undetermined X of knowledge. However, just as in a mathematical problem, where an unknown quantity can be resolved only if it is situated within the context of an equation that specifies the terms of the solution, so the object to be known must be located within the task of knowledge and this task specifies the terms of the 'solution'. Thus, Natorp argues that

It is necessary that knowledge have an original relation to the object if even the question concerning the object and the demand for knowledge to agree with the object are to have a specifiable meaning. And indeed, as the universal meaning (*Sinn*) of the X is predetermined by the form of the equation, in the same way the universal meaning of the object will be predetermined by that which we call the 'form' of knowledge.[20]

In essence, Natorp is arguing that the object to be known is projected or 'predetermined' by the task of knowledge. As we shall see in the last chapters a similar notion will become a hallmark of Heidegger's analysis of Dasein's understanding of being. Striking evidence of this similarity comes from Natorp's *Logische Grundlagen* (a work that Heidegger quotes from in 1919), where Natorp's description of the object of knowledge could practically have come from Heidegger's own pen. Natorp says,

> The word 'Object', a Latin term which in literal German would be 'Gegenwurf' (that which is thrown over against) or, more freely rendered, 'Vorwurf' (that which is thrown ahead), stands as the almost exact translation of the Greek 'pro-blema' (that which is thrown forward) ... The basic sorts of relation which makes knowledge possible are presupposed and already sketched in advance in the 'Vorwurf' of knowledge, they are 'cast forward' ('entworfen'). The object of knowledge becomes a project, the thrown-over-against that is thrown-ahead (das Objekt der Erkenntnis wird Projekt, das Gegenwurf Vorwurf).[21]

In many respects, Natorp's position does not display a radically new conception of philosophy, but is rather the rigorous application of Kant's own Copernican turn to philosophy understood as the science of knowledge. Indeed, Natorp simply applies to the theory of knowledge the same methodology that was able to set Greek mathematics and modern physics on the secure path of science.

What are the terms of the projection in this case? How is the undetermined determinable to be objectified? The equation of knowledge, Natorp contends, specifies that objectification be lawful, viz. that determination take place by the constructive application of lawful unities (concepts) to appearances.[22] As an illustration, think again of the lawful order that the geometrical concept of space imposes on external appearance. In essence, the task of knowledge projects that objectification according to law is the task of every special science, each of which lawfully objectifies experience according to its own particular subject matter. In relation to such scientific objectification, all other processes of objectification must appear as 'merely random groping'. Natorp sums this up by declaring that 'the law of *lawfulness itself* [is] the basic objective law of knowledge. This is the law that the view of things according to laws is the true and objective view. All specific laws of knowledge are only the specific concrete forms of this basic law'.[23]

Natorp believes that pure appearance, or what he calls 'pure subjectivity', can never be completely and thoroughly objectified by any *finite* process of objectification. In other words, the determinability of the undetermined determinable can never be exhausted. What follows from this is his characteristic claim that the task of knowledge is an infinite project.

In addition, even though the goal of knowledge is lawful objectification this does not mean that the subjective side of knowledge, viz. the activity and lived-experience of the subject in relation to knowledge, is simply set aside. As was earlier mentioned, Natorp believes that knowledge is two-sided. Consequently, he believes that there are two paths in which the task of knowledge proceeds towards objectification. On the one hand, there is the path of objectification which determines according to 'being', viz. objectification independent of the subject or what we may call extant objectification. On the other hand, there is objectification along the path of 'appearance'. This deals with the *objective* laws of subjective determination, i.e. the laws governing how subjects actively go about unifying and relating their lived-experience. Or, what we may very generally call objective psychology.

Again, objectification according to the concept of space is a good way to demonstrate what Natorp is getting at. When the concept of space has been imposed upon 'pure appearance' then a world of spatially locatable objects is constructed which includes the subject as also spatially located. The lawful relations governing such a spatially ordered world determines objectively the way in which any given object will appear to any given subject or, put differently, how the subject will experience the object, e.g. from a particular angle, etc. Of course, such spatial determination only partially characterizes the way in which the object will be experienced and is in need of further supplementation by the laws of physics, physiology, etc. By applying these laws one can objectively determine the elements of the subject's lived-experience of the appearing object. And from these elements, Natorp thinks, one can then lawfully 'reconstruct' the psychological processes, or, more correctly, the 'activity' (*Tätigkeit*) of the subject that would lead to the particular unification of the manifold by means of which the object was actively constructed in the first place. For instance, that such an object is constructed through the lawful unification of the manifold aspects of its appearance to a subject. Thus our *objective knowledge* of the activity and lived-experience of the subject is not just a construction, but a *reconstruction*. This is of course but a rough indication of the type of process that Natorp has in mind.

The general point is that there are two paths by which the undetermined determinable can be objectified. One path objectifies it according to its 'being' and the other according to the way in which it 'appears'. Thus, the being and appearance of the object of knowledge are merely two sides of the same coin. On the one hand, one may construct the object of knowledge from the side of its being and then, through a process of more refined objective determination, construct how that object would appear to a subject. On the other hand, one can proceed from the 'appearance' of the object to a subject in its lived-experience of that object and reconstruct the process by which the subject could have lawfully constructed the appearing object.

Moreover, given a more or less crude or refined degree of the objective determination of the being of the object, one would expect a correspondingly crude or refined determination of the appearance of the object to a subject and vice versa. Therefore, in the process of moving along one path to the other and back again the object itself becomes progressively determined, although, as was noted, a full determination of the object is an infinite project. That is, only in an infinite progression of such back and forth determinations would the object be completely determined. However, the two paths towards objective determination are always correlated with one another and thus are progressing in the same direction or, put differently, are seen as different objectifications of the same object. This is why Natorp says that in knowledge 'The object should be the object for the appearance; the appearance should be proven to be the appearance of the object'.[24]

Thus, the progress of knowledge comprises alternating processes of construction and reconstruction. Since both paths consist of objectification, Natorp sometimes refers to each of these processes, respectively, as objectification and objectifying subjectivity. He says,

> The *constructive* objectifying achievement of knowledge always comes first; from it we *reconstruct* as far as possible the level of original subjectivity which could never be reached by knowledge apart from this *reconstruction* which proceeds from the already completed objective construction. In this reconstruction we, so to speak, objectify subjectivity as such.[25]

As we have seen, these two paths work together in so far as each path helps refine the other and so on and so forth. However, as we said, the two paths of objectification and objectifying subjectivity are two aspects towards one and the same object of knowledge and therefore must converge in the infinite horizon of the absolute determination of the object or, as Natorp also calls it, the absolute 'concretization' of the object. Natorp believes this theory represents in a scientifically adequate fashion the 'double movement' of philosophical dialectic from particularity to universality and then from universality to particularity that was first conceived by Plato.[26]

3.   Methodological considerations and the role of questioning in Natorp's philosophy

Along with Rickert, Natorp maintains that knowledge is goal-oriented, but unlike Rickert, he maintains that the goal of knowledge is not the realization of a merely ideal value, but rather the progressive constitution of the object both from the perspective of objectivity or being and from the perspective of subjectivity or appearance. Contra Husserl, Natorp proposes a thoroughly 'logical' resolution of the problem of knowledge, i.e. one which does not rely on an experiential, intuitive foundation. Finally, contrary to both Rickert and Husserl, Natorp's resolution of the problem of knowledge depends on neither the immediacy of logical idealities nor the immediacy of absolute experiential intuition. Instead, according to Natorp, the conceptual and the experiential (which are both logical constructs for Natorp) mediate one another within the process of knowledge.

For this reason, Heidegger remarks that in Natorp's philosophy there are 'unmistakable connections with Hegel: everything unmediated is mediated' and that it represents 'the most radical absolutization of the theoretical and logical, an absolutization that has not been proclaimed since Hegel'.[27] However, this evaluation predates Heidegger's close personal interaction with Natorp that took place when Heidegger moved to Marburg. In addition, at the time that Heidegger wrote these words he also remarks that Natorp's position is 'so difficult'.

There is, without a doubt, a profound logical element in Natorp's philosophy. At the same time, however, Natorp maintains that his conception of knowledge, especially the correlation between lawfulness and objectivity, is not the result of mere speculation or a desire for system, but is borne out in the practice and activity of science itself. He says that it 'has been established not through the whim or the passion for system of this or that philosopher, but rather *through the action of science that everywhere constitutes the object in law*'.[28] Thus he is explicitly distancing himself from the systems of absolute idealism.

In fact, as a task, knowledge cannot be circumscribed by any finished system of knowledge, for these are only stages along the way of the endless task of knowledge. Any system of knowledge, no matter how thorough and complete it may be, is merely one stage of this unending task, i.e. one conceptual and experiential scheme of objectification. This applies even to systems of absolute idealism such as Hegel's. Having said this, one must keep in mind that this does not signify that Natorp endorses a relativistic stance towards such systems of knowledge. In truth, Natorp believes that every system of knowledge is an expression of the working out of the task of knowledge and that progress has been made toward realizing the goal of knowledge.

One witnesses this in Natorp's interpretation of the history of philosophy, which does exhibit a distinctly Hegelian approach in so far as that history is understood in relation to the task and goal of knowledge. As we have mentioned, Natorp believes that it was Plato (or perhaps the Eleatics) who first formulated the task of knowledge in so far as he was the first to differentiate being from appearance. Moreover, he was the first to formulate the task of knowledge as bringing being and appearance into a relational unity. According to Natorp, it was also Plato who took the next significant step by recognizing that being was characterized by universality while appearances were concrete and particular. More specifically, Plato realized that the being of an object is comprised of its universal determinations, viz. genus and species, while its appearance consists of particular instances of such universal determinations. Plato's mistake, however, was to reify these by arguing that being consists of rational, universal forms or ideas, on the one hand, and that appearance is circumscribed by the so-called sensible world which contains concrete, particular and imperfect instances of these ideal forms, on the other hand.

Natorp argues that modernity advanced beyond these pre-modern, reified conceptions of being and appearance by recognizing that they depended upon the activity of subjectivity. In other words, modernity was able to avoid the pre-modern, metaphysical interpretation of universality and particularity by understanding them in a more rigorous, epistemological fashion. This culminates in the genuinely critical view that being signifies the universal, nomological laws constructed by consciousness in order to unify a series of particular appearances, which in the end are themselves seen as concrete instantiations or determinations of those laws.

Natorp believes that if we adhere to the essence of knowledge itself and do not presuppose an uncritical concept of objectivity we see that what it seeks is laws and that, therefore, these are the true objects of knowledge. Furthermore, he believes that this view is not totally alien to ancient conceptions of objectivity since even Aristotle conceived of substance as the unity that underlies change. However, the true objects of knowledge are neither Platonic ideas nor Aristotelian substances, which to Natorp's mind are simply dogmatic, metaphysical notions of objectivity, but rather the laws that unify the manifold of appearances given to consciousness. Recognizing this was, in Natorp's mind, one of Kant's great achievements, and Natorp sees his own theory of knowledge as merely the extension of this to philosophy itself.

In fact, Natorp believes that he is able to resolve the critique of knowledge and, specifically, the distinction between subject and object, into the relation between universal and particular: a relation that he argues has dominated philosophy since its inception. That is, the problem of knowledge no longer needs to be dominated by ultimately dogmatic 'metaphysical' assumptions about the nature of the subject and object and the relation between the two. Rather, the problem of knowledge becomes a *logical* problem, i.e. the relation between law (the universal) and instance of law (the particular). In addition, Natorp thinks that this clarifies why objectivity and subjectivity are necessarily correlated to one another. That is, what we call objectivity and subjectivity are, properly understood, merely law and instance of law and so they *must* be correlated with one another in the simple sense that neither makes sense without the other.

In other words, Natorp views the history of philosophy as a unified progression towards a single goal, determined by the task of knowledge as it was originally formulated by the Greeks. It is interesting to note in this regard, that Natorp's approach fulfils one of the criteria of phenomenology, namely that it does not work from a preconceived standpoint or theory. All standpoints and all theories are, as far as Natorp is concerned, merely products of the task of knowledge, which precedes them all. Moreover, for him, the task of knowledge is the transcendental condition for the possibility of any possible system of knowledge precisely because all conceptual and experiential schemes, as we have called them here, are stages upon the way toward the completion of the task of knowledge. Finally, Natorp believes that the task of knowledge is ultimately what is *a priori* in knowledge, rather than a system of concepts or immediately given experiences.

Having said this, Natorp believes that 'pre-given' systems of concepts and experiences certainly have a role to play in furthering scientific knowledge. That is, in the infinite process of refining the objectifications of knowledge one is always developing previous conceptual and experiential schemes. In addition, he maintains that there is a natural, pre-scientific form of objectification. Prior to scientific examination, crude objectifications are constructed in everyday life, viz. intersubjective 'things'. Natorp holds that we naturally construct objects from out of the multitude of ways in which they appear to many different subjects. That is, we construct an intersubjective object.

This happens largely unconsciously and Natorp argues that it is in large part a function of language. He says, 'even common representations seek [univocal determinations of objects]; in its naming, in the unified meaning of words'.[29] Because this construction is so natural and unnoticed, one tends to assume that what has happened is that an independent object has passively affected a subject in such a way as to produce appearances in that subject. Subsequent to this, it is believed, the subject actively develops a *new* relation to these objects by reasoning from the appearances back to the object, most rigorously through knowledge. Natorp thinks that this explains the appeal of a subjective grounding for knowledge.

What is obscured in this natural process of objectification is that these intersubjective objects are in truth simply pre-scientific constructions of the activity of knowing. Explicit scientific knowledge represents a more exacting construction of objects, e.g. through lawful objectification. However, they are still part of one process, since these latter objectifications 'attempt to fulfil in a more developed and durable way the same tasks which language fulfils sufficiently for the immediate purposes of practical life'.[30] That is, both in everyday life and in our scientific activity we are engaged in the task of knowing in so far as we are objectively constructing the world around us. Philosophy, or transcendental critique of knowledge, is, according to Natorp, the most self-conscious form of engaging in the task of knowledge. For it proposes that the task of knowledge is itself to be lawfully carried out, namely that the law governing knowledge itself prescribes that science lawfully objectify the undetermined determinable in every case. Thus, we can see the various contours of the activity of carrying out the task of knowledge from its most primitive or natural form, to its scientific form, and finally to its critical-transcendental or philosophical form.

At this point, one can understand why Natorp thought that knowledge must be grounded in objectivity. As far as Natorp is concerned, this is merely the radicalization of the procedure that secured the validity of Greek mathematics and modern natural science and which Kant had explained in the preface to the second edition of the first *Critique*. Understood in this way, genuine scientific knowledge does not consist of a system, a theory, or a privileged set of judgements, but rather a *methodology*, viz. a way of proceeding scientifically.

According to Natorp, philosophy, as the most pre-eminent form of this, represents the most self-conscious application of this methodology. Indeed, it makes following this methodology into a law. This represents, in his mind, the perfection of knowledge, for 'it is precisely knowledge's business [*Sache*] to proceed with consciousness, *to know what it does and why*'.[31] At bottom then, Natorp's philosophy is clearly not a naively theoretical enterprise. It may rely exclusively on conceptualization in order to constructively objectify all lived-experience, which is certainly part and parcel of a theoretical approach, but ultimately Natorp's reflections on knowledge are guided by the activity of knowledge. He says, 'To question this consciousness of knowledge [i.e. the one that knows what it does and why] about its own activity was the direction indicated by our first considerations'.[32]

What guided the first considerations Natorp mentions? For one, the fundamental relation that knowledge bears to its object. We have seen that Natorp believes that this relation consists in the productive capacity of knowledge to construct its object according to lawful concepts. That is, the concept projects a lawful scheme through which objects can be actively formed in the process of knowledge. But a more important consideration is the way in which knowledge is able to *self-consciously* produce its object according to a determinate plan. And this is the function of a transcendental critique of knowledge. That is, by raising the activity of knowledge to self-consciousness a transcendental critique allows knowledge to proceed securely in its intended direction. This signifies that knowledge as a task finds its fulfilment in self-consciously carrying through this task, i.e. through its achievement. One could say that Natorp views the fulfilment of the task of knowledge as occurring in precisely the way that Husserl characterizes the pre-eminent living that takes place in the natural practical attitude, wherein 'the true and proper [*eigentliche*] performance lies in the willing and the doing', namely living 'in willful self-resolve or else in the activity of actually carrying out that resolve'.[33]

But, Husserl may reply, doesn't the fact that the task of knowledge must be carried out self-consciously require that one reflect upon the goal of the activity of knowledge? Broadly construed, yes. However, the reflection required is not theoretical reflection as Husserl understands this, viz. a form of reflection that is concerned purely with the 'what' of the goal to the exclusion of the practical considerations entailed in achieving the goal. That is, the de-vivifying character of theoretical reflection is appropriate only if one is concerned with directing doxic-theoretic acts towards the objectified goal that results from theoretical reflection. Such doxic-theoretic considerations are more or less useless if one is concerned with carrying out the task whose goal it is. In essence, Rickert makes the mistake of interpreting the primacy of the practical along theoretical lines by suggesting that this entails a theoretical science of values. Husserl also prejudices the theoretical attitude by giving primacy to the theoretical givenness of the objects of the practical attitude. The focus is then shifted toward the eidetic character of the goal and its evidential and intuitive givenness and away from the practical achievement of the goal.

In the end, the theoretical approach to knowledge will always be driven toward a privileged region of objects that are evidentially and intuitively given in an exemplary manner, and that, because of this, serve as the *a priori foundation* for all further knowledge. This is evident in Rickert and Husserl's philosophy to the extent that each reduced philosophy to the science of a privileged region, i.e. the science of value and the science of consciousness, respectively. Natorp's approach, on the other hand, seeks to formulate a philosophy that represents in an exemplary fashion the activity of science itself.

How, then, is the activity and task of knowledge given? When Natorp analyses the task of knowledge, specifically the relation that knowledge bears to its object, he argues that 'the meaning of this relation must be discoverable through analyzing what the questioner about the object intends, seeks, and since he seeks, presupposes'.[34] That is, it is questioning that sets forth and projects a task of knowing. Later, Natorp's student Gadamer will make something similar an essential aspect of his hermeneutic philosophy, i.e. questioning becomes the 'hermeneutical *Urphänomen*: No assertion is possible that cannot be understood as an answer to a question, and assertions can only be understood in this way'.[35] And, as we shall see, there are clear affinities between Natorp's focus on questioning and the centrality of questioning in Heidegger's philosophy. Finally, it is telling that Husserl, who took a traditional, theoretical approach to knowledge, consistently mistook the act of questioning for a doxic act, associating it with judgement, belief, doubt, etc.[36]

Natorp, therefore, makes the transition from knowledge as an equation to knowledge as scientific questioning. To discover the essence of knowledge one must look to what is sought after in scientific questioning. What is sought after in scientific questioning is objectivity. When one asks a question, moreover, the question is not *devoid* of meaning; rather, what is sought after in the question, analogous to the not yet determined X of the equation, is meaningful only to the extent that it is given in the context of the relations and constants of the question. The very fact that a question is asked necessitates that what is sought after in the question is contextualized according to the terms of the question, i.e. the basic possibilities of its determination are pre-given. As previously quoted, in the case of knowledge, '... The basic sorts of relation which makes knowledge possible are presupposed and already sketched in advance in the "Vorwurf" of knowledge [as an equation].' So inherent to any question is a general relation between that which is sought after in the question and that according to which it is questioned.

In this regard, and typical of the Marburg school of Neo-Kantianism, Natorp will assert that what the questioner intends and seeks in knowledge is the law. That is, he reduces the task of knowledge to an intensification of the task carried out by the natural sciences. However, this should not obscure the fact that Natorp has achieved a radical shift in the critical project away from a theoretical approach to a practical one. This of course has implications for the way in which a critical approach to knowledge is to be achieved. We have already indicated how Natorp sees this in terms of self-consciously carrying through the task of knowledge. How are we then to 'self-consciously' carry through the task of knowledge?

At this point, it seems clear that Natorp envisions that this self-consciousness is achieved through *deliberation* on the task of knowledge, i.e. a reasoned analysis with an eye towards action. Counterpose this to Husserl's theoretically oriented self-reflection. In the latter, self-reflection is geared towards *demonstration*, i.e. proof through intuitive fulfilment. Natorp on the other hand seeks to explicitly articulate the goal of knowledge through an examination of what the question of knowledge intends, seeks and presupposes, all with an eye towards tracing out the path for achieving this goal. For instance, Natorp argues that the 'objective' and 'subjective' paths of objectification are different though equally essential means for progressing towards the completion of the task of knowledge. Indeed, Natorp's entire account of knowledge consists of *how* to carry out the task of knowledge, rather than ascertaining 'what' it is.

4. Heidegger's criticism and appropriation of Natorp's philosophy

Given all of this, how does Natorp's philosophy hold up as primordial science? As we saw in Chapters 1 and 2, Heidegger believes that Rickert and Husserl's philosophies failed to satisfy the idea of philosophy as primordial science. Neither articulated a science that precedes the theoretical sciences. Rather, each in its own way developed an 'unproductive' science of an *Urregion*. Although in Husserl's case the *Urregion* of the pure stream of lived-experience is productive in so far as in it is constituted the world and everything therein, his phenomenological science of this primal region itself is merely a theoretical gazing upon and descriptive analysis of this primordial region.

Natorp, on the other hand, appears to have articulated something like a primordial science. It is certainly pre-theoretical in one important sense, viz. that it 'precedes' all objectification in so far as it represents the fully self-conscious carrying through of the task of knowledge which is to construct objects according to law. So, if a theoretical science is by nature objectifying, then Natorp has given us an idea of philosophy as a science that precedes the theoretical sciences. Moreover, it is the origin of the rest of the sciences precisely in so far as it is the exemplary form of the activity of science. In other words, it was latent in the original historical stirrings of the act of knowing as the perfection of that activity. This can be seen in the fact that it is in the end a result of deliberation upon this activity, i.e. an attempt to carry it through securely.

However, Natorp, as with Rickert and Husserl, leaves untouched the way in which knowledge and science are set in motion, viz. what enlivens the task of knowledge. For Rickert this was indicated by the metalogical factor that was necessary in realizing the sciences and in Husserl it was signified by the impossibility of excluding the living, pure Ego in the phenomenological *epoche* as well as phenomenology's inability to grasp and analyse it. What each leave in the background is philosophy as a full participant in life, as was mentioned in Chapter 2. Or, put another way, each miss *how* philosophy is lived.

On this count, Natorp comes closer than Rickert or Husserl to formulating philosophy as primordial science. Rickert saw philosophy as directed towards idealities that, in principle, bore no relation to the realities of life in so far as they existed in a separate realm from that of being. Husserl looked to philosophy to exhibit the being of pure lived-experience and all that is constituted through it, but because his phenomenology relied so heavily on theoretical reflection this became a lifeless, 'de-vivified', primal region of objects available for theoretical inspection. This necessitated a 'trans-phenomenological' principle to bring it back to life. Natorp, however, focuses on the activity of science and knowledge itself. That is, he did not relegate philosophy to the scientific study of some fundamental region of objects, but saw philosophy as primordial with regard to the activity of knowledge and science. In this respect, Natorp is able to unify the sciences by situating them all within a single primordial task of knowledge realized in scientific questioning, rather than in a transcendental realm.

In 1919, Heidegger criticizes Natorp's method of reconstruction because it too is objectifying and thus de-vivifying.[37] In particular, he says that Natorp's philosophy does not achieve what it set out to, viz. reconstruct lived-experience as it was prior to objective analysis. Heidegger notes that this is because it lacks a 'standard for reconstruction'. Since Natorp maintains that lived-experience cannot be given prior to objectification there is no justification for him claiming that a reconstruction represents lived-experience as it was prior to the reconstruction. Writing in 1919, it seems that Heidegger has misunderstood Natorp's philosophy. That is, he assumes that in criticizing Husserl's phenomenological approach to lived-experience, viz. that phenomenological reflection provides an unmediated disclosure of lived-experience, Natorp is setting out the purpose of his own philosophy, i.e. to disclose lived-experience just as it is prior to analysis. As Heidegger himself quite correctly shows, this cannot be achieved through an objective reconstruction of lived-experience.

On the other hand, Natorp never maintains that the reconstruction of lived-experience is supposed to reveal lived-experience as it was prior to all analysis. Rather, the reconstruction of lived-experience is the way in which the subjective path toward knowledge is objectively determined. In essence, this is simply a path that the task of knowledge must take if it is to progress towards its infinite goal of complete objective determination of the undetermined determinable.

Moreover, in his review of the first volume of Husserl's *Logical Investigations*,[38] he demonstrates that what he is really concerned about is that the subjective side of knowledge not become an 'uncomprehended, irrational surd'. He says,

> There also remains unresolved, in Husserl, the *opposition* between formal and material, *a priori* and empirical, and along with it that between the logical and the psychological, the objective and the subjective; or, to put it in one word and at the same time in his own terminology: the ideal and the real. The material, empirical, psychological i.e. the 'real' remains an uncomprehended, irrational surd.[39]

That is, the goal of Natorp's philosophy is not to reconstruct lived-experience as it was prior to all analysis, as Heidegger appears to interpret him, but that lived-experience not be left uncomprehended. Natorp's primary concern is to encompass subjectivity within the task of knowledge. Given this, it is clear what role the objective reconstruction of subjectivity is supposed to serve.

Although Heidegger's criticism misses the mark in this regard, one can see the trenchancy of his criticism when it is viewed in the larger context of the idea of philosophy as primordial science. Namely, is the critical, philosophical task of knowledge as Natorp describes it truly primordial science? Natorp indicates that the task of knowledge must be discoverable by analysing the questioner and what he or she intends, seeks and thus presupposes. Looking at Heidegger's criticism from a broader context, we can see that he is insinuating that Natorp's philosophy does not have the resources to do this. In this case, the fact that Natorp's method is objectifying poses problems for his analysis, for if objectification is de-vivifying then the activity and lived-experience of the questioner and the act of questioning has been stripped from its proper lived context, e.g. the motivational structures of life. Put differently, since Natorp himself maintains that the task of knowledge precedes every objectification, how can he make his way back to that which grounds the task of knowledge using an objectifying method?

Heidegger might ask, 'since the river flows' can Natorp use his proposed method to 'return to its source'? Heidegger does not think so.

To a large extent, the problem Natorp faces results from the fact that he relies so heavily on the natural sciences for his model of knowledge. That is, he is left with no resources for returning to what is, in essence, a historical phenomenon. Whether in construction or in reconstruction, his method proceeds according to the objectification that determines nature, namely the undetermined determinable X that is to be objectified according to law. Using this method it is impossible to return to the concrete phenomenon of the questioner and the act of questioning in order to examine what it means for the questioner to intend, seek and presuppose something. That is, how is questioning situated within life?

As we have already pointed out, Natorp is not alone in this regard. Rickert and Husserl face a similar problem. Rickert, Husserl and Natorp recognize the importance of situating their philosophy within life, but each formulates a philosophy that precludes an examination of life. This is why Heidegger turns to Dilthey and his analysis of life, lived-experience and historical method. Before turning to Dilthey, however, let us briefly examine the question of what Heidegger appropriated from Natorp.

It is not uncommon to see Heidegger's philosophy presented as a radicalization of Husserl's transcendental phenomenology.[40] And there are good reasons for such a reading. On the other hand, it is virtually unheard of to find a reading of Heidegger's philosophy as a radicalized version of Natorp's philosophy. One hopes that the account we have just given of Natorp's philosophy goes a little way towards making such a reading less startling.

For example, Heidegger's criticisms of Husserl certainly show the marked influence of Natorp's philosophical approach. That is, Heidegger, like Natorp, maintains a robust mistrust of phenomenology's self-assured reliance on the power of immediate evidence. In fact, he thinks that phenomenologists are frequently led astray by their trust in evidence.

For instance, Heidegger says that phenomenology frequently philosophizes 'without presuppositions' in a bad sense. Specifically, when 'One fails to see what is characteristic of all intuition, namely, that it actualizes itself in the context of a definite orientation and an anticipatory foreconception of the respective region of experience'.[41] Philosophy loses sight of this, as Husserl did, when it is driven towards immediate intuition, viz. a 'pure act of seeing'. In essence, one is so intent on achieving an immediate act of seeing, that one ignores the activity of thinking, or more specifically, the activity of inquiry that provided the anticipatory foreconceptions that made the supposed 'immediate' intuitions possible. Ironically, Husserl was so careful to emphasize the constitutive foreconceptions that lay behind the special sciences, while he simultaneously denied that any foreconceptions played a role in phenomenology itself. Consider this passage from Husserl's lectures on 'The idea of phenomenology':

> ... those forms of thought that I actually realize in thinking are given to me in so far as I *reflect* on them, accept them and posit them in a *pure act of seeing ... every experience whatsoever, can be made into an object of pure seeing and apprehension* while it is occurring. *And in this act of seeing it is an absolute givenness.*[42]

Is this act of seeing really 'pure' in the sense of being entirely unmotivated in such a way that it is not guided by any foreconceptions? Heidegger would argue that, as a living act, it clearly is caught up in the motivational tendencies of life. More significantly, Husserl's very notion of such a pure act of seeing is grounded in his foreconception of what philosophy should be and what it requires. Most specifically, Husserl's philosophy is driven by a desire for certainty, which he believes can only be fulfilled in immediate, intuitive givenness. This causes Husserl to 'fall prey to a certain blindness regarding the fact that [his philosophy's] motivational basis is itself in the end not primordial'.[43]

Ultimately, the importance of Natorp's approach to knowledge and his critique of Husserl is to point out that *all* givenness is a consequence of a prior act of foreconceptualization and, more fundamentally, a prior act of questioning. That is, according to Natorp, every inquiry seeks after something and, consequently, embodies a foreconception of what is sought. In other words, there is no 'pure' seeing or 'absolute' givenness or, put more exactly, such seeing and givenness is in truth guided by preconceptions and a determinate direction of inquiry. In the end, Natorp's philosophy truly captures the spirit of Kant's famous claim that 'intuitions without concepts are blind'.[44]

Moreover, in important respects, Heidegger's project of fundamental ontology is a radicalization of Natorp's task of knowledge. First, where Natorp was concerned with the question of the relation between knowledge and its object, Heidegger's project of fundamental ontology examines the question of the meaning of being, where being is always the being of a being. Second, Natorp specified that the relation between knowledge and its object was that of the construction of its object according to law. In the winter semester of 1921–2, Heidegger will appropriate this to fundamental ontology through his notion of philosophical definitions as 'formal-indications' or 'formal-indicative definitions of principle'.

As Heidegger describes it, a formal-indicative definition 'does not present fully and properly the object which is to be determined', but only gives 'in advance the principle of the object'.[45] Moreover, 'An indicative definition includes the sense that concretion is not to be possessed there without further ado but that the concrete instead presents a task of its own kind and a peculiarly constituted task of actualization'.[46] Finally, instead of the task of the concretization of the object of knowledge characteristic of Natorp's position, fundamental ontology will comprise Dasein's working out of its own concrete *Existenz*. In the coming chapters, we shall examine how Heidegger develops these ideas, and in the process we will see how they show clear signs of Natorp's influence.

Dilthey on Life, Lived-Experience and Worldview Philosophy

Although an early influence on Heidegger, Dilthey begins to play a more prominent role in the mid-1920s.[1] This is perhaps most evident in the second division of *Being and Time*, where the concepts of temporality and historicity are central. Heidegger praises Dilthey for his fundamental insights into life and the 'being of man'.[2] In this chapter, we will examine the way in which Dilthey attempts to situate the theory of knowledge and philosophy within life, lived-experience and history. Dilthey refuses to allow philosophy and knowledge to be extracted from life. In this way, he achieves what Rickert, Husserl and Natorp were unable to, viz. to see philosophy as a full participant in life and also as a condition of life. Moreover, he provides Heidegger with resources for determining philosophy as primordial science.

1.   Dilthey's critique of historical knowledge

In the end, Rickert, Husserl and Natorp do not have at their disposal the necessary resources for including within the range of their philosophical inquiries considerations of the living-context in which philosophy arises. Unless we can discover a science that precedes the theoretical sciences and the theoretical attitude, i.e. a pre-theoretical science, then we shall never understand how science and philosophy are situated within life. In this regard, Dilthey's critique of historical knowledge, viz. his critique of the *scientific* approach to history and historical phenomenon, moves us closer to seeing how thought is located in life. For Dilthey, the goal of a critique of historical knowledge is to reach a critical understanding of historical science that does not begin by taking up a theoretical perspective and, specifically, an objectifying approach.

In advance of his critique, Dilthey investigates the task and method of the human sciences. The reason for this particular starting point lies in the fact that the human sciences refer 'to human beings [and] their relations to one another and outer nature ... They are all founded in lived-experience, in the expressions for lived-experiences and in the understanding of these expressions'.[3] That is, the human sciences attempt to thematize human existence as lived, rather than as merely an object of theoretical sighting. Dilthey believes that precisely for this reason these studies must rely on a method and mode of 'reflection' (*Besinnung*) that is mediated. That is, in these disciplines one cannot simply step outside of life in order to gaze at it. Life and lived-experience is always operative.

Consequently, these disciplines require that one must indirectly, yet scientifically, come to an understanding of forms of life and of complexes of lived-experience that are not *immediately given* for inspection, but for which we have concrete expressions (texts, institutions, actions, etc.). This is accomplished partly by interpreting these expressions with regard to a unified nexus of expressions, i.e. by situating each individual expression within a larger, more *original* complex of expressions; for example, when a historical event or figure is situated within a larger historical context. However, in the end, expressions and complexes of expressions are understood only in so far as they can be traced back to the lived-experiences that produced them. This means for Dilthey that they must be traced back to what he calls the 'life nexus' (*Lebenszusammenhang*), i.e. the living 'reality' that expresses itself in these expressions. For example, in the science of history the understanding of historical expressions and complexes of historical expressions consists of interpreting them back into the life nexus that 'produced' them or, more exactly, that *expressed* itself in them.

A life nexus and its expressions are related to one another as one individual's lived-experiences are to their possible expression. That is, I *understand* someone's lived-experiences by *interpreting* his or her expressions of those lived-experiences. More generally, I understand the lived-experience(s) of another by interpreting them within the total context of that person's expressions. The ultimate goal would be to understand the whole of their life nexus, i.e. the unified totality of their lived-experiences, but of course, at any given time, we can only approximate this. The fact that this understanding is a form of interpretation already indicates that the proper method of the human sciences will be hermeneutic. That is, whereas the task of the natural sciences is to explain (*erklären*) phenomenon, the task of the human sciences is to understand (*verstehen*) the expressions of life.

The natural sciences explain the physical or natural realization of expressions, e.g. the writing on the page or the sounds that are made, by discovering the physical or natural *causes* of these. For instance, explanatory psychology investigates the *causal* connections between 'mental life' and its physical or natural effects. Like any natural science it investigates *only* causal structures. Dilthey argues that it accomplishes this by breaking experience down into fundamental elements and unifying them according to causal contexts (*Kausalzusammenhangen*). He argues that this defines the explanatory sciences in contradistinction from what he calls the 'descriptive sciences'.[4]

Explaining the causal mechanisms behind an expression, however, does not give us an understanding of what the person is trying to express, viz. what they *mean*. In fact, expressions can have an identical meaning while at the same time being brought about by radically different causal mechanisms. For example, if I am angry I can express this through any number of different causal mechanisms, e.g. I can write or say that 'I am very angry', or I can scream or make a gesture of anger. Grasping the meaning of an expression requires interpretation and understanding, not a causal explanation.

We have seen that for Dilthey the subject matter of the human sciences is lived-experiences, expressions of lived-experiences and our understanding of these expressions. However, within the human sciences a distinction must be made between psychology and the other human sciences. This distinction rests on two modes of expression. By 'subjective' expressions, Dilthey signifies all those expressions that express one's own peculiar life-nexus, i.e. the totality of one's own peculiar lived-experience. The scientific understanding of the life nexus of an individual, which Dilthey calls a 'psychic nexus', is accomplished through the science of descriptive psychology. On the other hand, the other human sciences have as their subject matter not the expressions of an individual psychic nexus per se but 'objective' expressions of intersubjective 'worldviews'. For example, the science of history has as its subject matter historical cultures, e.g. historical institutions of law, of government, of science, of literature, etc. which are not expressions of an individual psychic nexus, but of an intersubjective *worldview*.

Yet psychic nexuses and worldviews are by no means unconnected. Both are fundamental components of human existence and life and, for Dilthey, this means that they are components of a larger *life nexus*. That is, psychic nexuses and worldviews are always situated within a lifenexus of human existence, which consequently has both a 'subjective' and an 'objective' component. Moreover, within a life nexus the psychic nexus and worldview mutually affect one another. Each individual psychic nexus incorporates within itself a worldview and at the same time worldviews are shaped and modified by psychic nexuses. For example, every individual is situated within a historical context or historical epoch and likewise a historical context or epoch is, in many ways, a product of the many individuals within it.

This same interconnectedness manifests itself on the level of expression. An individual can typically only express himself or herself by means of an already expressed worldview that creates the intersubjective context for such expressions. Similarly, a worldview is expressed through the expressive action of many individuals. As an example, one can express one's pleasure or satisfaction by clapping only if the culture in which one finds oneself allows for this form of expression of pleasure or satisfaction. If I live in a culture for which clapping does not express pleasure or satisfaction, I should not be expressing my pleasure or satisfaction by clapping since no one (including myself) could interpret from the clapping of my hands that I feel pleasure or satisfaction. This is merely one instance of a more general principle that Dilthey describes as follows: 'In understanding we proceed from the coherent whole which is livingly given to us in order to make the particular intelligible to us. Precisely the fact that we live with the consciousness of the coherent whole, makes it possible for us to understand a particular sentence, gesture or action.'[5]

Earlier it was claimed that, for Dilthey, an individual must express himself or herself from within the context of an already existing worldview. For Dilthey, there are exceptional cases in which this is not true. Life, for him, is creative, spontaneous and 'free'. Indeed, new worldviews can be formed. Life produces new worldviews by means of exceptionally creative individuals. These exceptionally creative individuals can by the force of their 'objective' expression bring into existence a new worldview by embodying and bringing to expression an encompassing, unified view of life. Of course, transformations of worldviews can arise within more or less general spheres of life, e.g. transformation of religious worldviews, artistic worldviews and philosophical worldviews. However, Dilthey also believes that there are exemplary personalities who can bring about a transformation in the way we view every sphere of life. Illustrative for Dilthey in this regard is Goethe. Dilthey argues that such transformations of worldview, including the rupture that then exists between a present worldview and past worldviews, becomes the object of the study of history.

Dilthey takes it as evident that we have historical knowledge and even a scientific understanding of history. The question is: How is this knowledge possible? How can we come to a scientific understanding of a historical worldview and of historical individuals when their historical expressions are alien to us?

According to Dilthey, there is a common element in all worldviews which is human existence and human life. Following tradition, Dilthey argues that human life and existence can ultimately be understood as manifestations of human thought, feeling and will. In fact, every worldview includes these three aspects of human existence. Dilthey believes, therefore, that a scientific study of these, i.e. a 'descriptive psychology', is needed to ground the theory of worldviews and the critique of historical reason. Of course, the fundamental importance of psychology for understanding human life and existence is certainly not peculiar to Dilthey, but is an element of much nineteenth-century thought. What is peculiar to Dilthey is his analysis of the form that psychology must take if it is to ground a critique of historical reason.

Dilthey makes a distinction between what he calls explanatory or constructivist psychology, on the one hand, and descriptive psychology, on the other. Explanatory sciences are based on constructed hypotheses. That is, the elements and unifying principles of an explanatory science are not originally given to consciousness, but are rather constructed hypotheses whose purpose is to unify the data of sensation. For example, atoms and their causal relations are not given in experience, but are hypotheses that are constructed in order to explain and unify the manifold of sensation.

A descriptive or analytic science, on the other hand, begins with a unified nexus that is 'given originaliter' to consciousness. It then proceeds to describe and analyse the moments inherent in this unity. That is, it understands the parts in terms of the whole and the whole in terms of its parts. Dilthey argues that the human sciences, and in particular descriptive psychology, are just this sort of science. He argues that

> The human studies are distinguished from the sciences of nature first of all in that the latter have for their objects facts which are presented to consciousness as from outside, as phenomena and given in isolation, while the objects of the former are given originaliter from within as real and as a living continuum.[6]

This is particularly interesting in so far as it foreshadows Heidegger's own criticism that the theoretical sciences are de-vivifying, viz. that they set their object *outside* of lived-experience and isolate it from life.

Moreover, Dilthey's notion that the human sciences begin with something given originaliter, i.e. not something that is derivative, resembles in a less radical, or perhaps more concrete fashion the requirements of philosophy as primordial science. Dilthey emphasizes that, in the human sciences, '... the nexus of psychic life constitutes originally a primitive and fundamental datum ... The experienced [*erlebte*] whole [*Zusammenhang*] is primary here, the distinction among its members only comes afterwards'.[7] Importantly, Dilthey connects this to the fact that descriptive psychology is ultimately grounded in lived-experience:

In the [natural sciences], all connectedness [*Zusammenhang*] is obtained by means of the formation of hypothesis; in psychology it is precisely the connectedness which is originally and continually given in lived-experience [*Erleben*]: life exists everywhere only as a nexus or coherent whole.[8]

All descriptive sciences are ultimately grounded in an originally given unified nexus. This is significant in the present context, because it demonstrates from a different perspective why Husserl's use of theoretical reflection was inimical to his own expressed desire that phenomenology be a descriptive rather than an explanatory science. Namely, reflection destroys the originally given life-nexus in which lived-experiences are situated and therefore mitigates the possibility of a descriptive approach.

Since the unity necessary for descriptive psychology is given originarily and is not a hypothesized unity, Dilthey argues that it is capable of grounding a critique of knowledge in a way that no explanatory science can. For example, as we have already seen, because explanatory psychology utilizes hypothetical unities any attempt to give a critique based on it would be hypothetical as well. That is, Dilthey argues that any theory of knowledge is going to make some reference to psychology. However, if it attempts to ground knowledge through hypothetical explanations it will face the absurdity of being merely a hypothetical account of knowledge which again can be overturned by experience itself. If this were the case, it would frustrate the very purpose of a theory of knowledge which 'arose from the need to secure a firm ground in the midst of the ocean of metaphysical fluctuations, a generally valid knowledge of at least some scope. Were it to be uncertain and hypothetical it would vitiate its own goal'.[9] As our three previous philosophers also recognized, this would contribute 'enormously to the development of skepticism and a superficial and sterile empiricism, and thus to the increasing separation of life from knowledge'.[10] A genuine critique of knowledge, Dilthey maintains, cannot rest on a hypothetical foundation, for then the very conditions for the possibility of knowledge would be capable of being overturned by the progress of knowledge, a claim that Dilthey thinks is absurd. He laments, 'Hypotheses, everywhere only hypotheses!'[11]

Given their shared problematic, one can certainly understand why the elder Dilthey saw a strong affinity between the young Husserl's work and his own.[12] At the same time, it is also fairly evident how misguided Husserl was when he characterized Dilthey's philosophy as a 'historicism' that would inevitably lead to scepticism and relativism.[13] In truth, Dilthey does not attempt to ground validity in history. Quite the contrary, Dilthey grounds his theory of knowledge in human life and existence. That is,

Dilthey does not relativize knowledge to human history. This is made clear by the way in which he emphasizes inner experience and the psychic nexus in his account of knowledge. Dilthey maintains that the psychicnexus of lived-experience is originarily given as a unity and that it forms the basis of all cognition. For instance, he remarks that '*The psychic nexus forms the basis of cognitional processes*; one can therefore study the latter and determine its capacities only in the framework of this coherent nexus.'[14]

In other words, a critical theory of knowledge must be grounded in an analysis of the psychic nexus. At the same time, he emphasizes that this ground is not a transcendental realm insulated from life and lived-experience. Indeed, the analysis of this psychic nexus 'is a psychology in movement; to be sure, in movement towards a determined end'.[15] However, this does not signify that descriptive psychology cannot acquire 'universally valid descriptions' of the psychic nexus. In fact, it discovers the unifying structures that occur uniformly across the human psyche. It is 'in motion' because these structures are ones that can be 'concretely lived', rather than theoretical abstractions or idealities. Finally, unlike transcendental phenomenology it does not rely on theoretical reflection (*Reflexion*), but on self-consciousness (*Selbstbesinnung*).

Self-consciousness, unlike reflection, indicates an awareness of one's own living psychic nexus, which is, in a significant sense, one's very own self. Moreover, self-consciousness is not limited simply to a theoretical awareness of oneself, but can include practical and axiological awareness as well. Furthermore, self-consciousness is not an inert awareness of the structure of the psychicnexus, but in its living description and demarcation of the psychic nexus directs concrete living towards the finer articulation of that nexus.

In many respects, Dilthey's theory is a much broader and more substantial version of Natorp's attempt to grasp our self-consciousness of the task of knowledge. In large part, this is due to the fact that Natorp has a more limited, natural scientific outlook while Dilthey brings a keen awareness of the human sciences and their approach to human activity and lived-experience. As with Natorp, there is an essential developmental aspect to Dilthey's theory of knowledge and his psychology. We are always on the way to a 'complete' account of knowledge, although at any point along the way the living, uniform structures that govern knowledge are originarily given. The development of knowledge, according to Dilthey, is the result of the development of the psychic nexus in concrete life. And the development of the psychic nexus consists of a finer articulation of the originarily given structures of the psychic nexus. That is, Dilthey argues that '... the structural nexus does not grow together from discrete operations, but rather what occurs is that an even finer articulation is differentiated out of it, and behind this nexus one cannot go ... we find in the psychic structural nexus a unitary subject of psychic development'.[16]

Because the psychic nexus is developing in this way, part of the very process of understanding the psychic nexus is to trace this development. Furthermore, as we have already seen, the psychic nexus is intertwined with a worldview. So, for Dilthey, there is an intimate connection between the study of descriptive psychology and that of history. In order to do the former one must engage in the latter, and vice versa. Dilthey argues that

> Man does not apprehend what he is by musing over himself, nor by doing psychological experiments, but rather by history. This analysis of the products of human spirit – destined to open for us a glance at the genesis of the psychic nexus, of its forms and its actions – must, in addition to the analysis of historical products, observe and collect everything which it can seize of the *historical processes* wherein such a nexus becomes constituted.[17]

In addition, he argues that because the process of development for the psychic nexus is the ever finer articulation of the unitary 'structural nexus' of psychic life and not a development governed by physical causality, one can never predict what the next stage of psychic life will be. Rather, it is only *afterwards* that one can infer the *motives* that lead to it.[18] This inference is key for understanding the kind of interpretation through which understanding is achieved in descriptive psychology and history.[19]

In essence, Dilthey has provided a psychology and a theory of knowledge that is grounded in, as well as being fully participatory in, life and concrete lived-experience. It is not narrowly theoretical or objectifying but is, rather, hermeneutic. Consequently, he has attempted to give an account of subjectivity in its entirety. That is, the subject for Dilthey is not merely a cognizing subject but *equally* a willing and valuing subject, and he argues that the theory of knowledge and philosophy must respect this equality since these aspects are interwoven in the psychic nexus.[20] In addition, Dilthey has also grasped the historical and lived nature of our understanding of ourselves. Or, put another way, self-consciousness is always historically and livingly situated. That is, Dilthey has done away with merely reflective understanding. Indeed, he too moves in the direction that Natorp took by seeing that our understanding of ourselves is not immediate but mediated, i.e. it develops over time. However, unlike Natorp, Dilthey has the tools for understanding this mediated self-consciousness, viz. his descriptive psychology and his critique of historical reason.

One other aspect of Dilthey's views should be noted: that understanding and interpretation are realized by means of what he calls reliving (*Nacherle-ben*). In essence, one understands an expression of whatever kind by reliving the lived-experience of which it is the expression. That is, one reproduces in one's own psychic nexus, to the best of one's ability, the expressed lived-experience. This does not mean that one must get angry in order to understand another's expression of anger, but that one can only understand another's expression of anger because being angry and expressing it in the way it was expressed is part of one's own lived-experience or psychic nexus. Thus, Dilthey claims that if we are to understand life and lived-experience we can only do so by situating it within life. In other words, life and lived-experience must be understood according to those structures that are appropriate to life. The reason that reliving is so fundamental to Dilthey's philosophy is that such reliving is just the activity of situating what is to be understood in life, i.e. in its proper realm.

Clearly, then, Dilthey's view of understanding requires a certain degree of homogeneity in the psychic nexuses of the one who brings a lived-experience to expression and the one who tries to understand that expression by re-living the lived-experience that is expressed. Moreover, the degree of homogeneity determines the level of understanding. According to Dilthey, this homogeneity is brought about by similarities in the formations of the respective psychic nexuses, i.e. in how the psychic nexuses were 'acquired'. Dilthey claims that there are roughly two aspects of homogeneity in psychic nexuses. The first consists of the fact that everyone shares the same external world. The second is the degree of similarity in worldview, viz. 'the same ways of preferring and choosing, the same relationships between goals and means, certain uniform relations of values, certain similarities regarding the ideal of life, where it appears'.[21]

Therefore, Dilthey emphasizes shared contexts and shared environments in his analysis of the universalities present in psychic nexuses. For example, rather than grounding the universality of reason in the ability of consciousness to grasp idealities, e.g. as Husserl does, Dilthey grounds it in the fact that everyone shares the same external world and, at least in part, similar worldviews. In other words, the robust dichotomy between immanence and transcendence, viz. between the being of consciousness and being for consciousness, so prevalent in Husserl's transcendental phenomenology, is in large part absent from Dilthey's analysis.

From Heidegger's perspective this represents a marked improvement, viz. Dilthey has begun to break down the Cartesianism that remains latent in modern philosophy. However, although Heidegger praises Dilthey for his insights into life and lived-experience, he believes that Dilthey was unable to capitalize on his insights because 'he viewed his own work purely in terms of the traditional philosophy of his time'.[22] Because of this he was not able to inquire into the being of life as such. In part, this signifies that Dilthey tended to describe the psychic nexus as a self-contained entity that incorporates into itself that which lies outside of it. That is, Dilthey still sees human life as standing over against an external world. In other words, according to Heidegger, Dilthey failed to recognize the intentional structure of life, viz. that life transcends itself, and that intentionality is the living structure through which one comports oneself toward the world. In the coming chapters, we will examine how Heidegger attempts to overcome this shortcoming in Dilthey's philosophy.

Our guiding theme has been Heidegger's analysis of the idea of philosophy as primordial science. That is, it is in relation to this topic that Heidegger evaluates his predecessors. It is important, therefore, that we finish our examination of Dilthey's views by looking at how he understands the nature of philosophy.

2.   Philosophical worldviews, metaphysics and the 'world-riddle'

In his *The Essence of Philosophy*,[23] a work published just four years before his death, Dilthey gives a brief exposition of the nature of philosophy, specifically in comparison with religion and poetry, which, alongside philosophy, represent at this late stage in his thought the paradigmatic activities through which worldviews are formed.[24] Contrary to religious worldviews, a philosophical worldview strives to be universal and universally valid, i.e. it is not for a particular people at a particular time. And unlike poetic worldviews, it 'is a power which seeks to reform life'.[25]

Dilthey argues that a philosophical worldview develops out of experience (*Erfahrung*) and the sciences of experience (*Erfahrungswissenschaften*). Specifically, it articulates the way in which lived-experiences are to be objectified through conceptualization. In this way a philosophical worldview represents the conditions for the possibility of experience, which form the basis of the sciences of experience. Indeed, a philosophical worldview objectifies each of the 'general attitudes' of human existence, i.e. thought, feeling and will, by means of the fundamental concepts of being or reality, causation, value and purpose. For each of these it articulates a systematic structure that includes both logical and evidential components. That is, it specifies both a system of concepts and the conditions of intuition appropriate to each particular realm of human existence. The system of concepts characterizes the relations holding between concepts as well as a hierarchy of concepts. Thus, philosophical worldviews develop a concept of the ultimate ground, the absolute value and the highest good. The conditions of intuition specify the evidential requirements for knowledge of existence, i.e. knowledge of particular objects, values and goods. In sum, a philosophical worldview 'combines knowledge of the world, evaluation of life, and principles of action'.[26]

As with any worldview, a philosophical worldview is an admixture of these elements, viz. it includes conceptual objectifications of thought, feeling and will. For instance, a worldview could hypostasize each of these elements in an ideal form or in its material concretion, etc. Moreover, in many cases, one or more element is dominant within a philosophical worldview. However, there are also philosophical worldviews in which each element is given equal weight. Dilthey believes that these latter represent relatively undeveloped philosophical worldviews since they contain no unified principle of development, i.e. each sphere of conceptual objectification could with equal right be developed. As a philosophical worldview develops, one of the elements becomes dominant and the different spheres of objectification are ordered accordingly. For example, materialism emphasizes material causation and so feeling and purpose are reduced to this. Similarly, in Schopenhauer's philosophy, purpose or will is made dominant, and thought and feeling are interpreted to it. In other words, when a philosophical worldview develops then the kind of being according correlative with one of the fundamental attitudes of life is made exemplary.

In its fullest development, the formation of a philosophical worldview becomes metaphysics. That is, it strives to become universal and universally valid. In other words, for Dilthey, metaphysics is an 'attempt to conclusively express the world's coherency by using an interconnection of concepts'[27] and in a universally valid manner. More specifically, he believes that metaphysics is an attempt to solve what he calls 'the riddle of the world and of life' or simply the 'world-riddle'.[28] This consists of finding a 'point accessible to rigorous thinking' in 'the mystery of life' whereby one could unite life and the world. From a philosophical standpoint this signifies a position from which one could unite conceptual knowledge with its object. Dilthey imagines that this point of rigorous thinking would allow us to achieve a 'singular world-order' (*singuläre Weltzusammenhang*) in which life and the world are united.

One need not search far to find instances of what Dilthey is describing. Dilthey himself points to materialism, naturalism, positivism, 'objective idealism' (e.g. Schelling, Hegel) and the 'idealism of freedom' (e.g. Kant, Fichte). Materialism provides perhaps the most straightforward example.

That is, materialism unites life and the world through the 'singular world-order' of the materialistic, causal processes provided by the 'rigorous thinking' of the natural sciences. That is, both the world and our experience of that world are reduced to material, causal processes.

However, a less crude and more critical example of what Dilthey means by metaphysics can be found in Husserl's transcendental phenomenology. As was shown in Chapter 2, Husserl reduces life and the world to pure consciousness in so far as both the natural and the spiritual world are constituted in pure consciousness. Moreover, this is explicitly accessible by means of rigorous thinking, viz. through phenomenological analysis of pure consciousness as that is made possible by phenomenological reflection on the pure stream of lived-experience. Rickert also tried to unify conceptual knowledge and its object by means of the absolute value of truth. Similarly, Natorp projects the unity of the objective and subjective aspects of knowledge in the unending process of construction and reconstruction that is the purposeful task of knowledge.

Because Dilthey believes that *only* the originarily given unity of the life nexus can unify all experience, whether cognitive, practical or emotional, and serve as the ground for universally valid knowledge, he believes that metaphysics embodies a 'hidden contradiction in its very essence'.[29] In a critique quite similar to Heidegger's criticism of the theoretical objectification of lived-experience and the environing world, Dilthey believes that metaphysical attempts to unify life and the world will 'either unite the categories sophistically or distort the content of our consciousness'.[30]

In his critique Dilthey is relying on the fact that metaphysical systems are worldviews that privilege the system of conceptual objectification that arises in only one of the 'general attitudes' of the nexus of life, i.e. either thought, feeling or will. These metaphysical attempts to solve the world-riddle ultimately fail, as far as Dilthey is concerned, because thought, feeling and will are irreducible to one another. Each of these are distinct aspects of the nexus of life, *behind* which reason cannot go. He mentions that 'the subject has these various attitudes toward objects; one cannot go back behind this fact to a reason for it. So the categories of being, cause, value and purpose, originating as they do in these attitudes, can be reduced neither to one another nor to a higher principle'.[31]

In other words, the impossibility of a metaphysical solution to the world-riddle lies in the nature of the life nexus itself, i.e. that it is essentially a unity in diversity. Otherwise stated, the life nexus forms a unity of the fundamentally irreducible attitudes of life. Every metaphysical system necessarily 'distorts the content of our consciousness' because it tries to *univocally* determine the nexus of life and the world.

Dilthey claims that, in the end, metaphysics, just like serious poetry and art, merely 'discloses a feature of life, never before seen in this light, and ... thus reveals to us the various sides of life in ever new products'.[32] Because life is never exhausted by any one worldview, Dilthey believes that metaphysical systems are always in flux. That is, because life forever outstrips their conceptualizations and categorizations, metaphysical systems rise and fall in life and are continually being displaced by other metaphysical systems. This is how Dilthey conceives of the history of metaphysics, viz. it is the history of attempts at univocally *conceptualizing* life and the world by means of one or another of the fundamental attitudes of thought, feeling or will. He says that, in metaphysics, 'a world confronts us, as it appears when a powerful philosophical personality makes one of the general attitudes toward the world dominant over the others, and its categories over theirs'.[33] In the end, the history of metaphysics shows us various sides of life, but also demonstrates 'the unfathomable depth of the world'.[34]

Does this mean that Husserl was right when he criticized Dilthey's theory of worldviews as simply another version of historicism, viz. as a kind of historical relativism? Dilthey denies this charge both in the *Essence of Philosophy* as well as in his personal correspondence with Husserl. He argues that the theory of worldviews provides consciousness not of the relativity of all worldviews, but rather of 'the sovereignty of the spirit over and against every single one of them'.[35] That is, a survey of the history of worldviews demonstrates the freedom and autonomy of the spirit vis-à-vis all worldviews. This is a motif that Heidegger will utilize throughout his early philosophy. For example, he says that

> The existence which always makes up our being – though not the only determinant – is a matter of our *freedom*; and only a being which can be resolved and has resolved itself in such and such a way can have a world. World and freedom as basic determinations of human existence are most closely related.[36]

For Dilthey this means that the spirit is autonomous over all its products, i.e. over every worldview, whether poetical, artistic or philosophical. Thus, as far as Dilthey is concerned, although particular worldviews may not be absolute, the life of the spirit is.

In summary, Dilthey thinks that the theory of worldviews demonstrates the spirit's ability to autonomously reveal facets of life through its productive formation of worldviews. Philosophy embodies one form of this, viz. the spirit's ability to reveal facets of life by means of conceptualization. In this respect, what is peculiar to philosophy is not that it reveals life and the 'unfathomable depths of the world', for religion and poetry also do that, but the way it accomplishes this, viz. through the activity of conceptualization and the production of *philosophical worldviews*, and the fact that the spirit is sovereign over this activity and its products. To emphasize what is revealed and the products through which this is revealed is precisely what leads to historicist and relativistic interpretations of Dilthey's philosophy.

In essence, this is why Heidegger's attempt to explore the idea of philosophy as a primordial science should not be interpreted as the attempt to formulate a science of the pre-theoretical sphere of life, i.e. to gain non-objectifying access to primordial life. Dilthey had already accomplished that and more, both with his descriptive psychology and his theory of world-views. Because of this, Heidegger does not criticize Dilthey for having failed to gain access to pre-theoretical life. In fact, just the opposite is the case. Heidegger says that 'Dilthey penetrated into that reality, namely, human Dasein which, in the authentic sense, is in the sense of historical being. He succeeded in bringing this reality to givenness, defining it as living, free, and historical'.[37]

Furthermore, Heidegger maintains that the 'philosophical relevance' of Dilthey's work does not lie in the fact that he succeeded in bringing life and human Dasein to givenness, but that he was on the way towards the *question* of life.[38] Unfortunately, he was unable to escape from the constraints of 'traditional philosophy' which signified to Heidegger that he had not secured a proper method and a genuine formulation of the question.[39] If we think back to Natorp, we can interpret Heidegger's criticism as indicating that although Dilthey had gained access to life, he had failed to self-consciously engage in the task of life. In other words, he failed to understand the way in which the formation of a worldview could be part of the task of life.

At this point, let us situate the present chapter within the broader issue of Heidegger's project of examining the idea of philosophy as primordial science. Having scrutinized Dilthey's theory of worldviews we can now take into account the recurring context of Heidegger's discussion of philosophy. This is the relation between the two dominant conceptions of philosophy at the time, namely, philosophy as worldview and as scientific philosophy. Both in 1919 and 1927 Heidegger prefaces his lecture with a discussion of this issue. This is not at all surprising since, as we have seen, Rickert, Natorp and Husserl all characterize their own projects as attempts to work out a scientific conception of philosophy. Moreover, Husserl does so in conscious opposition to the idea of philosophy as worldview.

In his 1919 lecture on 'The idea of philosophy and the problem of worldview' it is clear that Heidegger is relying on Dilthey's discussion of the nature of philosophy in order to articulate his own problematic. When

characterizing the view that the formation of a worldview is the immanent
task of philosophy, Heidegger says,

> ... the efforts of the great philosophers are directed towards what is
> in every sense ultimate, universal, and of universal validity. The inner
> struggle with the riddles of life and the world seeks to come to rest by
> establishing the ultimate nature of these. Objectively stated: every great
> philosophy realizes itself in a worldview – every philosophy is, where its
> innermost tendency comes to unrestricted expression, metaphysics.[40]

Heidegger goes on to say that the formation of a worldview cannot satisfy
the idea of philosophy as primordial science.

Importantly, as we mentioned earlier, the philosophies of Rickert,
Husserl and Natorp remain instances of metaphysics understood as the
attempt to formulate a universal and universally valid philosophical worldview, viz. a unification of conceptual knowledge and its object. If, according
to Heidegger, the immanent task of philosophy as primordial science cannot
be the formulation of a worldview, then this indicates that Rickert, Husserl,
Natorp *and* Dilthey were wrong about the essence of philosophy: the first
three because they merely attempted to formulate a philosophical worldview and Dilthey because he identified philosophy with the various historical attempts to formulate philosophical worldviews. The question remains:
Is there a way to solve the world-riddle? That is, is there a way to unify life
and the world?

In his correspondence with Dilthey, Husserl argues that this can be
accomplished only through an analysis of the nature of intentionality,
which, according to Husserl, represents the most fundamental of all phenomenological inquiries. Since intentionality is essential to every one of the
general attitudes of life, it unifies life and the world by bringing them into
essential relation with one another. However, because Husserl systematically 'brackets' life and the world in order to examine how each is constituted in pure consciousness, Heidegger thinks that Husserl has concealed
the way in which intentionality is realized in life, i.e. the way in which life
comports itself towards a world.

Therefore, Heidegger takes a different approach to intentionality, viz.
one that remains fully engaged in life. In Heidegger's mind, Dilthey, contrary to Husserl's criticisms, points the way towards this. However, Dilthey
does not fully grasp the *task* of philosophy as primordial science and the relation of this to life. It is Natorp who lays the groundwork for understanding
philosophy as a task, but he similarly misses the connection between this and
life. Heidegger appropriates elements from each of Husserl, Natorp and

Dilthey, but only as indications, i.e. as paths to follow, toward a proper understanding of philosophy and its relation to life. For Heidegger, this signifies that 'philosophy can progress only through an absolute sinking into life as such, for *phenomenology* is never concluded, only preliminary, it always sinks itself into the preliminary'.[41] And this requires radicalizing aspects of Husserl, Natorp and Dilthey's views.

Toward a Fundamental Ontology

Heidegger rejects any philosophy's claim to be primordial science if it is not situated in life. The lack of primordiality in the philosophies of Rickert, Husserl and Natorp is indicated by the fact that one finds at the foundation of their philosophies a living element that they simply do not account for. Thus, according to Heidegger, the renewal of philosophy as primordial science requires exhibiting how philosophy is located in life as well as how it can be productive of life, most specifically, how it can be productive of the non-primordial sciences. This necessitates an investigation into philosophy as lived, i.e. philosophy as situated in life. In essence, philosophy as primordial science must be a 'philosophy of life' in the sense of belonging to life, but also as constitutive of life.

One step in this direction is already signified by Dilthey's analysis of the 'world-riddle', namely, the unity of life and world that he regards as the central concern of philosophy. Husserl believed that the unity of life and world consisted of the concrete connections realized in human intentional comportments. Heidegger maintains that if philosophy is to be primordial science then the concepts of world and intentionality must be resituated in life itself. They must be resituated in life because they have been removed from life by philosophical worldviews that conceptually objectify them. To this end, in 1919 Heidegger analyses the two fundamental lived-experiences of the environing world (*Umwelterlebnis*) and the lived-experience of the question: Is there something? (*Das frageerlebnis: Gibt es etwas?*) By doing so, he hopes to exhibit how both world and intentionality are situated within life. However, even as he was analysing these two lived-experiences he recognized that this term was inadequate to the task at hand, because it was a term of art in philosophy and, therefore, riddled with pre-conceptions.[1] By the middle of the 1920s and as his thought developed he referred to them simply as Dasein's 'being-in-the-world' and the 'question of the meaning of being'. With this preparatory analysis he was then able to investigate the way in which science, ontology, fundamental ontology and, ultimately, philosophy are situated within life and what constitutive role they play in life.

1.   Life and world

In his analysis of the lived-experience of the question 'Is there something?'
Heidegger wishes to recapture how intentionality is located in life and specifically how we living relate to our environing world. In addition, this question, as we shall later see, is the early precursor to the all-important question
of the meaning of being.

Heidegger begins by disabusing the question of its de-vivifying, theoretical interpretation. He does this by showing that it does not fit the traditional
dichotomy between a subject comporting itself towards an object. With
respect to the latter, Heidegger tries to show that what is questioned,
namely something in general, is not an object. With respect to the subjective
side, Heidegger demonstrates, first and foremost, that an Ego is not given
in the lived-experience of the question. That is, the question 'Is there
something?' cannot be captured by the traditional notion of intentionality
in which a subject comports itself towards an object. Rather, Heidegger
says that

> 'I comport myself' – is this contained in the sense of the experience? ...
> what is decisive is that simple inspection does not discover anything like
> an 'I'. What I see is just that 'it lives' [*es lebt*], moreover that it lives
> towards something, that it is directed towards something by way of ques-
> tioning, something that is itself questionable ... I do not find anything like
> an 'I', but only an 'ex-perience [*Er-leben*] of something', a '*living towards
> something*'.[2]

What is this something towards which the question is directed? Heidegger
argues that it is not something given either intuitively or conceptually,
i.e. it is not an intuitively given object or a conceptual objectification.
Rather, the 'something' in question *transcends* every objectification and
conceptualization.[3]

In this case, the question is whether there is 'anything whatsoever' (*etwas
überhaupt*). Heidegger says that 'It is asked whether there is *something*. It is
not asked whether there are tables or chairs, houses or trees, sonatas by
Mozart or religious powers, but whether there is *anything whatsoever*.'[4] That
is, it is not a particular object or something that can be given, however inde-
terminately, through intuition. Rather, according to Heidegger, intuition
always provides *something* under a determinate form, viz. as an object.

Moreover, Heidegger claims that the 'anything whatsoever' in question is
not 'something universal, one might say, indeed the most universal of all,
applying to any possible object whatsoever'.[5] That is, it is not the case that

'To say of something that it is something is the minimum assertion I can make about it.'[6] In other words, the something in question is not the highest or most general genus of all things, e.g. the concept that is applicable to anything whatsoever. Thus, the something in question is not that which can be given in what Husserl calls a categorial intuition. Categorial intuition always presents *something* under the auspices of a concept. Likewise, it is not the result of a 'constructive' conceptualization. It lies entirely outside the conceptual realm.

This is due to a peculiarity of the something that is asked about. It is neither an individual object nor a concept. In other words, every object is something, e.g. a chair, a table, a sonata by Mozart, etc. but at the same time every concept is something, e.g. natural thing, physical thing, psychical thing, etc. The 'something in general' is the index for any and all directedness, viz. directedness toward *something*. That is, it represents the pure possibility of objectivity or conceptuality. For any objectification and any conceptualization is a determination of 'something'.

Importantly, this signifies that the 'something' of the question 'Is there something?' is pre-theoretical in the sense that it *transcends* the theoretical. Heidegger illustrates this by pointing out that the something in general remains outside of the sphere of theoretical conceptualization. He says,

> Does not every theoreticized level of reality, in respect of the particular items of reality belonging to it, allow for the judgement, 'it is something'? And does not this ultimate theoretical characterization of the bare something in general fall out of the order entirely, such that any and every level can motivate it?[7]

If this is the case, then it raises the problem that if 'in the final analysis it belongs to the meaning of "something in general" to relate to something concrete ... the meaningful character of this "relating" still remains problematic'.[8]

Not coincidentally, this problem lies at the heart of Aristotle's discussion of being. In the *Physics*, Aristotle asks rhetorically, 'For who understands "being itself" [*auto to on*] to be anything but a particular substance [*on ti einai*]?'[9] More exactly, being is always understood in relation to a 'particular this'. In fact, Heidegger will develop this early notion of something in general into the 'ontological distinction' between being and beings. In other words, the issue that is raised in 1919 is the forerunner of the fundamental relation between being and beings that dominates Heidegger's concerns in the latter half of the 1920s and which is formulated explicitly in his *Basic Problems of Phenomenology*. There he says:

Being is essentially different from a being, from beings. How is the distinction between being and beings to be grasped? How can its possibility be explained? If being is not itself a being, how then does it nevertheless belong to beings, since, after all, beings and only beings *are*? What does it mean to say that being *belongs* [*gehört*] to beings?[10]

As in his 1919 lecture, Heidegger throughout the 1920s attempts to understand the relation between being and beings by focusing on a fundamental question. In 1919, it is the question 'Is there something?' while later on it will be the question of the meaning of being.

In essence, Heidegger has demonstrated that the something in question transcends objectification and conceptualization. In addition, he also argues that in the simple sense of the question there is no correlative subject that comports itself toward an object. The importance of this claim lies in the fact that Heidegger is refusing to import an external notion of subjectivity into the lived-experience of the question. In this way, he is preventing the subject/object dichotomy from being illegitimately introduced into this fundamental experience.

Heidegger claims that one does not experience an 'I' in the question, but merely a living towards something. What is this 'living towards' inherent to the question? How is this livingly-experienced in the context of the question? Heidegger argues that in the question 'Is there something?' what 'stands in questioning' is not the something, but rather the 'there is' (*es gibt*). Heidegger claims that 'In this experience *something* is questioned in relation to anything whatsoever. The questioning has a definite content: whether "*there is*" a something, that is the question. The "there is" stands in question, or, more accurately, stands in questioning.'[11] That is, 'It is not asked whether something moves or rests, whether something contradicts itself, whether something works, whether something exists, whether something values, whether something ought to be, but rather whether *there is* something.'[12]

As with the something in general, this 'there is' is an index that motivates innumerable other modes in which something is there, e.g. that something works, that something values, that something ought to be, etc. Each of these presupposes that something 'is there'. In other words, only if something is there can it be asked whether it works, or values, or ought to be, or can be thought or perceived. What stands in question then is the possibility of lived-experience as such. That is, any lived-experience of something represents a particular way in which something 'is there', i.e. a particular way of living towards something.

In essence, the lived-experience of the question 'Is there something?' represents the lived-experience of the possibility of intentionality, i.e. the possibility of living-towards something. In elucidating how 'something' 'is there' in life, Heidegger takes his cue from Husserl and Dilthey, for whom things are there in life and lived-experience in so far as they belong to the environing world. In other words, if anything is there, then it is there in the environing world.

Husserl understands the notion of the environing world in terms of objectivity. For example, he says that '*An object existing in itself is never one with which consciousness or the Ego pertaining to consciousness has nothing to do*. The thing is a thing belonging to the *environing world* . . .'[13] In the *Cartesian Meditations* he notes that the world and all worldly objects stand over against pure consciousness and the pure Ego. He says that 'neither the world nor any worldly object is a piece of my Ego, to be found in my conscious life as a really inherent part of it, as a complex of data of sensation or a complex of acts'.[14]

Dilthey, on the other hand, understands the world from the perspective of lived-experience. That is, he believes that the world is a unity to be found in life precisely as a unified nexus of lived-experiences. In other words, it is a structural unity of the life-nexus that pervades one's life and all of one's lived-experiences. In other words, it is a worldview. That is, it circumscribes all one's acts and sensations and makes them meaningful.

Heidegger utilizes Dilthey's understanding of world in opposition to Husserl's, precisely because he wants to investigate the environing world as it is lived. To do this he must work against Husserl's explicitly de-vivified interpretation of the world. That is, for Husserl, the world is essentially characterized as standing over against a transcendental subject and, therefore, the world itself is grasped by standing outside of it, by not being engaged in it, and by *perceiving and conceptualizing it*. Furthermore, from this perspective, the world is understood to comprise a totality of *objects* towards which the subject can actually or possibly comport itself in one way or another. Indeed, the world becomes a mere aggregate of objects.

In the terminology of *Being and Time*, this is equivalent to the ontic, present-at-hand notion of the world. Corresponding to this is an ontological, present-at-hand concept of world, which signifies the being of ontic, present-at-hand entities. Thus, this ontological concept of world embodies a regional ontology of objects;[15] for example, the 'world' of a mathematician, or a physicist, etc. In its broadest extension, this world represents the regional ontology of any experienceable object whatsoever or, as Husserl understands it, the environing world.[16]

In 1919, Heidegger attributes this understanding of the environing world to the fact that it has been interpreted from the perspective of the theoretical attitude. In essence, the being of the world and everything in it is constituted according to the way in which it is 'given' in the theoretical attitude. This is the reason that Heidegger writes that ' "Given" already signifies an inconspicuous but genuine theoretical reflection inflicted upon the environment. Thus "givenness" is already quite probably a theoretical form, and precisely for this reason it cannot be taken as the essence of the immediate environing world as environmental.'[17] Indeed, 'When I attempt to explain the environing world theoretically, it collapses upon itself.'[18]

Does this mean that Heidegger thinks that we should view the world through the practical or axiological attitudes? There is an all too common, although mistaken, interpretation of Heidegger's philosophy that sees it as giving 'primacy to practice'. As far as these interpreters are concerned, our relation toward the world and the things in it is based fundamentally on pragmatic considerations. On the other hand, Husserl, Dilthey and Heidegger fully recognize that life includes, and in fact precedes, all three of the basic attitudes, i.e. the theoretical, practical and axiological. As we saw in Chapter 2, Husserl argues that each of these basic attitudes is simply a different mode in which one can live pre-eminently. And even though he does privilege the theoretical attitude vis-à-vis the positing of being, he recognizes the irreducibility of each of these attitudes within spiritual life. And Dilthey and Heidegger agree.

In fact, Husserl suggests a more fundamental sense of 'practical'. Namely, he argues that there is a 'personal or motivational attitude' pertaining to spiritual life that circumscribes a broader sense of the practical, viz. 'the active or passive Ego and indeed in the proper intrinsic sense'.[19] This is the Ego in its activity and passivity, its spontaneity and affectivity; in essence, in how it lives. It is according to this more fundamental sense of the practical, rather than the 'practical attitude' in contradistinction to the theoretical and axiological attitudes[20] that Heidegger uses to capture the way in which we live toward our environing world or, later, Dasein *as* being-in-the-world.

Therefore, when Heidegger comes to describe the more primordial sense of world, he says that, in its ontic sense, it is 'that "wherein" a factical Dasein as such can be said to "live" '.[21] Its ontological sense is the 'worldhood of the world' and is characterized by involvement (*Bewandtnis*) and significance (*Bedeutsamkeit*). To use the previous example, the present-at-hand world of the mathematician that contains numbers, theorems, etc., viz. the world of mathematical objects, is not one in which we can live. Rather, the world in which Dasein can live provides a context for Dasein's activities. An example of this kind of world would be what is commonly expressed by the phrase 'the business world'. In this case, one certainly does not mean simply faxes, computers, copiers, etc. but rather the totality of business activities. Thus, this more primordial sense of world represents the factical context in which we carry out our activities.

Heidegger's redescription of the world is duly famous. However, an undue fascination with the active and spontaneous aspects of his descriptions of the world has led many to give voluntaristic readings of Heidegger's early philosophy.[22] When more carefully examined, however, one can see an interplay of spontaneity and affectivity in Heidegger's characterization of the world wherein Dasein lives. For instance, in 1919, when giving a concrete description of the lived-experience of the environing world, he says,

> I see the lectern in one fell swoop, so to speak, and not in isolation, but as adjusted a bit too high for me. I see – and immediately so – a book lying upon it as annoying to me (a book, not a collection of layered pages with black marks strewn upon them), I see the lectern in an orientation, an illumination, a background ... In the experience of seeing the lectern something is given *to me* [*gibt sich mir*] from out of an immediate environment.[23]

For many, passages such as these suggest that Heidegger is prioritizing our active comportment towards the world over the theoretical comportment of merely 'staring at' it. No doubt this is, to a certain extent, true. But more importantly Heidegger is pointing to the essential way in which, in life, something affects us, or as he will later say something 'touches' [*berühren*] us.[24] And he is contrasting this with the way in which transcendental philosophy relies one-sidedly upon the spontaneity of the Ego for the constitution or construction of the transcendent something, which makes it fundamentally something *for the Ego* or *for consciousness* rather than something *given to me*.

Furthermore, things are given to me *from out of* an environing world, rather than being constituted in pure consciousness, as Husserl would have it, or being constructed by the transcendental Ego as the Neo-Kantians contend. Accordingly, Heidegger says, 'Living in an environment, it signifies to me everywhere and always, everything has the character of world. It is everywhere the case that "*it worlds*" [*es weltet*] ...'[25]

Having said this, it certainly does not mean that Heidegger wishes to downplay the active or spontaneous aspects of life. In our concernful dealings (*besorgenden Umgang*) with things, the things dealt with, the *pragmata*, the ready-to-hand, are gauged with respect to their serviceability, conduciveness, usability and manipulability.[26] That is, through understanding (*Verstehen*) Dasein projects possibilities of being onto things in its concernful dealings.

What is overlooked in voluntaristic accounts of our being-in-the-world is that such projections can fail and things that we deal with can be conspicuous, obtrusive and obstinate. When this happens their worldly character 'announces itself', i.e. the world becomes conspicuous, obtrusive and obstinate to one extent or another.[27] Thus, there is both a spontaneous and affective component to the way in which we live in and toward our environing world.

More significantly, the 'being-there' (*Das Da-sein*) of Dasein is a function of state-of-mind (*Befindlichkeit*), which '*has already disclosed, in every case, Being-in-the-world as a whole, and makes it possible first of all to direct oneself towards something*'.[28] Moreover, this '*implies a disclosive submission to the world, out of which we encounter something that matters to us*'.[29] Only in this way can something be serviceable or unserviceable, inconspicuous or obtrusive, useful or obstinate. In fact, state-of-mind is the way in which Dasein can factically have a world wherein it can live, i.e. it captures what Heidegger calls Dasein's 'thrownness' (*Geworfenheit*).

State-of-mind is not a spontaneous act on Dasein's part; rather the phenomenon of state-of-mind has 'long been well-known ontically under the terms "affects" and "feeling" '.[30] But Heidegger notes that no progress has been made on its ontological interpretation since Aristotle's work on rhetoric. Rather, it has simply been interpreted as a psychical phenomenon alongside cognition and volition, i.e. as one of the three fundamental attitudes that characterized the Kantian legacy in transcendental phenomenology and Neo-Kantianism.

Pervading Heidegger's early philosophy is a sensitivity to the affectivity and passivity involved in life and lived-experience. Namely, that human life is characterized by the lived-experience that 'there is something', i.e. that in life we *encounter* something, and that this is made possible by our being thrown into a factical environing world. One must hold fast to this in order to avoid succumbing to purely voluntaristic distortions of human life and activity. However, we must also be wary of falling into the contrary misinterpretation, which tends to see in Heidegger's philosophy the view that human beings are at the mercy of some primordial, creative life-force.

Kisiel is no doubt correct when he says that 'Heidegger indicates that he understands such impersonals [e.g. it worlds (*es weltet*)] more in terms of the intransitive verb instead of the substantifying "it" ', and that ' "It" is a sheer action, both subjectless and objectless'.[31] However, he proceeds to virtually substantize this 'it', since he goes on to interpret it as 'this obviously primary but mysterious "something" of life and sheer being which "takes place", happens to me . . . Life befalls me, anonymously, impersonally. I am of It, I find myself in It willy-nilly, already under way in existence.'[32] Although it is neither a subject nor an object, for Kisiel life is merely the ineffable and indefinable something in which meaning is constituted, i.e. it is the indefinable and inscrutable 'event' of meaning. More to the point, Kisiel appears to reduce life to a purely spontaneous power of meaning creation, i.e. the movement of life is a creative, historical event, a productive break-ing-forth that one can only absorb. This is simply the counter-position to the voluntaristic interpretation.

Contrary to both interpretations, Heidegger maintains that life, i.e. Dasein as being-in-the-world, is essentially an interplay of spontaneity and affectivity. Dasein is, Heidegger says, a 'thrown projection'. One can see in this Aristotle's continued influence on Heidegger's thought, for it was Aristotle who argued that all motion, including that of life, is an interplay of spontaneity and affectivity.

Thus, Kisiel is quite right that in using the impersonal 'it worlds' Heidegger wants to focus on the intransitive verb. For instance, in the winter of 1921–2, Heidegger will note that 'to live' has an intransitive sense, e.g. 'to live "in" something, to live "out of" something, to live "against" something, to live "following" something, to live "from" something'.[33] And he goes on to argue that this something 'whose manifold relations to "living" are indicated in these prepositional expressions ... is what we call "world"'.[34] That is, the affectivity of life consists of its necessary contextualization in a factical world. For instance, *in the world* something exists, something works, something fails, something values, something ought to be, etc. In essence, life requires a factical world wherein Dasein can live.

However, 'to live' also has a transitive sense. Heidegger says that this transitive sense is embodied in the expressions 'to live life' and 'to live one's mission in life' and that 'here for the most part we find compounds: "to live through [*durchleben*] something", "to live out [*verleben*] one's years idly", and, especially, "to have a lived-experience [*erleben*] of something."'[35] This transitive sense of 'to live', viz. to comport oneself towards something, represents the spontaneity of life. In *Being and Time*, this is characterized by the 'in-order-to' (*das Um-zu*), the 'towards-which' (*das Wozu*), and the 'for-the-sake-of-which' (*das Worumwillen*). That is, that nature of Dasein's existence is not exhausted by its 'disclosive submission' to the world, but it is also characterized by the fact that it actively comports itself in and towards the world and 'innerworldly beings'.

Heidegger says that the transitive and intransitive senses of the verb to live are ambiguously nominalized in the term 'life' and that rather than eliminating the ambiguity we must 'let it remain' and 'seize hold of it'.[36] Furthermore, in life '... we always move [*bewegen*] in an understanding of being'.[37] We are now in a position to see what this signifies. In essence, it means that Dasein is (1) affected by its world and things in this world, i.e. it is 'factically thrown' into a world wherein it can live and (2) it comports itself towards its world. Therefore, to a significant extent, Husserl's contribution to Heidegger's analysis of being-in-the-world lies in Heidegger's appropriation of Husserl's insights into the 'life of the spirit' and its motivational structure, i.e. the way in which we actively and passively encounter entities within the world. At the same time, it was Dilthey who recognized the fundamental role that the notion of world played within the structure of life.

2.   *Techne*, science, ontology and fundamental ontology

Turning back to what has been our primary focus, we must examine how Heidegger resituates philosophy in life. If our interpretation of philosophy is to be guided by the idea of primordial science, which by the mid-1920s had become, in Heidegger's thought, inseparably connected with the notion of a fundamental ontology, then we will also need to investigate the way in which Heidegger resituates science in life, both what he calls the sciences of beings, i.e. the special sciences, and the science of being, viz. ontology. However, this requires that we look at how Heidegger understands our technical dealings in the world. That is, in his approach to philosophy and science, Heidegger appropriates Aristotle's own analysis in the first book of his *Metaphysics*,[38] where Aristotle claims that *sophia* arises from *episteme*, which arises from *techne*, which, in turn, arises from *empeiria*. However, Heidegger appropriates Aristotle's account from within the context of the broadly Kantian perspectives that we have examined in the preceding chapters.

What we shall see is that for Heidegger each 'stage' in the analysis of the living character of *techne*, science, ontology and finally fundamental ontology correspond to different levels in which *something is there* for us, i.e. in which Dasein encounters something. Moreover, each successive stage is achieved by means of our transcending the previous stage in a 'transcendental turn'. In other words, the higher stages are not merely refined or specific versions of earlier stages, but rather each stage represents a wholly original comportment toward being. This is contrary to those who view Heidegger through a pragmatic lens, i.e. to those who claim that Heidegger holds to the thesis that meaning is ultimately grounded in and through our pragmatic engagement with the world and who uphold the thesis of the 'primacy of practice'.[39] The truth is, for Heidegger our 'technical comportments' (*technischen Verhalten*) toward entities are simply the most ontic of Dasein's comportments, i.e. those in which we deal with entities 'unthematically'. In its technical comportments, Dasein encounters what is ontically closest, but ontologically furthest away. Our scientific, ontological and finally fundamentally ontological comportments are wholly original comportments wherein we transcend our purely ontic, technical comportments to levels of ontological thematization and comportment.

The first question we will consider, then, is how does science arise from out of our technical comportments? More broadly, how does science arise in the context of life? Heidegger calls this the question of the 'existential concept of science'. With Natorp, Heidegger argues that science is predicated on our everyday dealings in life.[40] Heidegger says that 'The basic structures of any such area [of scientific research] have already been worked out after a fashion in our pre-scientific ways of experiencing and interpreting that domain of Being in which the area of subject-matter is itself confined.'[41] Thus, we need to scrutinize these pre-scientific ways of experiencing and interpreting beings.

As with all of life, our technical dealings are infused with both active and passive components. For instance, we are passively affected by something, which leads to an active reaction to it, and this in turn leads to a counter-reaction in which it either yields to our purposes or resists us in some way.[42] As we have seen, Dasein's dealings in the world presuppose that it is passively affected by the world, viz. that 'Dasein *exists* factically, i.e. *is in a world* ... and [that] beings always already lie before Dasein as somehow revealed',[43] and in this way Dasein is able to actively comport itself towards those beings. At the lowest level, this represents 'the world as it is immediately accessible to practical Dasein'.[44]

In this world, we predominantly comport ourselves towards innerworldly beings through our 'practical' or pragmatic dealings with them. These innerwordly beings of our practical dealings can be either natural or spiritual entities. Most significantly, our comportment towards them does not primarily consist of merely staring or gazing at them and passively perceiving them. Rather, in the case of nature, Heidegger claims that we encounter beings in a technical manner. That is, we encounter natural beings by the resistance that they offer to our technical comportments, e.g. producing, manipulating, organizing, measuring, etc. In these technical comportments, we utilize tools or equipment (*Zeug*) and we use these *on* something. Both our understanding of equipment and that upon which we employ equipment arise from within the context of our dealings with them. We get to know (*kennen*) equipment by using or employing (*gebrauchen*) it.[45] Thus, our 'pre-ontological understanding' of equipmental beings comes from using them. More specifically, we get to know equipment by understanding a possible use to which they could be put and employing them in that manner. In the world of Dasein's technical dealings, equipment is, in Heidegger's words, 'ready-to-hand'.

Likewise, that upon which we employ equipment, i.e. what in an everyday sense is called 'nature' and, correspondingly, 'natural beings', are also not understood by gaping at or reflecting on them, but by the way in which we encounter them in our artful dealings. More specifically, nature is that which stands over against our technical comportments. Thus, Heidegger says, '. . . we do not reveal nature in its might and power by reflecting on it, but by struggling against it and by protecting ourselves from it and by dominating it.'[46] This includes the natural beings that are used as equipment, those natural beings upon which we use the equipment, and simply the 'might and power' of nature that intrudes into our practical lives. That is, at the lowest level, nature is simply what resists our practical purposes or impinges upon us. In the world of Dasein's technical dealings, nature represents what is broadly 'present-at-hand'.

In essence, in all our technical dealings and comportments 'there is something'. Specifically, innerworldly beings are encountered in a preconceptual and pre-objective way. Moreover, in these dealings we are absorbed exclusively with beings and only in so far as they manifest themselves in such dealings. In this case, we ourselves and that which stands over against us are there in a thoroughly ontic manner. So much so that many times the two are hardly distinguishable from one another. Even when our technical dealings are momentarily suspended and we survey the practical situation this is still done for the sake of resuming our technical comportments toward the world, and not primarily in such a way that we distinguish ourselves from that with which we are dealing.

For this reason, Heidegger says that the transition to the scientific comportment does not result from the mere secession of our technical dealings. In addition, he also believes that the scientific comportment is not achieved through the mere contemplation of beings. In fact, Heidegger maintains that our scientific comportment 'demands and includes technical arrangements and manipulations'. And that 'This is borne out by every construction of an experimental arrangement in the natural sciences, by editorial work and philological investigations, by archeological excavations, and by the history of art.'[47] Thus, he says that neither the absence of technical comportments, i.e. *'praxis'*, nor mere contemplation characterizes the scientific comportment.

Similar to what we saw in Husserl's analysis of science, Heidegger says that what characterizes an ontic scientific comportment, i.e. a scientific comportment toward beings, is its purpose, viz. to reveal beings as beings by disclosing them in their what and how, and *for the sake of this very revealing*. That is, ontic science is a kind of activity that is done for its own sake. Far from signifying an absence of *praxis*, Heidegger's characterization of the comportment characteristic of ontic science corresponds precisely to Aristotle's description of the kind of activity that he calls *praxis*. For example, in the *Metaphysics* Aristotle remarks that, in *praxis*, '. . . the action is the end, and the actuality is the action'.[48]

One must be clear about what this means. For one can easily succumb to the mistaken notion that a scientific comportment *merely* produces something, e.g. a scientific articulation of innerworldly beings. This may be one of its essential accomplishments, but this is not its proper end. To think that its end is to *produce* something would be to interpret scientific comportment as itself a kind of technical comportment, viz. as a comportment whose for-the-sake-of-which is to produce *something*. In this case, it would not be a *praxis*, but a *poeisis*, i.e. an activity of making or producing. This is also why it is not a pragmatic form of activity. In other words, it cannot be evaluated on the basis of whether it works or not, whether it is efficacious or not. In other words, it is not as if ontic science is a tool that could be dispensed with if it doesn't fulfil the use or purpose for which it is employed.

As a *praxis*, the activity of science is done for its own sake. As Aristotle says, 'All men by nature desire to know',[49] and Heidegger says that 'science [is] a kind of knowing. But we do not mean knowing in the sense of the known, but rather as a knowing comportment.'[50] Properly understood, then, the ontic scientific comportment is a way in which Dasein *can be*, i.e. a possible way for Dasein to exist. Thus, Heidegger remarks that '. . . *scientific* knowing is characterized by the fact that the existing Dasein sets before itself, as a freely chosen task, the uncovering [*Enthüllung*] of the beings which are already somehow accessible, *for the sake of their being uncovered*.'[51]

That it is a freely chosen task indicates that this task has not been imposed on Dasein from without, e.g. it is not merely a reaction to practical exigencies, but is rather a task that Dasein chooses for itself. In other words, Heidegger argues that in this 'free projection' Dasein has chosen for itself a 'task of existence'.[52] In his explication of the task of existence that is science, it is clear that Heidegger is relying on Natorp's conception of science as a model. For, as we noted in Chapter 3, Natorp believed that what is *a priori* to knowledge, and more specifically scientific knowledge, is its task. Furthermore, Natorp argues that this task is carried out by means of progressively determining the object of knowledge and this means projecting a conceptual objectification of the being and appearance of the object. In other words, one projects a conceptual determination of the object such that the concepts can be seen to be the being of the object, i.e. that by which it is known, and that the appearances can be seen to be appearances of the object, i.e. that by which it is experienced.

Heidegger follows Natorp in this regard. For Heidegger maintains that 'the basic act which accomplishes [*vollziehen*] the conversion of prescientific to the scientific comportment' is the act of objectification.[53] Because of his epistemological commitments, Natorp construed this act of objectification fairly narrowly in so far as he restricted the concepts at work to merely those that are lawful. Heidegger broadens the range and scope of the concepts that must be employed in carrying out our scientific comportment, and he also recognizes that the 'appearances' correspond to our preontological understanding of beings as revealed through our technical and practical comportments.

That is, in carrying out the task of science we project an objectification of the pre-scientific something by employing concepts that are appropriate to our pre-objective, pre-scientific understanding of the being that is to be objectified. In other words, the objectification that an ontic science projects must use concepts that are appropriate to what Heidegger calls our preontological understanding of the realm of beings that comprises the subject matter of the science. He also refers to these as the 'basic concepts' of the science. In other words, the conceptual objectification accomplished in science must be seen to *be* that very being which we were dealing with in our pre-scientific, pre-objective comportments. Or, put another way, the object must be seen *as* the being that we were dealing with pre-scientifically and pre-objectively.

In this way, it is clear that the accomplished objectification is a consequence of a new scientific comportment towards the *very same* being towards which we had comported ourselves in our technical and practical dealings. Thus, we see that Heidegger is making use of two meanings of the term 'projection'. On the one hand, the projection of scientific comportment is the plan or design by which the task embodied in such a comportment is carried out. On the other hand, this task is accomplished by projecting *an* objectification in such a way that the resulting object can be seen to unify all of our pre-scientific, pre-objective dealings, analogous to the way in which an artist projects a single point in order to capture perspective.

In addition, the projection and articulation of the conceptual objectification of beings that takes place in science will itself lead to new technical and practical comportments towards those beings, which will, in turn, eventually lead to a new projection of a conceptual objectification, and so on and so forth. In just this way, we can see how the scientific comportment is a *praxis*, i.e. an activity whose for-the-sake-of-which is that very activity.

To make this clear, Heidegger uses the example of Galilean natural science. Heidegger argues that the scientific comportment underlying Galilean natural science consisted of projecting a conceptual objectification of nature in such a way that it can be seen to be the very same being with which we were dealing in our technical comportments towards nature and through which our pre-ontological understanding of nature arose. At the time, those technical comportments included most prominently mathematical measurement and calculation, whose products were 'facts (*Tatsachen*) of nature'.[54]

In Galileo's time, the pre-modern conception of nature as natural *substance* no longer corresponded with the technical comportments by which nature was being dealt with. That is, the pre-modern notion of a natural substance was simply not amenable to mathematical measurement or calculation. Galileo therefore recognized that nature must be objectified using concepts appropriate to the modern technical comportments through which nature was increasingly being mastered. Thus, by projecting an objectification of nature according to the basic concepts of motion, velocity, body, place and time, viz. by projecting nature as moving bodies located in space and time, the scientifically achieved conceptual objectification of nature was revealed to be the very same being with which we were dealing in our pre-scientific comportments. As Heidegger puts it, 'It is only in light of the mathematical opening and projection of nature, i.e. by delimiting [nature] through such basic concepts as body, motion, velocity, place, and time, that certain *facts* of nature become accessible as facts of *nature*'.[55]

The proper task of an ontic science, then, is to work with the basic concepts of its subject matter as circumscribed by our pre-ontological understanding of that realm of beings. For example, the task of the natural objectification of beings requires the elucidation and explication of the basic concepts of nature. Likewise, the task of the historical objectification of beings requires the elucidation and explication of the basic concepts of history.[56] Heidegger says that this working out of the basic concepts of an ontic science is the elucidation and explication of the 'ontological constitution' of a realm of beings.[57] At the same time, this consists of working out the *objective meaning* of those beings. That is, in so far as an ontic science is a *new* comportment towards beings, as those beings are already accessible through technical comportments, it also brings about a new 'stratum' of meaning for those beings. In this case, it reveals the *objective* meaning of beings or what Heidegger calls 'beings as beings'.[58]

Put differently, an ontic science will project a *world* of objects, e.g. the physical world, the historical world, etc. In many respects, Heidegger's account of the scientific comportment towards beings is familiar from Husserl's own investigations into the constitution of the positive sciences. However, there is a fundamental difference. Namely that Husserl argued that the constitution of the objective meaning of beings can only take place in the primal region of pure, transcendental consciousness. Heidegger's appropriation of Natorp's conception of scientific knowledge allows him to demonstrate that such a primal region is not necessary. What is needed is the recognition that science is a kind of activity that human beings engage in and which accomplishes the meaningful objectification of beings through its use of concepts. That is, the constitution of meaning in science occurs in life itself, not in a pure region of consciousness.[59] And this is why Heidegger can claim that it is a 'task of existence' for Dasein.

It is worth noting that beings can resist our scientific attempts at objectification. That is, science cannot easily and wilfully impose its concepts upon beings. A perfect example of this is the *Methodenstreit* between the natural and human sciences. The attempt to project the conceptual structures appropriate to the natural sciences onto beings that are encountered in our pre-ontological dealings with spirit, e.g. historical beings, failed or at least became exceedingly difficult and forced. The human sciences require their own basic concepts and thus their own form of objectification as is appropriate to our pre-understanding of the beings towards which these sciences comport themselves. Moreover, even within its appropriate subject matter, a science must struggle with and against beings in so far as it must work out the concepts that are appropriate to our pre-ontological understanding of beings.[60] In essence, the spontaneity and affectivity of life pervades the ontic sciences.

Finally, this new scientific comportment *transcends* our everyday technical and practical comportments and it does so by working out the transcendental source of those comportments. That is, science comports itself conceptually towards the very being that the corresponding technical and practical comportments were pre-scientifically directed towards. In this way, the objectification accomplished in science represents the transcendent source which unifies our pre-ontological understanding of beings as they arose in numerous technical and practical comportments. That is, it is *the* unity that transcends (i.e. lies beyond, not behind) those technical and practical comportments. Put differently, only our ontic, scientific comportments reveal the objects that we in fact were struggling against, manipulating, protecting ourselves against, etc. in our technical and practical dealings. As an objective, unifying source of these technical and practical dealings, it is also a transcendental condition for the possibility of these technical and practical comportments. Interestingly, then, the objectifications accomplished through ontic science represent the transcendent, transcendental condition for the possibility of our technical and practical comportments.

Given the limits of their task, Heidegger says that the ontic sciences cannot inquire into their own 'self-founding' (*Selbstbegründung*), i.e. they cannot investigate their own ability to project, as a task, the conceptual objectification of beings. For Heidegger, an indication that such a founding is necessary is evidenced by the fact that the ontic sciences undergo crises in their basic concepts.[61] This signifies that the ontic sciences need a founding discipline. An ontic science can elucidate and explicate its basic concepts and can apply these concepts so as to objectively determine beings, but it cannot inquire into the being of its conceptual objectification of a region of beings. For example, Heidegger says that '. . . whereas the physicist defines what he understands by motion and circumscribes what place and time mean – whereby he relies in part on ordinary concepts – still, however, he does not make motion's way of being a theme of his investigation'.[62]

For Heidegger, *ontology* is the task that accomplishes the founding of the ontic sciences. That is, it is ontology that inquires into the 'ontological constitution' that takes place in the ontic sciences. Moreover, Heidegger notes that ontology investigates the 'ontological constitution' of any region of beings, i.e. any *regional ontology*, whether it is the subject matter of a 'factual science' or not. Therefore he says that

> . . . the question concerning the ontological constitution of beings is not solely limited or primarily referred to a being which is just the object of a factual science. Rather, all beings . . . can and must be explicated with respect to their ontological constitution – e.g. the world as it is immediately accessible to practical Dasein.[63]

In addition, Heidegger maintains that ontology is itself a science, in this case, the science of the being of beings. Thus, it too accomplishes its task through objectification. In this case, however, what is being objectified are not beings, but the being of beings: 'All ontological inquiry objectifies being as such. All ontic investigation objectifies beings.'[64] Indeed, as a science, ontology shares with the ontic sciences the scientific comportment as was described above. For this reason, ontology is similarly a freely projected task, viz. a 'task of existence' for Dasein. Hence, ontology is a possible way of being for Dasein, which is at least in part why Heidegger can assert that '*Understanding of Being is itself a definite characteristic of Dasein's Being*. Dasein is ontically distinctive in that it *is* ontological.'[65]

Ontology's projected task is to objectify the being of beings and therefore, analogous to the ontic sciences, it too must have a pre-understanding of that with which it deals. This signifies that we have a pre-understanding of the being of beings and this arises from our dealings with the ontological constitution of beings. Since ontology founds the ontic sciences we can look to these for an indication of the ways in which we deal with the being of beings. The question is then, in our conceptual objectification of beings, how do we comport ourselves towards that conceptual objectification? In this we are not asking how we thematize the process of conceptual objectification, which is what the science of ontology does, but rather what we employ and use in our conceptual objectification of beings and through which we encounter in a technical and practical way the ontological constitution of beings, analogous to the way in which the ontic sciences rely on measurement, calculation, experimentation, etc.

Certainly, the most systematic way in which this happens is in the accomplishments of ontic science itself, i.e. in the ontic scientific process of conceptually objectifying beings. In this process, we encounter the conceptual determination and objectification of beings through our formation of judgements, opinions, hypotheses, etc., which then get taken up into the ontic sciences. Moreover, we also deal with the conceptual determination of beings when we evaluate something, i.e. in our axiological reasoning, and when we deliberate about means and ends, i.e. in our volitional reasoning. These too can be taken up systematically by an ontic science. In essence, we deal with the ontological constitution of beings in what Rickert, Husserl, Natorp and Dilthey called our cognitive, evaluative and volitional lived-experiences. And it is by employing and using these and, systematically, by taking them up into an ontic science that we ontologically constitute beings. Thus the science of ontology itself has its own *praxis* akin to the ontic sciences, which is, very broadly understood, our conceptual dealings with beings.

The science of ontology, then, is the task of projecting an objectification of that which we already encounter in our practical and technical dealings with the ontological constitution of beings, i.e. our dealings with the being of beings. As with the ontic sciences, we can say that the task of the science of ontology is characterized by the fact that the existing Dasein sets before itself, as a freely chosen task, the uncovering of the being of beings which is already somehow accessible to us, for the sake of its being uncovered. In this way, it too is a *praxis* for Dasein, i.e. an activity whose for-the-sake-of-which is that activity itself.[66] In the course of accomplishing its task, the science of ontology formulates ontologies, i.e. objectifications of the being of beings.

What are these objectifications? In order to answer this, we must inquire into what it is that our cognitive, evaluative and volitional lived-experiences struggle with and what it is that ontic science struggles with. In essence, in these we struggle with ways in which a subject can relate itself conceptually towards an object or a region of objects. Or, most generally, the ways in which subjectivity comports itself towards its world. In the case of the theoretical ontic sciences, this is specifically the knowing relation between subjectivity and its world. However, in these lived-experiences themselves and in ontic science, of course, this is what is struggled with, not what is thematized and uncovered. In sum, we struggle with how we relate ourselves toward the world. It is the task of the science of ontology to project an objectification of this.

Analogous to the requirement of objectification in the ontic sciences, the projected objectification in the science of ontology must be seen to be the objectification of what was encountered in our pre-understanding of the being of beings, i.e. in our dealings with the being of beings. This means that the projected objectification must realize in a unifying and objectifying fashion what it was that was being struggled with in our formation of judgements, in ontic science, etc. This projected objectification should be the *objective meaning* of the ways in which subjectivity is related to its world in so far as this is already accessible in our comportments towards it.

Traditionally, these objectifications have been called categories. Therefore, we can also say that the science of ontology will work out the categories of being. Of course the projection and articulation of the objective meaning of the relation between subjectivity and its world will itself lead to new concrete lived-experiences and new ontic sciences, etc. This will, in turn, eventually lead to a reworking of the objective relation between subjectivity and its world, and so on and so forth. That is, our understanding of the relation between subjectivity and the world will change and develop.

At first sight, this may seem a peculiar way of characterizing the science of ontology. For, after all, the 'traditional' notion of the discipline of ontology is that it works out the highest and most general concepts of all beings and, therefore, works out the most general ontological constitution of beings.[67] We cannot fully examine this claim here, but needless to say, Heidegger thinks that this merely collapses the distinction between being and beings. The result is that ontology simply becomes the *über* ontic science and, even if there were such a thing, it would not be able to account for its own self-founding any more than the other ontic sciences could. That is, it could not inquire into its own ontological constitution of beings and, therefore, it would need to be founded in the science of ontology.

Heidegger's notion of ontology can perhaps best be exemplified by examining his unorthodox and controversial claim that the 'positive outcome' of Kant's *Critique of Pure Reason* was an ontology of nature, rather than a theory of knowledge.[68] According to Heidegger's interpretation, Kant predicated his first critique on the fact that we have synthetic *a priori* knowledge of nature. That is, he began with the fact that there is a certain exemplary relatedness between subjectivity and the natural world. This is embodied, for Kant, in the ontic sciences of theoretical geometry and theoretical physics, which for Kant represent the foundation for all of our scientific knowledge of nature. In other words, these two ontic sciences elucidate and make explicit the basic concepts of nature presupposed by every science of nature. However, neither the science of theoretical geometry nor theoretical physics is capable of investigating the being of their basic concepts and the way in which they objectively determine nature.

As an *ontological* inquiry, the first *Critique* investigates the way in which nature is dealt with in these ontic sciences, viz. how it is that they engage with the task of and accomplish a conceptual objectification of nature. What is striking to Kant about these sciences is that they are able to conceptually objectify nature in an *a priori* fashion. In order to ontologically found these ontic sciences of nature, he turns to the forms of judgement, i.e. to the ways in which the ontic sciences accomplish their task. In these forms of judgement, he discovers the pure concepts of the understanding or, simply, the categories. However, these, in turn, are the result of the unity of apperception or transcendental subjectivity, which uses them in its constitution of objective experience. In this, Heidegger argues that Kant has worked out the objective meaning of the relation holding between subjectivity and the world which lays the foundation for the ontic sciences of nature. Thus, on Heidegger's account of ontology, Kant's first critique accomplishes an ontology of nature.

In this regard, Husserl's transcendental phenomenology is a much more ambitious ontology than Kant's in so far as the former takes as its task not merely the objectification of the ontological constitution of beings by the sciences of nature, but rather the ontological constitution of every possible region of beings. Correspondingly, Husserl engages in an ontological inquiry into the totality of ways in which we can meaningfully intend any being whatsoever. The resulting categories of being are the absolute being of pure consciousness, viz. the pure stream of lived-experiences, on the one hand, and being as manifested in consciousness, on the other hand. That is, it is in pure consciousness that all the regions of beings as manifested in consciousness are meaningfully constituted. Finally, it is the pure Ego that lives through pure consciousness towards beings. According to Heidegger, then, this too is an ontology, since it specifies the *objective meaning* of what is already encountered in our intentional dealings with beings.

In like manner, Rickert's philosophy of value and Dilthey's early critique of historical reason are ontological inquiries. Specifically, Rickert's philosophy of value attempts to project an ontological objectification based on the normative character of our judgements, and Dilthey inquires ontologically into our ability to achieve understanding (*verstehen*) in the human sciences.

As is the case in the ontic sciences, the attempts at categorial objectification in the science of ontology can fail. Heidegger certainly did not have to look far to find supposed instances of this failure, namely psychologism, naturalism and historicism. As has been mentioned, these were criticized for their relativistic implications. But if we examine them from the perspective of Heidegger's account of ontological inquiry, we can perhaps see more perspicuously in what way they exemplified for him failed ontological projects. From this vantage point, the crux of the issue is not whether they devolve into relativism, but whether their objectification of the subject's comportment toward its world corresponded in the proper way to the pre-understanding of the being under consideration. From this perspective, Husserl's celebrated critique of psychologism is not directed fundamentally at its relativistic implications, but at the fact that it fails to adequately found the ways in which we meaningfully intend beings. That is, Husserl argues that what psychologism took to be the objective meaning of, for example, mathematical or logical judgements was factual psychological processes. But, because a factual psychological process could never ground the evident, necessary character of our mathematical or logical judgements, psychologism fails as an ontology of the basic concepts of mathematics or logic.

Finally, the objectifications accomplished in the science of ontology *transcend* the ways in which we deal with our relatedness to the world in lived-experience and through the ontic sciences. That is, the science of ontology projects the objective meaning of the relation between subjectivity and the world as it was dealt with in our lived-experiences and in our active engagement in the ontic sciences. This objective relation between subjectivity and the world is the transcendent source that unifies the ways in which we have a pre-understanding of the being of beings as that arose in our lived-experiences and through the ontic sciences. That is, it is a unity that transcends (again, that lies beyond, not behind) any possible lived-experience or ontic science; for instance, the 'unity of apperception' in Kant's philosophy. Only the science of ontology reveals this objective meaning, which is, as an objective, unifying source of these lived-experiences, also the transcendental condition for their possibility.

Having said that Husserl's transcendental phenomenology represents for Heidegger an ontological inquiry, it must be borne in mind that Husserl would not have recognized it as such. As we saw in Chapter 2, Husserl denies that pure consciousness or beings as manifested in that pure consciousness are *projected* objectifications. Rather, he believes that these are *immediately* accessible to us in an objective fashion through phenomenological reflection. That is, as far as Husserl is concerned, the method of the science of phenomenology is entirely different from that of the other sciences. It was on this key point that Heidegger and Natorp criticized Husserl.

We can now see better what Heidegger had in mind when he criticized Husserl. Husserl, Heidegger claims, conceived of pure consciousness or the pure stream of lived-experiences as absolutely existing, i.e. as simply being there regardless of how and whether we comport ourselves towards it – and Husserl was certainly not alone in this respect. What Natorp demonstrated, as Heidegger recognized, was that this was not the case and that our related-ness to the world as that is embodied in our lived-experience cannot be had *immediately* through a simple act of reflective inspection. Contrary to Husserl's account, Heidegger argues that lived-experiences are ways in which we deal with and through which we struggle with our relatedness to the world. In essence, lived-experiences as they are lived are analogous to our everyday technical comportments. Whereas the latter exhibit our pre-scientific dealings with beings, the former display our pre-ontological deal-ings with our relatedness to the world.

Therefore, according to Heidegger, the *objective* meaning of our related-ness to the world is an objectifying projection from out of our living engage-ment with the world, just as the objective meaning of beings is the result of an objectifying projection from out of our living engagement with innerworldly beings. Moreover, the former founds the latter. In both cases, this projection is an achievement of a 'task of existence' of Dasein, i.e. a way of being of Dasein. Going back to our earlier discussion, we can see that the activity of science and of ontology is characterized by thrown-projection, i.e. they project a task from out of a pre-understanding of being. To a significant extent, Dilthey had already glimpsed this in his analysis of philosophical worldviews. Namely, Dilthey saw philosophical worldviews as attempts to solve the 'world-riddle', i.e. the riddle of the unity of life and world, and to do so by conceptually objectifying the relation between life and the world.

He also recognized that these worldviews arise from out of life, viz. that they are unities of life that have their origin in life itself. Thus, the produc-tion of a worldview is a fundamental aspect of life. That is, life projects for itself a world in which we can live concretely, i.e. a world of objects to be thought, valued and used, as well as the ways in which we are related to these. That is, Dilthey's conception of a worldview embodies what Heideg-ger believes to be the accomplishment of the science of ontology and the ontic sciences, viz. an objectification of beings and of our relatedness to those beings. However, Dilthey also argues that the history of world-views demonstrates our 'sovereignty' over any particular worldview. That

114   *Heidegger and Aristotle*

is, the rise and fall of worldviews, i.e. of ontologies, demonstrates that life is sovereign over these worldviews, i.e. that life is autonomous of any one worldview. Interestingly, Dilthey's theory of the history of worldviews demonstrates that ontology goes through crises just as the ontic sciences do. Put differently, the history of ontology demonstrates Dasein's sovereignty over any particular ontology.

For Heidegger this indicates that ontology itself needs to be founded: a founding that, because of the limitations of ontology's task, ontology cannot itself perform. Thus, Heidegger says, '*Laying the foundation of a science of beings means founding and developing the ontology which underlies this science.* In turn, these ontologies are grounded in *fundamental ontology*, which constitutes the *center of philosophy*.'[69] When Heidegger came to criticize Husserl and Kant, among others, he argued that they had not asked the question of 'the being of subjectivity' or the 'being of Dasein'. We now understand that this signifies that Heidegger thought that they had not founded their own ontological accomplishment, i.e. their own objectification of the subject's comportment towards the world, just as the ontic sciences had failed to found their conceptual objectification of beings. Therefore, what is needed is a *fundamental* ontology, viz. an inquiry into the being of our comportments toward the world. Or, put differently, ontology needs to be founded upon an inquiry into Dasein as being-in-the-world. This will require that we exhibit the ways in which we pre-understand our being-in-the-world, i.e. we need to 'destroy' the history of ontology by tracing ontology back to our 'fundamental experiences' of our being-in-the-world.[70]

Fundamental ontology will found both ontology and the sciences of beings in so far as each of these *are* comportments toward the world, i.e. ways of being-in-the-world or 'tasks of existence'. Indeed, fundamental ontology's task will be to project a world in which Dasein can live. Within the context of such a world we can technically comport ourselves towards beings, the ontic sciences can objectify beings, and ontology can objectify our comportments toward the world. But, as a task, fundamental ontology is itself a way of being, a 'task of existence', for Dasein. Thus, fundamental ontology is Dasein's way of existing in which it projects for itself a world in which it can exist. In this regard, fundamental ontology is not just any *praxis*, e.g. the *praxis* of science, but the *praxis of life itself*, which is the source of every other *praxis*.

In this manner, fundamental ontology represents primordial science because it is both the source of every science, whether of beings or of the being of beings, and is itself situated in life as well as formative of life. Moreover, it is a pre-objective, pre-theoretical inquiry, precisely because it is the source of ontology and the sciences of beings in which all objectification take place. Finally, whereas the ontic sciences ask about the meaning of beings and ontology asks about the meaning of the being of beings, both of which can have an objective meaning, fundamental ontology asks simply about the meaning of being. In Chapter 6 we will turn to Heidegger's analysis of fundamental ontology and its relation to philosophy and life.

Philosophy as Praxis

In this final chapter we will examine Heidegger's understanding of philosophy as praxis. We ended Chapter 5 by exhibiting the task of fundamental ontology. Our discussion there was set specifically in the context of Heidegger's appropriation of fundamental ontology from out of the broadly Kantian context of his predecessors. However, we also mentioned that Heidegger's analysis of the way in which science, ontology and fundamental ontology are interrelated and the way in which they arise in and out of life was, in large part, inspired by Aristotle's own account.

Now we will look at Heidegger's account of the task of fundamental ontology, but this time principally from the context of his engagement with and appropriation of Aristotle's discussion of *proto philosophia*. It is important in this regard to elucidate, from Heidegger's perspective, how Aristotle's own notion of first philosophy was developed in the history of philosophy. Heidegger believes that in the process of this development the very task of fundamental ontology became concealed. Moreover, this was no perversion of Aristotle's own aims, but rather the result of following out a direction of inquiry that Aristotle himself indicated. Heidegger sees, therefore, the possibility of a renewal and reappropriation of first philosophy through a hermeneutic return to Aristotle. That is, Heidegger finds in Aristotle the setting forth of the task of fundamental ontology.

From Chapter 5, we know which elements Heidegger will be looking for when he examines Aristotle's articulation of first philosophy. That is, as with the task of the ontic sciences and of ontology, fundamental ontology must have its own peculiar pre-understanding of being. In this latter case, what is required is a pre-understanding of the meaning of being, i.e. how we encounter the meaning of being in our dealings with it. Secondly, as a task of inquiry, fundamental ontology projects something out of this pre-understanding of the meaning of being. Unlike ontic science and ontology, fundamental ontology does not project an objectification, but rather a world in which Dasein can exist, i.e. a world in which we can live. To accomplish this, fundamental ontology must employ non-objectifying categories, or what Heidegger will call in the early 1920s 'the categories of life'. These categories don't objectify life, but rather indicate structures in which Dasein can live. Finally, we shall look at the way in which Heidegger resituates philosophy in the *praxis* of life through his attempt to go beyond the two dominant conceptions of philosophy in his time, viz. philosophy as worldview and as scientific philosophy.

1. Aristotle on first philosophy and its modern development

When Heidegger comes to describe our pre-understanding of being in *Being and Time*, he notes that 'We do not *know* what "Being" means. But even if we ask, "What *is* 'Being'?" we keep within an understanding of the "is", though we are unable to fix conceptually what that "is" signifies.'[1] Thus, the question arises as to what is the relation between the *meaning* of being and being. The answer, Heidegger believes, lies in *living discourse* [*Rede*], though this certainly should not be understood solely as a 'vocal proclamation in words' which is merely discourse 'when fully concrete'.[2] Rather, discourse represents Heidegger's appropriation of the Greek *logos*.[3] He says, '*Logos* as "discourse" means rather the same as *deloun*: to make manifest what one is "talking about" in one's discourse.'[4] That is, through living discourse about being we have *a* pre-understanding of being.

On Heidegger's interpretation, Aristotle also believed that metaphysics was grounded in discourse about being, for Aristotle famously poses the problem of metaphysics as whether or not there can be a science of being, given that being is '*said* in many ways'. That is, according to Heidegger, Aristotle recognized that we could only approach first philosophy from the manifold ways in which we address being in our discourse about it.

On the other hand, Aristotle also believed that any science requires a univocal first principle. Thus, it appears at first sight that there cannot be a science of being since being does not have a univocal meaning. Famously, Aristotle says that there can be a science of being because, although 'being is said in many ways' [*to de on legetai men pollachos*], it is always said 'towards one and some one nature' [*pros hen kai mian tina phusin*].[5] Aristotle demonstrates this by showing that the ten categories of being are all *analogically* said of substance (*ousia*).[6] Thus, a science of being is possible for Aristotle in so far as all discourse about categorial being is centred upon substance. This has profound ramifications for the history of metaphysics.

Heidegger argues that Aristotle understood *ousia* primarily through the domain of objects capable of being produced and employed. Heidegger writes,

The domain of objects supplying the primordial sense of being was the domain of those objects *produced* and put into use in dealings. Thus the toward-which this primordial experience of being aimed at was not the domain of being consisting of *things* in the sense of objects understood in a *theoretical* manner as facts but rather the world encountered in going about dealings that produce, direct themselves to routine tasks, and use.[7]

That is, Heidegger claims that the primordial sense of being for Aristotle is the sense of being of those things that we deal with in our practical and technical comportments toward the world. Moreover, Heidegger goes on to argue that Aristotle understands by this primordial sense of being something that one possesses:

> With the objects it addresses, *legein* takes beings in their beingness (*ousia* [substance]) of their look into true safekeeping. But in Aristotle and also after him, *ousia* still retains its original meaning of the household, property, what is at one's disposal for use in one's environing world.[8]

That is, *ousia* is something possessed which is to be used and employed. On the other hand, Heidegger notes that *ousia* does not exhaust the manifold ways in which being is spoken of. Because Aristotle argues that being primarily indicates *ousia*, this signifies to Heidegger that Aristotle understood all being to be fundamentally geared towards what is possessed in order that it can be used or employed.

This becomes decisive in the history of philosophy when Aristotle turns his attention to the being of human beings. At one point, Aristotle says that *logos* is a *hexis* in the human soul. That is, it is a way in which the movement of the soul comes 'to take a stand'. This is exemplified in Aristotle's famous metaphor concerning the soul's movement toward knowledge. He says that

> We conclude these states [*hexis*] of knowledge are neither innate in a determinate form, nor developed from other higher states of knowledge, but from sense-perception. It is like a rout in a battle stopped by first one man making a stand [*stantos*] and then another, until the original formation [*arche*] has been restored. The soul is so constituted as to be capable of this process . . . When one of a number of logically indiscriminable particulars has made a stand, the earliest universal is present in the soul.[9]

That is, a universal is a *logos* that is a *hexis* of the soul.[10] In essence, we see Aristotle suggesting that discourse (*legein*) results in a *hexis* of the soul, i.e. a 'having', 'possessing' or 'habit' of the soul. Consequently, discourse about being, in this case in coming to know beings, results in a hexis of the soul.

However, as Heidegger points out many times, Aristotle understood human being as the *Zoon logon echon*, i.e. the living being which possesses discourse.[11] In this case, *logon* is not a *hexis* of a human being, but is an *echon*. The Greek word *echon* means 'to have or possess something'. Aristotle's discussion of the distinction between *echon* and *hexis* is significant and illuminating. He says that *echon* has a number of meanings, the most important of which are: (1) in an active sense or 'to treat a thing according to one's own nature or according to one's own impulse; so that fever is said to have a man, and tyrants to have their cities, and people to have the clothes they wear'[12] and (2) in a passive sense, viz. 'that in which a thing is present as in something receptive of it is said to have the thing; e.g. the bronze has the form of the statue, and the body has the disease'.[13] The active sense of *echon* is a '*tropon kata ten autou phusin*', i.e. it is to have something in a direction, way or approach (*tropon*) that is in accordance with one's own nature. Thus, human being (as *Zoon logon echon* in its active sense) is the living being who essentially *possesses* discourse for the sake of its own proper end, e.g. as one has clothes that one wears. However, one should not discount the passive sense of *echon* either. That is, human being is the living being that possesses discourse as 'something receptive of it', e.g. as the 'bronze has the statue' or the 'body has the disease'. In this passive sense, human being possesses discourse as being formed by it. This ambiguity in Aristotle's definition of human being, namely, as having discourse for the sake of its own end, i.e. as something to be employed for its own end, and as having discourse as that which informs it, is an ambiguity that Heidegger will use in his own analysis of Dasein. That is, discourse can be something that we can spontaneously use, but we can also be affected by it.

Hexis has an analogous, though quite different, meaning from *echon*. Aristotle says that *hexis* means

> A kind of activity [*energeia*] of the haver [*echontos*] and of what he has [*echomenou*] – something like an action [*praxis*] or movement [*kinesis*]. For when one thing makes [*poie*] and one is made [*poietai*], between them is a making [*poiesis*]; so too between him who has [*echontos*] a garment and the garment which he has [*echomenes*] there is a having [*hexis*]. This sort of having [*hexis*], then, evidently we cannot *have* [*echein*]; for the process will go on to infinity, if it is to be possible to have the having of what we have.[14]

A *hexis* for Aristotle is a possessing or having that itself cannot be possessed. It is the activity or movement (*praxis* or *kinesis*) that is the having itself.

Importantly, this activity or movement is *not* an instance of categorical being, i.e. it is not directed towards *ousia*. This is explicit in Aristotle's under-standing of the categories in so far as *echon* is one of the categories, but *hexis* is not.[15] That is, one has (*echon*) something, an *ousia*, and is had by an *ousia*. However, the very having itself is a *hexis* that is 'between' these. Interest-ingly, production (*poiein*) is likewise one of the categories, since only an *ousia* can be produced. However, neither action (*praxis*) nor movement (*kin-esis*) is a category. That is, *praxis* and movement are utterly different from *poiesis*, viz. producing which has its telos in an *ousia*, or what is to be pro-duced. As we saw in Chapter 5, for Aristotle, a *praxis* is a movement in which the end or 'for-the-sake-of-which' is the *praxis* itself:

> Since of the actions which have a limit none is an end but all are relative to the end, e.g. the removing of fat, or fat-removal, and the bodily parts themselves when one is making them thin are in movement in this way ... this is not an action or at least not a complete one (for it is not an end); but that movement in which the end is present is an action. E.g. at the same time we are seeing and have seen, are understanding and have understood, are thinking and have thought (while it is not true that at the same time we are learning and have learnt) ... At the same time we are living and have lived well.[16]

Praxis transcends the categorical structure centred on *ousia*. Furthermore, according to Aristotle, the activities of life, seeing, understanding and think-ing are all *praxis*, not *poesis*.

Therefore, when Aristotle says that a human being is a living being (*Zoon*) that possesses (*echon*) discourse, this is a substantival definition of human being, i.e. a definition of the *substance* human being. Human being is the *ousia* that has discourse as something possessed (in both the active or passive sense). In this definition of human being, the living character of human being as *praxis* has become subordinated to the categorical structures of thought. In other words, at one point, Aristotle says that a human being is a *living* being characterized by its *praxis*, but when it comes to defining human being, he gives a substantial definition.

Moreover, because of this, discourse has become a possession of a sub-stance and the connection between human life and discourse about being is covered over. Heidegger argues that

> The domain of being consisting of objects of dealings (*poioemenon* [what has been produced], *pragma* [a thing done], *erlon* [a work], *kineseos* [what has been set in motion]) and the mode of addressing these objects

in such dealings, namely, a particular 'logos' or more precisely the objects of such dealings in the how of their being-addressed, mark out the fore-having from which Aristotle drew the basic ontological structures and also the modes of addressing and defining for approaching the object 'human life'.[17]

Significantly, Heidegger argues here that Aristotle took his cue for the analysis of human life from a *particular 'logos'*. Namely, that *logos* for which being is primarily addressed as *ousia*. In this way, both human life and discourse are understood substantially. A human being is therefore understood as a substance that deals with, produces and uses things, and does so primarily by manipulating and using speech. At the same time, however, Aristotle glimpses something that transcends this, namely, the activity of discoursing about being – of which *ousia* is but one particular manifestation. Aristotle, however, does not directly grasp life itself (*praxis*) and its relation to being, discourse and world. Put differently, Aristotle glimpsed that a fundamental way of being of Dasein is to discourse about being. However, by focusing on one way in which Dasein addresses being, i.e. as substance, he covered over the relation between Dasein and its activity of discoursing about being as a kind of *hexis*.

Heidegger believes that this is a profoundly important ambiguity in Aristotle's thought, for Heidegger argues that modern philosophy is characterized by its *intensification* of Aristotle's *substantial* interpretation of human being. That is, Heidegger claims that modernity understands human being primarily and exclusively as a *substance* and moreover, primarily as one whose proper activity is *knowing*. According to Heidegger, when it comes to understanding human life, modernity interprets it in accord with Aristotelian *ousia*, i.e. as a subject of predicates and in a peculiarly modern, epistemological sense. He argues that

Kant adopts [the] definition of the ego as *res cogitans* in the sense of *cogito me cogitare* except that he formulates it in a more fundamental ontological way. He says the ego is that whose determinations are representations in the full sense of *repraesentatio* . . . The ego is a *res*, whose realities are representations, *cogitationes*. As *having* these determinations the ego is *res cogitans* . . . The ego which has the determinations is, like every other something, a subjectum that has predicates. But *how* does this subject, as an ego, 'have' its predicates, the representations? . . . The *having* of the determinations, the predicates, is a *knowing* of them.[18]

Heidegger believes that Kant, and others after him, characterized the subject as that which *possesses* (*echon*) representations and that this is a development of Aristotle's own analysis of human being as *Zoon echon logon*, wherein *echon logon* has been reduced to the mere possession of representations rather than discourse. Moreover, Heidegger argues that the modern subject possesses its attributes by means of self-consciousness: 'The ego is a subject in the sense of self-consciousness. This subject not only is *distinct* from its predicates but also *has* them as known by it, which means as *objects*. This *res cogitans*, the something that thinks, is a subject of predicates and as such it is a subject *for* objects.'[19]

In what way does the ego *have* its predicates? The ego has its predicates, viz. representations, by knowing them. Therefore, for modernity, the activity of knowing is the *hexis* characteristic of human being. *Knowing* is the peculiar *praxis* and *kinesis* of the modern theoretical subject. Once again, we see how influential Natorp's insight into the modern problematic was for Heidegger's own destruction of the modern subject. That is, Natorp understood that knowledge was the pre-eminent *task*, activity and movement of the self. According to Heidegger, modernity's understanding of human being went only so far as what is required to ground knowledge. In other words, for modernity there was nothing more fundamentally important to our being than our knowing comportment towards the world. Moreover, it could never understand the peculiar human activity of first philosophy, i.e. discoursing about being, because this could not be reduced to our knowledge of objects within the world.

In essence, for Heidegger modernity failed to recognize the task of fundamental ontology, because they could not see further than an ontological account of our being-in-the-world. According to Heidegger, this was due to the fact that they could only see one way of addressing being. Everything, including human being, was interpreted according to the *logos* of *ousia*. This reduction was already latent in Aristotle's own first philosophy, but modernity developed and extended it in such a way that even *ousia* was reduced to that of a mere object for knowledge. So much so, that even the subject who knows was comprehended entirely within the horizon of an object known through self-reflection. This very movement from discoursing about being towards *ousia* and, finally, towards mere objectification is an instance of what Heidegger calls Dasein's 'ruinance' (*die ruinanz*) or, later and more famously, the fallenness (*Verfallenheit*) of Dasein into the world.

By raising anew the question of the meaning of being, Heidegger attempts to renew our discoursing about being and our articulation of the meaning of being. This he thinks can be achieved by means of a fundamental ontology, i.e. by inquiring after the being of that which is objectified in ontology or, which is the same, our comportment towards the world. This brings into focus the way in which we have a pre-understanding of our comportment towards the world, i.e. how we encounter the world. That is, Heidegger thinks that we encounter our world by means of our living discourse concerning being, e.g. that of the world's, our own and innerworldly beings.[20] This represents Heidegger's genuine appropriation of Aristotle's insight into the foundations of first philosophy. But Heidegger's approach to this issue involves a hermeneutic that is illuminated not only by Aristotle, but one that is deeply influenced by his reading of Husserl, Natorp and Dilthey.

A first step toward renewing fundamental ontology is to examine how it is that we 'address and discuss' (*legein*) being or, which amounts to the same, how we have a pre-understanding of being. Heidegger argues, appropriating Dilthey, that all expression and meaning are grounded in Dasein's being-in-the-world. However, given that being as such transcends such meaning, how can we address and discuss it? The answer lies in the fact that living discourse [*Rede*] is not limited to that which is meaningful in this way. In elucidating this, Heidegger turns both to Husserl's analysis of meaning and expression in the *Logical Investigations* and also to Aristotle's understanding of philosophical definition.

At the very beginning of his discussion of expression and meaning, Husserl makes a distinction that is fateful both for the development of his own thought and for its impact on Heidegger's thought. Husserl remarks that 'Every sign (*Zeichen*) is a sign for something (*etwas*), but not every sign has "meaning", a "sense" that the sign "expresses".'[21] There are two types of signs, namely those that are merely indications [*Anzeichen*] and which do not express anything, and those that have both an indicative and signitive function [*Bedeutungsfunktion*].[22] Husserl mentions as examples of the former a flag as the sign of a nation, Martian canals as signs of the existence of intelligent beings, etc. These, Husserl argues, do not *express* anything because they have no meaning. That is, for someone who understands these indicative signs they '. . . "mean" something to him in so far as he interprets [*deutet*] them, but even for him they are without meaning in the special sense in which verbal signs [*sprachlicher Zeichen*] have meaning: they only mean in the sense of indicating'.[23] The latter 'verbal signs' (as Husserl refers to them), i.e. expressive signs that have both an indicative and signitive function, would be any meaningful expression that discloses the world and innerworldly beings. These, for Husserl, have their meaning grounded in pure consciousness. That is, 'In virtue of [sense-giving] acts, the expression is more than a merely sounded word. It *means* something, and in so far as it means something, it relates to what is objective'.[24]

Because of this, mere indications are not instances of intentionality, i.e. they are not meaningful unless given meaning through a sense-bestowing act of pure consciousness. Moreover, according to Husserl, everything that can be meaningfully intended is objective. For this reason, he argues that mere indications and merely indicative connections 'lack insight'. If this merely indicative connection is transformed into a meaningful connection by means of a further sense-giving act then this latter connection is capable of leading to insight or intuitive fulfilment.

Accordingly, merely indicative relations play no fundamental role within Husserlian phenomenology and, correspondingly, in a genuine scientific philosophy. Phenomenology, according to Husserl, must rely solely upon *meaningful* connections and intuitive insight, i.e. on immanent structures of consciousness. In essence, this is the only way that meaning, intentionality and objectivity could remain intact after the required phenomenological *epoche*.

Heidegger, on the other hand, argues that meaning is not constituted in pure consciousness. Rather, for him, meaning is grounded in Dasein as being-in-the-world. How, then, can he account for such fundamental 'signs' such as 'being', which, although it has meaning in worldly contexts, also appears to indicate something that transcends all worldly contexts? In other words, our use of the term 'being' is not limited to the way in which it can be used to intend worldly beings. In the living discourse of first philosophy we employ the term 'being' in such a way that it transcends worldly contexts. Most terms are, one could say, 'saturated' by their worldly meaning. That is, in discussing them we are always directed towards the world. However, for a term like 'being' this is not the case. What it indicates cannot be exhausted by any worldly meaning it may have. This certainly does not signify that it has no relation to the world, but it seems to transcend any particular being or even the being of beings.

In 1922, Heidegger calls this kind of term a 'formal indication'. This arises in the context of Heidegger's analysis of philosophical definition:

> A philosophical definition is one of principle [*Die philosphische Definition ist eine prinzipielle*], so that philosophy is indeed not a 'matter of fact' ['*Sache*']; 'possessing in principle'. Therefore this definition must be one that 'indicates': what is at issue; that is only a more precise explication of the specific character of a principle. The philosophical definition occasions a pre-'turning' to the object, such that I do indeed not 'turn' to the content. The definition is '*Formally*' indicative – the 'way', the 'approach'. What is pre-given is a bond that is indeterminate as to content but determinate as to the way of actualization.[25]

In essence, philosophical definitions are living discourse at the limit of what is meaningful. The living discourse embodied in formal indications transcends the world and worldly meaning. It accomplishes this by pointing the way or approach towards *something*, although not through a determinate content. As formally indicative in this way, the term 'being' points the way or approach towards the categorization of being and, subsequently, towards the conceptualization of beings. Or, as we saw in Chapter 5, it points the way toward the task of ontology. It is, Heidegger says, fundamental ontology's task to found ontology. Therefore, by inquiring into the formally indicative term 'being', fundamental ontology sets itself the task of projecting Dasein as being-in-the-world. In accomplishing its task, fundamental ontology realizes a meaningful world towards which Dasein can comport itself and in which it can pursue ontology, the sciences of beings, or technical and practical dealings.

In his own way, Aristotle understood the term 'being' as formally indicative. For the investigation of first philosophy, as he understands it, is predicated on the question whether or not there can be a science of 'being', i.e. a unified approach to all the different ways in which something can be said 'to be'. Moreover, the fundamental ways in which things are said 'to be' is expressed in a philosophical definition. Aristotle argues that all scientific knowledge, i.e. every determination of being, proceeds demonstratively from first principles. However, the first principles are indemonstrable. Thus, Aristotle maintains that it is by means of definitions that the first principles are acquired. He says that 'the basic premises of demonstrations are definitions, and it has already been shown that these will be found indemonstrable'. Therefore, 'the primary truths will be indemonstrable definitions'.[26] He goes on to argue that 'definition is an indemonstrable statement [*logos*] of essential nature'.[27]

The 'primary truths' embodied in philosophical definitions certainly cannot, Aristotle believes, be the truth that applies to judgements, since the latter are *synthetic combinations* that presuppose the categories and so have a derivative sense of truth. Thus, Aristotle distinguishes between the sense of 'truth' whose contrary is error and another sense of 'truth' whose contrary is not error, but ignorance.[28] This latter sense of 'true' is 'primary truth', which 'causes derivative truths to be true [and which] is most true ... so that as each thing is in respect of being, so is it in respect of truth'.[29] That is, from Heidegger's perspective, philosophical definitions as 'primary truths' disclose a meaningful sphere or, more concretely, a region of being that is capable of further inquiry and determination for the disclosure of 'derivative truths'.

He says, 'With respect to an indicational or referential characteristic, the determination "formal" signifies something decisive! Object "emptily" meant: and yet decisively! Not arbitrarily and without a sound approach, but precisely "emptily" and determinative of direction: indicative, bind-ing.'[30] At the level of philosophical definition, truth is, as Heidegger says, the accomplishment of an 'uncovering' (*entdecken*) for its own sake. How-ever, the task of uncovering, even for its own sake, requires a way or approach. At the most fundamental level, this is provided by means of the formally indicative term 'being'. The task of following out the path pro-jected by this formally indicative term is fundamental ontology which accomplishes a meaningful articulation of being by projecting Dasein as being-in-the-world for its own sake.

In other words, fundamental ontology must be understood as a *praxis*, an activity done for the sake of that activity. In this case, this signifies that fun-damental ontology is the task that uncovers, for its own sake, Dasein in its living, i.e. in its way of existing. This will include, but is not limited to, Dasein's possession (*echon*) of a world. However, according to the dual active and passive senses of *echon*, this means that Dasein possesses its world in such a way that it is something through which Dasein can further its own 'for-the-sake-of-which', i.e. its own possibilities of being, and that it pos-sesses its world in the sense of that which it itself is determined by. Therefore, it is by being-in-the-world that being becomes meaningful, both in the case of Dasein's own being and also in the case of those beings that are not Dasein.

The task of fundamental ontology, on the other hand, is not possessed (*echon*) by Dasein but is a state or disposition (*hexis*) of Dasein, i.e. it is a kind of activity by which Dasein has something and by which something is had by it. In the present case, this signifies that it is through its activity of fundamental ontology, namely by inquiring into the meaning of being, that Dasein has its world and the world is had by Dasein. This, in turn, sig-nifies that Dasein exists by living in a world.

Furthermore, life is for Heidegger a *praxis*, as it was for Aristotle. It was Dilthey who brought to Heidegger's attention the intimate connection between life and world. However, the connection between the *praxis* of phi-losophy and that of life was brought to Heidegger's attention by the corre-spondence between Count Yorck and Dilthey. Heidegger says that Count York was already on the way to '. . . raising up "life" into the kind of scien-tific understanding that is appropriate to it'.[31] For Yorck, 'to philosophize is to live'. This directs Heidegger toward the peculiar nature of philosophy, i.e. that which distinguishes it from every other inquiry. Heidegger remarks, 'In discussing the question, "What is philosophy?", we are accustomed to say: the question should not be posed in this form; we can only state what "philosophizing" is. We cannot teach and learn philosophy but only "phi-losophizing".'[32] However, with regard to other scientific disciplines such as biology, it is different. Heidegger says that, 'With regard to biology, we can speak of "pursuing biology", but we have no corresponding word "bio-logize". We can form such words, but we recognize immediately that the term "philosophize" expresses "more". It does not mean "to pursue philosophy", "to busy oneself with philosophy".[33] The ontic sciences and ontology have as their accomplishment an objectification of beings or of the being of beings, respectively. Philosophy, on the other hand, has as its accomplishment not an objectification of being, but rather a world in which one can live. Philosophy, therefore, occurs in and for life.

2. The categories of life

As with ontology and the ontic sciences, fundamental ontology must have its own structures through which it accomplishes its task. Heidegger believes that this requires structures that are not tied to the objectifying and worldly categories that are employed in the former activities. One cannot project life by objectifying it because that is de-vivifying. Rather, new kinds of categories are needed, viz. categories of life. These categories are not to be understood as ways in which we have 'access' to life, if this signifies a way in which life is 'given to us', i.e. a way in which we 'see' or 'glimpse' life. Rather, these are structures through which we *live* life. Moreover, they are projected from out of the ways in which we deal with life and encounter our own lives. Heidegger calls these *Grundkategorien*, viz. 'fundamental' or 'basic' categories.

By 1922, Heidegger had already begun to identify Dasein with life.[34] He states that in the terms 'life' and 'to live', 'a peculiar prevailing sense now resounds: life = existence, "*being*" in and through life [*Leben = Dasein, in und durch Leben »Sein«*]'.[35] We saw in Chapter 5 that 'to live' has both an intransitive and transitive sense.[36] These two senses of 'to live' will be represented in fundamental ontology by the structures that Heidegger calls 'world' and 'concern' (*Besorge*), respectively. In addition to these, Heidegger lists a third sense of 'life', namely, its relational (*Bezugssinn*) sense. In fundamental ontology, this is that structure of Dasein that Heidegger terms 'care' (*Sorge*).

The expression 'to live' in its intransitive sense indicates Dasein as thrown into a 'factical' world. That is, the intransitive sense of 'to live' 'takes explicit form in phrases such as to live "in" something, to live "out of" something, to live "for" something ... The "something", whose manifold relations to "living" are indicated in these prepositional expressions ... is what we call "world"'.[37] World, therefore, is a basic category of life that, in every case, primarily indicates *what* is lived, the content of life. In other words, it indicates a context in which the *praxis* of life can occur. This intransitive sense of 'to live' in fundamental ontological terms corresponds to the fact that Dasein is being-in-the-world, i.e. being-in-the-world is a state or disposition (*hexis*) of Dasein, or what Heidegger calls an *existentiale*. That is, Dasein is being-in-the-world in such a way that it does not possess (*echon*) this, rather it is simply a way in which Dasein can live, i.e. a way in which Dasein can exist (*existieren*).[38] On the other hand, It is that activity through which Dasein possesses its world. Put differently, Dasein is being-in-the-world in the sense that it lives within a world by possessing a world.

These particular, 'factical' worlds in which life takes place are, according to Heidegger, 'historical' worlds, and not just in the sense of a 'past' world. Rather, a factical world is always historical *because* it is essentially part of the activity or movement of life, of Dasein's existence. Heidegger makes this clear when he distinguishes the basic category of world from objective interpretations of the world. He says that the fundamental category of 'world' is not 'a place wherein living beings happen to be found. On the contrary, we are determining the concept of world precisely by beginning with the phenomenon indicated in the verb, "to live" . . .'[39]

Furthermore, the articulation of the objective meaning of a world is carried out in ontology and the ontic sciences. That is, ontology carries out the objectification of the ways in which we comport ourselves towards the world. And the ontic sciences objectify the innerworldly beings in a particular, factical world. Heidegger remarks that 'factical life itself is compelled to interpretation'.[40] The objective articulation of a factical world is a preeminent way in which Dasein *concerns* itself with its world. That is, the concrete working out of its world, which includes the *tasks* of science and ontology, is an *existentiell* of Dasein. Heidegger states that 'The question of existence never gets straightened out except through existing itself. The understanding of oneself which leads *along this way* we call "*existentiell*". The question of existence is one of Dasein's ontical "affairs".'[41] That is, Dasein *concerns* itself with its world, i.e. it lives towards its world. However, this is predicated on Dasein's possessing a world.

Dasein's activity of possessing a world is the 'relational' sense of the expression 'life'. This indicates life as *praxis* or, in the terminology of fundamental ontology, Dasein as *Existenz*. This represents Heidegger's appropriation of the Greek term '*hexis*' into fundamental ontology. In its broadest signification, the relational sense of life is governed by care, the most important of the fundamental categories of Dasein according to Heidegger. He will claim that 'caring, indicated formally, and so without laying claim to it [is] *the* basic relational sense of life in itself'.[42] Moreover, Heidegger says that ' "*Privation*" (*privatio, carentia*) is both the relational and the intrinsic basic mode and sense of the Being of life.'[43]

In other words, for Heidegger life is a *praxis* because its being is intrinsically that of 'privation', viz. incompleteness. Hearkening back to ancient concepts, we could say that life is intrinsically *becoming* – a being that is between being and non-being. The very purpose of Aristotle's treatise on movement, the *Physics*, is to understand becoming in such a way as to resurrect it from the oblivion of non-being into which it had sunk because of Parmenides' absolute dichotomy between being and non-being.[44] In essence, every movement exists because of a privation with respect to something's own proper nature.[45] The essence of movement is the attempt to overcome this privation. If this overcoming succeeds then movement ceases and it comes to rest. If, however, privation is *intrinsic* to something's own proper nature, then its movement never ceases, i.e. this movement is a *praxis*. However, intrinsic privation is not total and utter privation, it is rather part of the nature of something whose being is such that it can always be 'filled' with more. This, Heidegger argues, is the ancient sense of 'care'. He famously quotes Seneca: 'Now when it comes to these [God and man], the good of the one, namely God, is fulfilled by his Nature; but that of the other, man, is fulfilled by *care* . . .'[46]

To live is, in its broadest relational sense, caring in the context of the intrinsic privation that is the basic mode of the being of life. Heidegger states that 'living, in its verbal meaning, is to be interpreted according to its relational sense as *caring*: to care for and about something; to live from [on the basis of] something, caring for it . . .'[47] This basic category of care has an essential relation to the first category of life, namely world. Understanding this relation will give us insight into how Heidegger understands care. Specifically, Heidegger says that 'What we care for and about, what caring adheres to, is equivalent to what is meaningful. *Meaningfulness* is a categorial determination of the world; the objects of a world, worldly, world-some objects, are lived inasmuch as they embody the character of meaningfulness.'[48] That is, Dasein, in care, lives in and toward a *meaningful* world. That is, Dasein's care is its activity of *living in a world and towards that world*. In essence, care is the *hexis* between the intransitive sense of 'to live', to have a world, and the transitive sense of 'to live', to live towards something, i.e. to have concern for beings within that world.

Concern is, in fact, Heidegger's fundamental ontological analogue of Husserl's 'intentionality'. As we saw in Chapter 2, Husserl had characterized intentionality as *living towards*, but his grasp of the being of this, i.e. the way it was situated in life, was hampered because of his own overriding theoretical concern for the universal structures of immanent consciousness. Heidegger thus goes on to argue that living towards something, namely intentionality as it is lived, is an *encountering* (*begegnen*). What makes this possible, however, is care, because in the activity of care Dasein possesses a world and can live towards that world. In other words, Heidegger states that 'The world and worldly objects are present in the basic mode of life as relational, namely caring. An act of caring encounters them, meets them as it goes its way. The objects are encountered.'[49] In essence, this is the way in which something 'is there' for us, namely we meaningfully encounter it within a world. Only at this point can we concern ourselves with inner-worldly beings. Thus, Heidegger will say in 1923, 'These beings-which-are-there are being encountered in the how of their being-of-concern, i.e. in their there which has been placed into *concern* ... when care has finished with it and made it ready, when it stands there at our disposal.'[50] In Chapter 5 we came across numerous instances of this, namely concern for beings in those activities that are comprised of our technical comportments, our ontic scientific comportments and our ontological comportments.

3.   Beyond worldview philosophy and scientific philosophy

In his writings up to the late 1920s Heidegger contextualizes his own work on the nature of philosophy by means of the debate between two apparently different and competing views of philosophy, namely scientific philosophy and worldview philosophy.[51] In many ways, Heidegger is work-ing within the problematic that Husserl sets out in his lecture 'Philosophy as Rigorous Science', wherein Husserl is keen to avoid subordinating philo-sophy to the natural sciences or reducing it to (what he sees as) the histori-cism of Dilthey's worldview philosophy. Throughout much of his early work, Heidegger is concerned to go *beyond* these two traditions to a radical rethinking of both; a rethinking that resituates them both in life.

In 1923 Heidegger presents in stark contrast the two driving forces of late nineteenth-century philosophy, namely 'historical consciousness' and scien-tific philosophy.[52] These two currents of thinking are manifested in the methodological reflection concerning the nature of the special sciences, that is, in the debates over the respective methodologies of the *Geisteswis-senschaften* and the *Naturwissenschaften*. None of the figures that we have looked at in detail fall neatly on one side or the other of this *methodological* debate. There is, rather, considerable overlap. This is true for Rickert. For even though he is explicitly concerned with concept formation in the *Geistes-wissenschaften*, he is at pains to maintain the universalism characteristic of the theoretical sciences in general and avoid any hint of historicism. It is also evident in Dilthey, to an extent, in so far as he still views his own later project as an attempt to give a *critique* of the *Geisteswissenschaften* and is therefore concerned with grounding these sciences in the universal typologies of his 'descriptive psychology'.

It is also true of those thinkers who tended to emphasize the natural sciences. Natorp, for example, allows for the historical development of the lawfulness that is so essential to the natural sciences and the theory of knowledge. Finally, Husserl's transcendental phenomenology is meant to be a universal science and, thus, foundational for all of the special sciences.

As Heidegger remarks in *Being and Time*, these debates have become all the more urgent given the radical upheaval in the 'basic concepts' of the special sciences that occurred at the beginning of the twentieth century. 'In such immanent crises,' he argues, 'the very relationship between positively investigative inquiry and those things themselves that are under interrogation comes to a point where it begins to totter.'[53] From a methodological perspective, the division between philosophical approaches in the latter half of the nineteenth century can also roughly be divided into those that predicated philosophy on 'historical consciousness' or 'worldviews' and those striving to be scientific philosophy.

What is clear is that Heidegger's thinking emerges in a time where philosophy is facing an upheaval in its own 'basic concepts', analogous to the upheaval in the special sciences. Again, in his own approach Heidegger turns to Aristotle for guidance, but he reappropriates Aristotle's thought through his contemporary, hermeneutic situation, i.e. through Husserl, Natorp and Dilthey's conceptions of the essence of philosophy. We have seen Heidegger's understanding of the concept of 'world', which also plays such an integral role in Dilthey's worldview philosophy. In this regard, Heidegger believes he has properly grounded Dilthey's insights by understanding the concept of world in relation to the *praxis* of life, which Dilthey had failed to do. What is characteristic of scientific philosophy? Scientific philosophy is, following Husserl, characterized by its focus on 'intuition'.

When Heidegger looks to Aristotle, he also finds that *nous*, i.e. 'intuition', is central to Aristotle's own view of our ability to 'scientifically' grasp the *arche* of *episteme*. In the *Posterior Analytics*, for instance, Aristotle argues that 'it will be intuition that apprehends the primary premisses' and, furthermore, 'intuition will be the originative source of scientific knowledge'.[54] However, we should pay careful attention to why Aristotle thinks this. His argument in the *Posterior Analytics* runs, 'no other kind of thought except intuition is more accurate than scientific knowledge, whereas primary premises are more knowable than demonstrations, and all scientific knowledge is discursive [*meta logou*]'.[55] It is because scientific knowledge is *meta logou*, viz. within discourse, that intuition is more accurate than scientific knowledge. This applies more broadly than just to *episteme*. In the *Nicomachean*

Ethics, Aristotle argues that not only *episteme*, but also *techne* and *phronesis*, are *meta logou*, because each of these involves demonstration which is essentially *meta logou*. Aristotle argues, on the other hand, that there must be more than mere discourse.

What is the primary source from which *episteme*, *phronesis* and *sophia* spring? Aristotle argues that *nous* is itself an originative source (*arche*) and that *nous* grasps the first principles (again, *arche*). That is, there is an ambiguity in *nous* in so far as it is an *arche*, namely, that it is both an originative source and it is that by which we grasp first principles. This ambiguity in *nous* is, for Aristotle, a necessary aspect of *nous*, but only inasmuch as it is realized in human beings, namely *Zoon echon logon*. In other words, it is because *logon* is essential to human beings that our *nous* is *dianoein*, i.e. a thinking through or thinking by means of *nous*. More specifically, *nous* is realized in human beings only in so far as it is mediated by and through discourse (*logos*). Heidegger makes this plain in his own analysis of Aristotle:

> ... it must be said that *nous* as such is not a possibility of the Being of man. Yet insofar as intending and perceiving are characteristic of human Dasein, *nous* can still be found in man ... This *nous* in the human soul is not a *noein*, a straightforward seeing, but a *dianoein*, because the human soul is determined by *logos*. On the basis of *logos*, the assertion of something *as* something, *noein* becomes *dianoein*.[56]

Put differently, in human beings, *nous* is caught up in the movement and activity of life. That is, human life in its full philosophical realization is a *nous echon logon*. In essence, Heidegger believes that *dianoein* is the activity of life comprised by the indication that occurs in living discourse. In an every-day sense, such living discourse indicates worldly things and these things become meaningful through that discourse. This certainly is not limited to pointing out something to be 'seen', but rather is a structure that pervades all of our everyday comportments towards innerworldly beings. For instance, living discourse is involved in our practical and technical comportments. These comportments are predicated on an articulated, meaningful context that indicates the use to which something can be put.

However, there are also those forms of living discourse in which we carry out and accomplish science and philosophy. Namely, in the case of the ontic sciences this is our *explicit* understanding of the technical and practical comportments that provide the context for our dealings with beings. That is, in the task of ontic science we must first explicitly elucidate and articulate through discourse our technical and practical comportments toward beings so that we may have a meaningful context that indicates a direction and a path towards the objectification of those beings. This objectification, as was said, transcends the meaningful context provided by our practical and technical comportments, but is nonetheless indicated in that context. In essence, ontic science follows the path towards the conceptual objectification of beings precisely from an explicit articulation of our technical and practical dealings with beings.

In the case of ontology, the living discourse is circumscribed by the ways in which we deal with our own comportments toward the world, i.e. the being of beings. This indicates a path towards the objectification of the being of beings which is carried out in the task of ontology.

Finally, fundamental ontology is similarly predicated on living discourse. In this case, however, the living discourse includes the totality of what is meaningful. Thus, what is indicated through this living discourse is something that transcends the factical world in which we find ourselves. For example, a formally indicative term like 'being' utterly transcends whatever meaning it may have within a factical world. Thus, these formally indicative terms indicate not the objectification of beings or the being of beings, but something beyond the factical world in which we live. In essence, they indicate the possibilities of life, i.e. the possibility of factical worlds in which one can concretely live. Put differently, the living discourse upon which fundamental ontology is predicated points beyond our present factical world. It opens up other possible forms of life, namely other factical worlds in which we can live. Fundamental ontology opens up these possibilities of Dasein's existence and in carrying out its task it projects a concrete, factical world in which Dasein can live.

In each case, we see that there is *logos*, i.e. a living discourse related to our factical world, i.e. either living discourse about beings within the world or living discourse that transcends the limits of what is meaningful in that world. But, there is also something else, namely *nous*. In this case, *nous* represents the 'sighting' of the task, i.e. what is to be accomplished or carried out in the task. In technical comportments this is what is to be produced, manipulated, etc. In ontic scientific comportments this is the revealing of beings for its own sake by means of an objectification of beings, i.e. by revealing the objective meaning of beings. In ontology, it is the revealing of the being of beings, i.e. the objective meaning of the ways in which we comport ourselves towards beings. In fundamental ontology, the *nous* that is indicated by the living discourse is a projected possibility of Dasein's being-in-the-world, i.e. a concrete form of life or a *praxis* of life. In each case, the indicative relationship circumscribes the living movement between *logos*, i.e. living discourse, and *nous*, i.e. the way or path ahead. Or, put more directly, human activity always occurs from out of a meaningful, linguistic context and towards something that we 'sight' only from out of this context.

Dilthey had grasped this discursive character of life. That is, he had seen that the movement of life always takes place within a meaningful context, viz. within a worldview. As Heidegger puts it, in life '. . . we always move [*bewegen*] in an understanding of being'.[57] For Dilthey, as for Heidegger, this indicates the historicity of life. That is, that the context of life is always a factical world. Dilthey, however, did not genuinely and primordially grasp the role of *nous* in life. This is why his worldview philosophy was always in danger of becoming *historicism*. In essence, he had failed to understand the 'futural' aspect of life, namely, that it is directed towards *nous*, i.e. towards something 'sighted'. Put differently, Dilthey understood only the dialectical (*dialektikos*) moment of life, and missed the projection that is embodied in *nous*, namely the *futural* task of life.

Husserl, on the other hand, understood that *scientific* thought was always directed towards intuition, specifically intuitive fulfilment. That is, Husserl sees the activity of thought as the movement from meaning intention towards its intuitive fulfilment, i.e. the movement from *logos* towards *nous*. This very movement he understood as truth, since truth just is the activity of the intuitive fulfilment of meaning intention. However, because of the limitations Heidegger finds in Husserl's notion of truth, namely that it is understood only as the unity of thought and evidence and, thus, entirely from within a critical, epistemological framework, Heidegger fundamentally reworks Husserl's analysis of truth in his own understanding of the fundamental concept of *aletheia*, i.e. uncovering or disclosure.

In large part this was due to the influence of Natorp, who had recognized that knowledge was not grounded in immediately given evidence, but in the accomplishments of the task of knowledge. In other words, for Natorp, the truth of knowledge is the objectifications it accomplishes. Heidegger extends Natorp's insight. That is, Heidegger argues that every revealing or disclosure whether technical, scientific, ontological or fundamental ontological is a movement that takes place 'between' a given *logos* and a projected *nous*. In this way, Heidegger argues that *aletheia* is the movement that follows out a projection from a given *logos*, viz. a given living discourse, towards its accomplishment as sighted in *nous*, i.e. the 'for-the-sake-of-which' of a task.

Aristotle similarly realized that the notions of *logos* and *nous* were not limited solely to scientific knowing, but applied to all human endeavours. Thus, Heidegger returns to Aristotle's account of the four modes of *aletheia*, each of which are both *dialego* and *dianoein*, i.e. they are mediated both by *logos* and *nous*. These are *techne, episteme, phronesis* and *sophia*. *Techne* is directed towards production and use. *Episteme* is directed toward 'what cannot be otherwise', viz. what is invariable or 'universal'. And *phronesis* is directed towards what is variable, i.e. 'what can be otherwise'. More specifically, it is directed toward life. We will look at *sophia* later.

Nous is, as we have seen, what *aletheia* is moving towards. However, what it is moving towards is always a projection *from* out of something, viz. *logos*, and *towards* something, whether this is production and use, conceptual objectification, or life itself. In essence, *nous*, for Heidegger, is Dasein's projecting (*Entwurf*) of being from out of its facticity. In the case of the tasks of ontic science, ontology and fundamental ontology these never have a finished 'product', i.e. they are not brought to completion. Rather, what they accomplish is yet another *logos* that indicates. That is, they accomplish a new context toward which we comport ourselves. For instance, ontic science articulates the objective meaning of beings to which we comport ourselves technically and practically. Ontology articulates the objective meaning of our comportment towards beings towards which we in turn comport ourselves by means of our lived-experiences, e.g. through judgements, etc. Finally, fundamental ontology accomplishes an articulation of Dasein's being-in-the-world, i.e. a factical world in which we can live. That is, the 'accomplishment' of *nous* sets yet another task in motion, i.e. yet another movement between a *logos* and a corresponding *nous*. The *praxis* of this movement is *aletheia* or 'truthing'.[58]

The *aletheia* of *phronesis* is living itself. Many authors have highlighted the significance of *phronesis* in Heidegger's fundamental ontology.[59] Specifically, they have pointed out the phronetic character of Dasein's being-in-the-world. From our present perspective, we can see why this is the case. Dasein lives, i.e. exists, only in so far as it is in a factical world. Thus, the structure of Dasein's understanding of its factical world should be phronetic, i.e. directed towards life. The *aletheia* of *phronesis* then is Dasein as factically living, i.e. as factically existing.

What, on the other hand, is the *aletheia* of *episteme*? Aristotle suggests that it deals with 'what cannot be otherwise' or what is invariable. Aristotle thought of this as what is universal. Much of the history of philosophy follows him in this. Significantly, Husserl realized that grasping the universal requires a peculiar form of intuition or *nous*, viz. 'categorial intuition'. Heidegger believes that this was an important step forward in the history of thought. Contrary to Husserl, Heidegger understands the *aletheia* of *episteme* along the lines of his own fundamental appropriation of Aristotle. That is, he sees it as a movement that is predicated on living discourse, i.e. *logos* that is situated within a factical world. Already in 1919, Heidegger realized that 'universality of word meanings primarily indicates something originary: worldliness [*Welthaftigkeit*] of experienced experiencing'.[60] Thus, the universality of the subject matter of *episteme* is not, as the tradition would have it, a grasping of something that transcends the world. Rather, it indicates the fact that *episteme* is always situated within a factical world. Thus, from the perspective of that world, certain structures are 'universal', i.e. are inter-subjectively common.

Put another way, the *aletheia* of *episteme* is the movement *within* a world, from the living discourse that is meaningful in that world and towards a pro-jection of its objective meaning. The fact that it is always situated within a world means that what it relates to will be meaningfully 'universal'. From this it becomes clear why Heidegger would argue that the mode of *aletheia* of *episteme* is derivative with respect to the *aletheia* of *phronesis*: for innerworldly meanings must be disclosed by *phronesis* before any *episteme* is possible.

There is another mode of *aletheia* that is even more primordial than either *phronesis* or *episteme*, namely *sophia*. Aristotle says that *sophia* takes place only when there is an opportunity for leisure, 'for it was when almost all the necessities of life and the things that make for comfort and recreation had been secured that such knowledge began to be sought'.[61] Dilthey also recog-nized this. He says, 'If we step aside from chasing after goals and calmly turn in upon ourselves, then the moments of life appear in their significance.'[62] For, in philosophy, we transcend the world. By turning towards the *praxis* of life itself, i.e. by setting aside our busy engagement with the world, we turn towards the movement of *aletheia* itself, i.e. the movement between *logos* and *nous*. Though, as is clear from the above, this does not mean that we 'escape' from life. It is rather an intensification of life. The traditional view of philosophy is that its subject matter 'transcends' life. On the con-trary, according to Heidegger, philosophy is the intensification of life. It is, he argues, *philosophizing*. And philosophizing is just a pre-eminent form of the *praxis* of life. That is, it is the activity of moving from *logos* toward *nous*, and for which there is no completion.[63]

Put differently, philosophizing takes place when Dasein is no longer 'fallen' into its world, i.e. busying itself with its world. Philosophizing occurs when Dasein steps back from its world. But this does not mean that it steps back and gazes upon the world. Rather, it is that stepping back from our engagement within the world that allows us to project anew our being-in-the-world. This is precisely the task of fundamental ontology as we have been describing it.

However, fundamental ontology per se is not philosophizing. What expresses the *praxis* of philosophizing? Heidegger answers, 'With the ques-tion of the meaning of Being, our investigation comes up against the fundamental question of philosophy.'[64] This is the question that instigates the task of fundamental ontology. In other words, raising the question of the meaning of being is that which motivates us to inquire into our being-in-the-world, which in turn leads us to project a factical world in which we can live from out of our living discourse. Philosophizing is just the *questioning* of the meaning of being. Thus, Heidegger will say that 'To grasp philosophy authentically means to encounter absolute question-ability and to possess this questionability in full awareness. The fixed ground ... lies in grasping the questionability; i.e. it lies in the radical maturation of questioning.'[65]

Looked at from a different perspective, philosophizing is simply the unending movement of *Aletheia*, i.e. the movement characterized as *dialogos* and *dianoia*. This explains why Heidegger remarks that '*Dasein is 'in the truth'*. This assertion has meaning ontologically. It does not purport to say that ontically Dasein is introduced 'to all the truth' either always or just in every case, but rather that the disclosedness of its ownmost being belongs to its existential constitution.[66] This, therefore, is the primordial notion of *aletheia* and correspondingly of *logos* and *nous*. However, this does not rule out that there are derivative movements of *aletheia*. Of course there are, but all of these are simply movements within the broader *praxis* of *aletheia*.

Heidegger sees in the expression 'phenomenology' a statement of philoso-phizing. That is, 'This expression does not characterize the what of the objects of philosophical research as subject-matter, but rather the *how* of that research.'[67] In pulling apart this term 'phenomenology', we get the two moments of *aletheia*, namely *dianoia* and *dialogos*. As to the former, Heidegger remarks that ' "*Phenomenon*", the showing-itself-in-itself, signifies a distinctive way in which something can be encountered'.[68] And with respect to the latter he says, 'The *logos* lets something be seen (*phainesthai*), namely, what the discourse is about.'[69] This is why he goes on to say that the question of the meaning of being 'must be treated *phenomenologically*'.[70]

That is, philosophy is the unending movement, i.e. the *praxis*, between *logos* and *nous*, between living discourse and possibilities sighted in that discourse, and between Dasein's thrown-facticity and its projection of new possibilities for being.[71] However, this unending movement is just the *praxis* of life. That is, this movement circumscribes all our lived comport-ments, namely our fundamental ontological comportments, our ontologi-cal comportments, our ontic scientific comportments and our technical comportments. Moreover, as we saw in the last section, these movements are structured by the fundamental categories of life, viz. world, concern and care. It is in this way, then, that Heidegger conceives of philosophy as primordial science, i.e. it is a full participant in life and is also constitu-tive of life.

Notes

Introduction

1. Martin Heidegger, 'Phenomenological interpretations in connection with Aristotle: An indication of the hermeneutical situation', trans. John van Buren, in Martin
   Heidegger, *Supplements: From the Earliest Essays to 'Being and Time' and Beyond*, ed.
   John van Buren (2002). Albany: SUNY Press, p. 112.
2. Hans-Georg Gadamer, *Philosophical Apprenticeships*, trans. R. Sullivan (1985).
   Cambridge, Mass.: The MIT Press, p. 49.
3. See Charles R. Bambach, *Heidegger, Dilthey, and the Crisis of Historicism* (1995).
   Ithaca: Cornell University Press, pp. 1–55.
4. This is not to be confused with Dilthey's 'theory of worldviews', which we shall discuss in Chapter 4.
5. Dilthey is, in many respects, an exception.
6. This course was titled 'The Idea of Philosophy and the Problem of Worldview' and
   is included in Martin Heidegger, *Towards the Definition of Philosophy*, trans. Ted
   Sadler (2002). London: Continuum.
7. John van Buren, *The Young Heidegger: Rumor of the Hidden King* (1994). Bloomington:
   Indiana University Press.
8. There are many and various versions of this kind of interpretation. Perhaps most
   famous is Theodore Kisiel, *The Genesis of Heidegger's Being and Time* (1993). Berkeley: University of California Press. But there is also Steven Crowell's interpretation,
   wherein Heidegger's early philosophical project is seen as the attempt to extend
   Husserl's own transcendental phenomenology of meaning beyond its objective
   boundaries by formulating a pre-objective, pre-theoretical transcendental phenomenology of meaning as it is situated in factical life. See Steven Galt Crowell,
   Husserl, Heidegger, and the Space of Meaning (2001). Evanston, IL: Northwestern
   University Press.
9. Martin Heidegger, 'The Theory of Categories and Meaning in Duns Scotus', trans.
   Roderick M. Stewart and John Van Buren, in Martin Heidegger, *Supplements: From
   the Earliest Essays to Being and Time and Beyond*.
10. Martin Heidegger, *Ontology: The Hermeneutics of Facticity*, trans. John van Buren
    (1999). Bloomington: Indiana University Press, p. 1.
11. See, for instance, Franco Volpi, 'Being and Time: A translation of the Nicoma-
    chean Ethics?', trans. John Protevi in *Reading Heidegger From the Start: Essays in His
    Early Thought*, ed. Theodore Kisiel and John van Buren (1994). Albany: SUNY

Press, pp. 195–211; Walter Brogan, 'The place of Aristotle in the development of Heidegger's phenomenology', in *Reading Heidegger From the Start: Essays in His Early Thought*, pp. 213–27; Walter Brogan, *Heidegger and Aristotle: The Twofoldness of Being* (2005). Albany: SUNY Press, Ch. 5; Jacques Taminiaux, 'Heidegger and *praxis*', in *The Heidegger Case: On Philosophy and Politics*, ed. Tom Rockmore and Joseph Margolis (1992). Philadelphia: Temple University Press; Jacques Taminiaux, *Heidegger and the Project of Fundamental Ontology*, trans. Michael Gendre (1991). Albany: SUNY Press; Robert Bernasconi, 'Heidegger's destruction of phronesis', *The Southern Journal of Philosophy*, Vol. 48 supplement (1989), pp. 127–53; and Hans-Georg Gadamer, *Truth and Method*, trans. Joel Weinsheimer and Donald G. Marshall (1989). New York: Continuum, especially part II, II, 2 (B).

Chapter 1

1. Rüdiger Safranski, *Martin Heidegger: Between Good and Evil*, trans. Ewald Osers (1998). Cambridge, Mass.: Harvard University Press, p. 63.
2. There are excellent, although sadly too few, studies in Rickert's philosophy. See, for instance, Herbert Schnädelbach, *Philosophy in Germany, 1831–1933*, trans. Eric Matthews (1984). Cambridge: Cambridge University Press, Ch. 6; Charles R. Bambach, *Heidegger, Dilthey and the Crisis of Historicism* (1995). Cornell: Cornell University Press, especially Ch. 3; Guy Oakes, *Weber and Rickert: Concept Formation in the Cultural Sciences* (1988). Cambridge, Mass.: The MIT Press; Guy Oakes, 'Introduction' to Heinrich Rickert, *The Limits of Concept Formation in Natural Science*, trans. Guy Oakes (1986). Cambridge: Cambridge University Press; and Jeffrey Andrew Barash, *Martin Heidegger and the Problem of Historical Meaning* (2003). New York: Fordham University Press, Ch. 1.
3. Heidegger, *Towards the Definition of Philosophy*, trans. Ted Sadler (2002). London: Continuum, p. 121.
4. Ibid. See also Hans-Georg Gadamer, *Gadamer in Conversation*, trans. Richard E. Palmer (2001). New Haven: Yale University Press, pp. 89–90.
5. Ibid. pp. 30, 121.
6. J. G. Fichte, *The Science of Knowledge*, trans. Peter Heath and John Lachs (1982). Cambridge: Cambridge University Press.
7. Daniel Breazeale, 'Check or checkmate? On the finitude of the Fichtean self', in *The Modern Subject: Classical German Idealist Conceptions of the Self*, ed. Karl Ameriks and Dieter Sturma (1995). Albany: SUNY Press, p. 87.
8. For Rickert's critique of voluntarism, see Heinrich Rickert, *The Limits of Concept Formation in Natural Science*, trans. Guy Oakes (1986). Cambridge: Cambridge University Press, p. 229.
9. Heidegger, *Towards the Definition of Philosophy*, p. 118.
10. See Heinrich Rickert, *The Limits of Concept Formation in Natural Science*, pp. 101–5.
11. Heidegger, *Towards the Definition of Philosophy*, p. 33.

12. Ibid.
13. Ibid. p. 31.
14. Ibid.
15. Ibid. p. 33.
16. Ibid. pp. 31, 34.
17. Ibid. p. 36: 'Experience clearly shows that, in order to fulfil the demands of true thinking, I do not always need an explicit consciousness of the ideal of thought. Thousands of people think factually and correctly without any consciousness of this ideal.'
18. Martin Heidegger, *History of the Concept of Time*, trans. Theodore Kisiel (1985). Bloomington: Indiana University Press, p. 17.
19. Wilhelm Windelband, 'History and natural science', trans. Guy Oakes, *History and Theory* 19 (1980), pp. 165–85.
20. Ibid. p. 175.
21. Ibid.
22. Heidegger, *Towards the Definition of Philosophy*, p. 144.
23. Heinrich Rickert, *The Limits of Concept Formation in Natural Science*, p. 38.
24. Ibid. p. 78.
25. Ibid. p. 64.
26. Ibid. p. 89.
27. Ibid. p. 88.
28. '... in historical reality, individuals are never *isolated*. All objects of history are rather parts of a larger whole with which they stand in a real nexus. As we have seen, the abstractions of natural science destroy this nexus and isolate instances. History cannot proceed in this way. It becomes the science of the unique, real event only by means of a representation of the *historical nexus*' (Ibid. pp. 62–3).
29. Ibid. p. 39.
30. Heidegger, *Towards the Definition of Philosophy*, p. 145.
31. Rickert, *The Limits of Concept Formation in Natural Science*, p. 50.
32. Ibid. p. 52.
33. John McDowell, *Mind and World* (1996). Cambridge, Mass.: Harvard University Press, p. 18.
34. Rickert, *The Limits of Concept Formation in Natural Science*, pp. 43–4.
35. Ibid. p. 230.
36. Ibid.
37. Ibid. italics mine.
38. Ibid.
39. Ibid. p. 37.
40. Ibid. p. 45.
41. Ibid. p. 231.
42. Ibid. p. 232.
43. Ibid. p. 231.
44. Bambach, *Heidegger, Dilthey, and the Crisis of Historicism*, pp. 229–30 and Barash, *Martin Heidegger and the Problem of Historical Meaning*, pp. 102–3.

45. Ingo Farin, 'Heidegger's critique of value philosophy', *Journal of The British Society for Phenomenology*, Vol. 29, No. 3 (October 1998), 273–4.

46. Steven Galt Crowell, *Husserl, Heidegger, and the Space of Meaning: Paths Toward Transcendental Phenomenology* (2001). Evanston: Northwestern University Press, p. 132 and Bambach, *Heidegger, Dilthey, and the Crisis of Historicism*, p. 229.

47. Heidegger, *History of the Concept of Time*, p. 17.

48. Martin Heidegger, 'The theory of categories and meaning in Duns Scotus', trans. Roderick M. Stewart and John van Buren in Martin Heidegger, *Supplements: From the Earliest Essays to Being and Time and Beyond*, ed. John Van Buren (2002). Albany: SUNY Press, p. 62.

49. Martin Heidegger, 'Comments on Karl Jasper's *Psychology of Worldviews*', trans. John van Buren, in Martin Heidegger, *Supplements: From the Earliest Essays to Being and Time and Beyond*, p. 80.

50. Heidegger, *History of the Concept of Time*, p. 18.

51. Heidegger, *Being and Time*, trans. John Macquarrie and Edward Robinson (1962). New York: Harper & Row, pp. 30–31.

52. Heidegger, *Towards the Definition of Philosophy*, pp. 11–14.

53. Jürgen Habermas, *Moral Consciousness and Communicative Action*, trans. Christian Lenhardt and Shierry Weber Nicholsen (1990). Cambridge, Mass.: The MIT Press, pp. 1–20 and Richard Rorty, *Philosophy and the Mirror of Nature* (1979). Princeton: Princeton University Press, Ch. 8.

54. Heidegger, *Towards the Definition of Philosophy*, p. 50.

55. Aristotle, *Metaphysics*, trans. W. D. Ross in *The Basic Works of Aristotle*, ed. Richard McKeon (1941). New York: Random House, Book I, Ch. 9.

56. Martin Heidegger, 'The theory of categories and meaning in Duns Scotus', p. 65.

57. 'We cannot at all see logic and its problems in their true light if the context *from which they are interpreted is not a translogical one. Philosophy cannot for long do without its authentic optics: metaphysics.*' (Martin Heidegger, 'The theory of categories and meaning in Duns Scotus', p. 65.)

58. Aristotle, *Metaphysics*, 1005b: pp. 10–12.

59. Heidegger, 'The theory of categories and meaning in Duns Scotus', pp. 65–6.

60. In 1916, Heidegger takes as his model of this mediaeval thought, in which 'The scale of values does not therefore gravitate exclusively toward the transcendent but rather is as it were reflected back from the fullness and absoluteness of the transcendent and comes to rest in the individual' (Ibid. p. 67). Cf. Hans-Georg Gadamer, *Reason in an Age of Science*, trans. Frederick G. Lawrence (1981). Cambridge, Mass.: The MIT Press, p. 81.

61. Heidegger says, 'One has not in the least understood consciousness if it is neutralized into the concept of a blind, biological faculty' (Ibid. p. 66). Cf. Gadamer, *Reason in the Age of Science*, pp. 69–87.

62. Ibid. p. 68. In the first instance, Heidegger is clearly thinking of Rickert and value-philosophy. In the second, he is thinking of Emil Lask. Of all of the Neo-Kantians, the relation of Lask's philosophy to Heidegger's development has been treated most extensively. The most influential of these studies include: Theodore Kisiel, *The*

Genesis of Heidegger's Being and Time; Theodore Kisiel, 'Why students of Heidegger will have to read Emil Lask', *Man and World* 28 (1995), 197–240; and Steven Galt Crowell, *Husserl, Heidegger, and the Space of Meaning*.

63. Heidegger, *Towards the Definition of Philosophy*, p. 20.
64. Heidegger, *Being and Time*, pp. 116–17.

Chapter 2

1. For other accounts of the relation between Husserl and Rickert, see the already mentioned works by Bambach, Barash and Crowell, and also see John Jalbert, 'Husserl's position between Dilthey and the Windelband-Rickert school of Neo-Kantianism', *Journal of the History of Philosophy* 26 (1988), 279–96.

2. Husserl's classic statement of this with regard to naturalism and historicism is Edmund Husserl, 'Philosophy as Rigorous Science', trans. Quentin Lauer in Edmund Husserl, *Phenomenology and the Crisis of Philosophy* (1965). New York: Harper & Row, pp. 71–147.

3. Edmund Husserl, *Logical Investigations*, trans. J. N. Findlay (2001). London: Routledge.

4. Crowell, *Husserl, Heidegger, and the Space of Meaning*.

5. From Emil Lask, *Die Logik der Philosophie und die Kategorienlehre; Eine Studie über den Herrschaftsbereich der logischen Form* (1911). Tübingen: J. C. B. Mohr (P. Siebeck), as quoted and translated by Steven Crowell in his 'Emil Lask: Aletheiology as Ontology', *Kant-Studien* 87 (1996), 69–88.

6. Husserl gives his first sustained critique of psychologism in the first part of the *Logical Investigations*.

7. Since we are primarily concerned with Husserl's philosophy in its relation to Heidegger's early philosophy, we will not consider whether Husserl in the early to mid-1920s perhaps rejected his own earlier Cartesianism, since Heidegger, rightly or wrongly, gives no indication of this. For examinations of Husserl's 'Cartesianism' and/or lack thereof, see Ludwig Landgrebe, 'Husserl's departure from Cartesianism', in *The Phenomenology of Edmund Husserl*, ed. Donn Welton (1981). Ithaca: Cornell University Press; Donn Welton, *The Other Husserl: The Horizons of Transcendental Phenomenology* (2002). Bloomington: Indiana University Press; and Steven Galt Crowell, 'The Cartesianism of phenomenology', *Continental Philosophy Review* 35 (2002), 433–54.

8. Edmund Husserl, *Ideas Pertaining to a Pure Phenomenology and to a Phenomenological Philosophy*, trans. F. Kersten (1983). The Hague: Martinus Nijhoff Publishers, p. 36. Hereafter referred to merely as *Ideas I*.

9. Cf. Karl Ameriks, 'Kant's transcendental deduction as a regressive argument', *Kant-Studien* 69 (1977), 273–85. Reprinted in Karl Ameriks, *Interpreting Kant's Critiques* (2003). New York: Oxford University Press, pp. 51–66.

10. In his translation of *Ideas I* Kersten translates *Umwelt* as 'surrounding world'. I have modified this translation, because in most of the translations of Heidegger's

work, *Umwelt* is translated using one of the terms environment, environmental, environing world, etc.

11. Husserl, *Ideas I*, p. 53.

12. Ibid.

13. Ibid. p. 54, footnote 9. See also, Edmund Husserl, *Ideas II: Studies in the Phenomenology of Constitution*, trans. Richard Rojcewicz and André Schuwer (1989). Dordrecht: Kluwer Academic Publishers. Hereafter referred to as *Ideas II*.

14. Husserl, *Ideas I*, p. 52.

15. This is, unfortunately, a widely held position, but it is perhaps no more clearly evident than in 'neo-pragmatic' interpretations of Husserl as Heidegger's 'cognitivist' foil. See, for example, Hubert L. Dreyfus, *Being-in-the-World: A Commentary on Heidegger's 'Being and Time', Division I* (1991). Cambridge, Mass.: The MIT Press and Mark Okrent, *Heidegger's Pragmatism: Understanding, Being, and the Critique of Metaphysics* (1988). Ithaca: Cornell University Press.

16. For the sake of simplicity, we will be setting aside throughout this chapter any consideration of what Husserl calls the eidetic sciences of transcendencies, e.g. pure mathematics. That is, Husserl mentions in addition to the environing world the 'ideal environing worlds' (cf. *Ideas I*, § 28).

17. Frederick Copleston, S. J., *A History of Philosophy*, Vol. 7 (1963). New York: Doubleday, p. 40.

18. Husserl, *Ideas Pertaining to a Pure Phenomenology*, p. 126.

19. Ibid. p. 171.

20. Ibid. p. 142.

21. Ibid. § 38.

22. Ibid. p. 177.

23. Ibid. p. 174. Cf. Heidegger, *Towards the Definition of Philosophy*, p. 83.

24. Ibid. p. 178.

25. Ibid. p. 114. Translation modified.

26. Kant, *Critique of Pure Reason*, trans. Norman Kemp Smith (1965). New York: St Martin's Press, B68.

27. Husserl, *Ideas I*, p. 175. Translation modified.

28. Ibid. p. 110.

29. Ibid. p. 112.

30. Ibid. p. 115.

31. Ibid. p. 129.

32. See the translator's introduction to Husserl, *Ideas II*, pp. xi–xvi.

33. Husserl sent Heidegger a copy of the manuscript of *Ideas II* early in 1925 and Heidegger refers to this work in 1925 (cf. *The History of the Concept of Time*, pp. 93, 121) and in *Being and Time* (Division One, Chapter 1, footnote ii) and he mentions that these ideas were commonly known to many from Husserl's lecture course entitled 'Nature and Spirit' that he repeatedly gave in Freiburg starting in 1916 (cf. *The History of the Concept of Time*, p. 121).

34. Husserl, *Ideas II*, p. 10.

35. Ibid. p. 12.

36. Ibid. p. 191.
37. Cf. Husserl, *Ideas II*, pp. 4–6 and Heidegger, *Towards the Definition of Philosophy*, p. 74.
38. Husserl, *Ideas II*, pp. 6–7.
39. Ibid. p. 9.
40. Cf. Ibid. § 11.
41. Ibid. p. 195. Translation modified.
42. Cf. Ibid. § 50.
43. Husserl, *Logical Investigations*, Investigation one, Chapter 1, § 3.
44. Husserl, *Ideas II*, p. 231.
45. Husserl, *Ideas I*, pp. 106–7. Translation modified.
46. Husserl, *Ideas II*, p. 232.
47. Ibid. p. 228.
48. Ibid. p. 199.
49. Ibid. pp. 27–9.
50. Ibid. p. 28.
51. Husserl, *Ideas I*, p. 13.
52. Heidegger says, '*Existentialia* and categories are the two basic possibilities for characters of Being. The entities which correspond to them require different kinds of primary interrogation respectively: any entity is either a "*who*" (existence) or a "*what*" (presence-at-hand in the broadest sense)' (*Being and Time*, p. 71).
53. *Ideas I*, p. 191.
54. Ibid. p. 133. For this reason he also holds that the personal Ego cannot take the place of the pure Ego. Cf. *Ideas II*, § 57 and Supplement X.
55. *Ideas I*, p. 191, note 22. Husserl at first resisted positing a pure Ego and criticized Natorp for doing so precisely because it could not be descriptively analysed. See Husserl, *Logical Investigations*, Vol. 2, trans. J. N. Findlay (2001). London: Routledge, investigation V, § 8. However, he later agreed with Natorp. See Husserl, *Ideas I*, 'author's footnote' on p. 133 and Husserl, *Logical Investigations*, investigation V, § 8, footnote 6.
56. Quoted from Theodore Kisiel, 'Husserl and Heidegger', in *Encyclopedia of Phenomenology*, ed. Lester Embree et al. (1997). Dordrecht: Kluwer, p. 335.
57. Martin Heidegger, *Ontology: The Hermeneutics of Facticity*, trans. John van Buren (1999). Bloomington: Indiana University Press, p. 37. Translation modified.
58. For further discussion of Husserl's *Ideas II*, see *Issues in Husserl's Ideas II*, ed. T. Nenon and L. Embree (1996). Dordrecht: Kluwer.
59. Heidegger, *Towards the Definition of Philosophy*, p. 107.
60. Kisiel, *The Genesis of Heidegger's Being and Time*.
61. Ibid. p. 47 and Theodore Kisiel, 'From intuition to understanding: On Heidegger's transposition of Husserl's phenomenology', in Theodore Kisiel, *Heidegger's Way of Thought: Critical and Interpretive Signposts*, ed. Alfred Denker and Marion Heinz (2002). New York: Continuum.
62. Paul Natorp, *Allgemeine Psychologie Nach Kritischer Methode, Erstes Buch: Objekt und Methode der Psychologie* (1912). Tübingen: J. C. B. Mohr, pp. 190–91. Cf. Heidegger, *Towards the Definition of Philosphy*, p. 85.

63. Ibid. p. 189. Cf. Heidegger, *Towards the Definition of Philosophy*, pp. 85, 93–4.

64. See Kisiel, *The Genesis of Heidegger's Being and Time*. For more on formal indication see also John van Buren *The Young Heidegger: Rumor of the Hidden King* (1994). Bloomington: Indiana University Press; Daniel Dahlstrom, 'Heidegger's method: Philosophical concepts as formal indications', *Review of Metaphysics*, Vol. 47, No. 4 (1994), 775–95; Daniel Dahlstrom, *Heidegger's Concept of Truth* (2001). Cambridge: Cambridge University Press; and Ryan Streeter, 'Heidegger's formal indication: A question of method in *Being and Time*', *Man and World*, 30 (2007), 413–30.

65. Crowell, *Husserl, Heidegger, and the Space of Meaning*, pp. 115–28.

66. For an account that interprets Heidegger along these lines see George Kovacs, 'Philosophy as primordial science in Heidegger's courses of 1919', in *Reading Heidegger from the Start: Essays in His Earliest Thought*, ed. Theodore Kisiel and John van Buren (1994). Albany: SUNY Press.

67. Husserl, *Ideas II*, pp. 5–6.

68. Crowell, *Husserl, Heidegger, and the Space of Meaning*, p. 117. Cf. Kisiel, *The Genesis of Heidegger's Being and Time*, p. 17 and especially p. 457 where Kisiel remarks that: 'We find Heidegger at the end of 1927 thoroughly convinced of being within the reach of the goal of a scientific philosophy. The bold claims induced by the spell of the Kantian transcendental philosophy apparently lead Heidegger to believe that something like a Kantian schematism of human existence is capable of *definitively articulating the evasive immediacy of the human situation, that is, of "saying the unsayable"* ' (Italics mine).

69. Martin Heidegger, *The Concept of Time*, trans. William McNeill (1992). Oxford: Blackwell. See also Heidegger, *History of the Concept of Time*, pp. 1–7.

70. Heidegger, *History of the Concept of Time*, § 13.

71. Heidegger, *Towards the Definition of Philosophy*, p. 13.

72. We did not examine this aspect of Heidegger's critique of value philosophy in the last chapter. Heidegger's criticism appears in *Towards the Definition of Philosophy*, pp. 35–9.

73. Cf. Dan Zahavi, 'How to investigate subjectivity: Natorp and Heidegger on reflection', *Continental Philosophy Review* 36 (2003), 155–76.

74. Heidegger, *Towards the Definition of Philosophy*, p. 85.

75. Ibid. p. 74.

76. Ibid. p. 20.

77. Ibid. p. 20.

Chapter 3

1. Cf. Kisiel, *Heidegger's Way of Thought*, p. 30. On the 'double objection', see Kisiel, *The Genesis of Heidegger's Being and Time*; Zahavi, 'How to investigate subjectivity: Natorp and Heidegger on reflection'; and Crowell, *Husserl, Heidegger, and the Space of Meaning*. More extensive studies have been done on the relation between Husserl and Natorp. For example, Iso Kern, *Husserl und Kant* (1964). The Hague: Martinus

Nijhoff and Sebastian Luft, 'A hermeneutic phenomenology of subjective and objective spirit: Husserl, Natorp, and Cassirer', *The New Yearbook for Phenomenology and Phenomenological Philosophy IV* (2004), 209–48. Additional treatments of Natorp include Vasilis Politis, 'An introduction to Paul Natorp's *Plato's Theory of Ideas*', in Paul Natorp, *Plato's Theory of Ideas: An Introduction to Idealism*, trans. Vasilis Politis and John Connolly (2004). Sankt Augustin: Academia Verlag; Vasilis Politis, 'Anti-Realist interpretations of Plato: Paul Natorp', *International Journal of Philosophical Studies* 9 (2001), 47–61; Adolf Reinach, 'Concerning phenomenology', *Personalist* 50 (1969), 194–221; Thomas E. Willey, *Back to Kant: The Revival of Kantianism in German Social and Historical Thought* (1978). Detroit: Wayne State University Press; and Klaus Christian Köhnke, *The Rise of Neo-Kantianism: German Academic Philosophy Between Idealism and Positivism* (1991). Cambridge: Cambridge University Press.

2. Hans-Georg Gadamer, *Philosophical Apprenticeships*, trans. R. R. Sullivan (1987). Cambridge, Mass.: The MIT Press, p. 10.
3. Ibid. p. 26.
4. Paul Natorp, 'On the objective and subjective grounding of knowledge', trans. Lois Phillips and David Kolb, *Journal of the British Society for Phenomenology*, 12 (1981), 245–66.
5. Paul Natorp, Einleitung in die Psychologie nach kritischer Methode (1888). Freiburg i.B.
6. Paul Natorp, *Allgemeine Psychologie nach kritischer Methode* (1912). Tübingen: Mohr.
7. Paul Natorp, 'On the objective and subjective grounding of knowledge', p. 248.
8. Ibid. p. 246.
9. Ibid. p. 249.
10. Ibid. p. 250.
11. This, Natorp says, is an infinite task.
12. Natorp, 'On the objective and subjective grounding of knowledge', p. 262.
13. Ibid. p. 262.
14. Ibid. p. 263.
15. Ibid. p. 261.
16. Ibid. p. 263.
17. Ibid. p. 263.
18. Ibid. p. 262.
19. Ibid. p. 262.
20. Ibid. p. 247.
21. Paul Natorp, *Die Logischen Grundlagen Der Exakten Wissenschaften* (1910). Leipzig: B. G. Teubner, pp. 32–3, as translated by Lois Phillips and David Kolb in footnote 11 of 'On the objective and subjective grounding of knowledge', pp. 265–6, with my own additional translation of the complete last sentence.
22. Natorp, 'On the objective and subjective grounding of knowledge', p. 248.
23. Ibid. p. 264.
24. Ibid. p. 247.
25. Ibid. p. 263.

26. Cf. Paul Natorp, *Plato's Theory of Ideas: An Introduction to Idealism*, trans. Vasilis Politis and John Connolly (2004). Sankt Augustin: Academia Verlag.

27. Heidegger, *Towards the Definition of Philosophy*, p. 91.

28. Natorp, 'On the Objective and Subjective Grounding of Knowledge, p. 248, italics mine.

29. Ibid. p. 263.

30. Ibid. p. 263.

31. Ibid. p. 253, italics mine.

32. Ibid.

33. Husserl, *Ideas II*, p. 12.

34. Natorp, 'On the objective and subjective grounding of knowledge', p. 247.

35. Hans-Georg Gadamer, *Philosophical Hermeneutics*, trans. David E. Linge (1976). Berkeley: University of California Press, p. 11.

36. In *Ideas I*, Husserl says, '. . . The mode of *"certain" belief* can change into the mode of mere *deeming possible* or *deeming likely*, or *questioning* and *doubting*; and, as the case may be, that which appears and which, with regard to the first dimension of characterizations is characterized as "originary", "reproductive" and the like has taken on now the *being-modalities* of *"possible"*, of *"probable"*, of *"questionable"*, of *"doubtful"* ' (p. 250). And even in the 1930s he remarks that 'The phenomenon of *questioning* has its origin in the domain of modalized certainty and is found there in close association with doubt' (Edmund Husserl, *Experience and Judgment*, trans. James S. Churchill and Karl Ameriks (1973). Evanston: Northwestern University Press, p. 307).

37. Cf. Heidegger, *Towards the Definition of Philosophy*, pp. 90–92.

38. Paul Natorp, 'On the question of logical method in relation to Edmund Husserl's Prolegomena to Pure Logic', trans. J. N. Mohanty in *Readings on Edmund Husserl's Logical Investigations*, ed. J. N. Mohanty (1977). The Hague: Martinus Nijhoff, pp. 55–66.

39. Ibid. p. 65.

40. For instance, just two of many who read Heidegger in this way are: Crowell, *Husserl, Heidegger, and the Space of Meaning* and Jacques Taminiaux, *Heidegger and the Project of Fundamental Ontology*, trans. Michael Gendre (1991). Albany: SUNY Press, Ch. 1.

41. Martin Heidegger, 'Comments on Karl Jaspers' *Psychology of Worldviews*', trans. John van Buren, in Martin Heidegger, *Supplements*, p. 74. See also 'Phenomenological interpretations in connection with Aristotle: An indication of the hermeneutical situation', trans. John van Buren, in Heidegger, *Supplements*, p. 122.

42. Edmund Husserl, *The Idea of Phenomenology*, trans. by Lee Hardy (1999). Dordrecht, the Netherlands: Kluwer, p. 24.

43. Heidegger, 'Comments on Karl Jaspers' *Psychology of Worldviews*', p. 74.

44. Kant, *Critique of Pure Reason*, A51/B75.

45. Martin Heidegger, *Phenomenological Interpretations of Aristotle: Initiation into Phenomenological Research*, trans. Richard Rojcewicz (2001). Bloomington: Indiana University Press, p. 26.

46. Ibid.

Chapter 4

1. A few of the vital resources on Dilthey's thought include: Michael Ermarth, *Wilhelm Dilthey: The Critique of Historical Reason* (1978). Chicago: University of Chicago Press; H. P. Rickman, *Wilhelm Dilthey: Pioneer of the Human Studies* (1979). Berkeley: University of California Press; and Rudolf Makkreel, *Dilthey: Philosopher of the Human Studies* (1992). Princeton: Princeton University Press. On the relation between Heidegger and Dilthey's thought see Robert C. Scharff, 'Heidegger's "appropriation" of Dilthey before *Being and Time*', *Journal of the History of Philosophy* 35, no. 1 (1997), 105–28; Kisiel, *The Genesis of Heidegger's Being and Time*, Ch. 7; Charles Bambach, *Heidegger, Dilthey, and the Crisis of Historicism*, Chs 4 and 5; Charles Bambach, 'Phenomenological research as "destruction": The early Heidegger's reading of Dilthey', *Philosophy Today* 37 (1993), 115–32; and Barash, *Martin Heidegger and the Problem of Historical Meaning*.

2. For example, Heidegger lauds Dilthey for his 'disclosure of new horizons for the question of the being of acts and, in the broadest sense, the being of man' (*History of the Concept of Time*, p. 119). See also, Martin Heidegger, 'Wilhelm Dilthey's research and the struggle for a historical worldview', trans. Charles Bambach, in Martin Heidegger, *Supplements: From the Earliest Essays to Being and Time and Beyond*, p. 162.

3. Wilhelm Dilthey, 'Studies toward the foundation of the human sciences', trans. Rudolf A. Makkreel and John Scanlon, in Wilhelm Dilthey, *Selected Works III: The Formation of the Historical World in the Human Sciences*, ed. Rudolf A. Makkreel and Frithjof Rodi (2002). Princeton: Princeton University Press, pp. 91–92.

4. Wilhelm Dilthey, 'Ideas concerning a descriptive and analytic psychology', in Wilhelm Dilthey, *Descriptive Psychology*, trans. Richard M. Zaner (1977). The Hague, Netherlands: Martinus Nijhoff, p. 23. There he says, 'The distinction between explanatory sciences and descriptive sciences on which we here rely corresponds to the common usage. By explanatory science is to be understood every subordination of a domain of experience to a system of causality by means of a limited number of well-determined elements (i.e. the components of the system). This concept characterizes the ideal of such a science, formed in particular from the development of atomic physics. Explanatory psychology thus seeks to subordinate the manifestations of mental life to a causal system by means of a number of well-determined elements.'

5. Ibid. p. 55.

6. Ibid. p. 27.

7. Ibid. pp. 27–8.

8. Ibid. p. 28.

9. Ibid. p. 30.

10. Ibid. p. 29.

11. Ibid. p. 27.

12. Cf. Martin Heidegger, 'Wilhelm Dilthey's research and the struggle for a historical worldview', pp. 147–76. On p. 154 Heidegger remarks, 'Perhaps this [a new strain

in Dilthey's thought] can be traced back to the effect of Husserl's *Logical Investigations*, which Dilthey read at that time and called an epochal work, holding seminars on it for years with his students.'

13. Cf. Husserl, 'Philosophy as rigorous science', pp. 186–7.
14. Dilthey, 'Descriptive and analytic psychology', p. 35.
15. Ibid.
16. Ibid. p. 104.
17. Ibid. p. 63.
18. 'Seen more closely, the nature of psychic development, different from that of physical development, presents first of all a negative character. We are incapable of predicting, in effect, what in the unfolding of psychic life will follow a given state. It is only subsequently that we can disengage the reasons for what has happened. We cannot predict the acts from their motives. We can analytically ascertain the motives only after the acts ... Historical development, moreover, shows the same character, and precisely in the great creative periods an enhancement comes about which cannot be derived from the previous stages' (Ibid. p. 104).
19. It is also quite likely that Husserl's own analysis of the motivational structure of spiritual life that we scrutinized in Chapter 2 was influenced by his reading of Dilthey. In the section on spiritual life in *Ideas II*, Husserl prefaces his discussion by placing Dilthey in the 'first rank' of those who have investigated the topic and goes on to describe his project of formulating a descriptive psychology.
20. As became clear in Chapter 2, Husserl recognized this intertwining of the three fundamental attitudes of 'pre-theoretical' experience, but gave pride of place to the theoretical attitude when it came to reflection and, therefore, to the theory of knowledge and philosophy.
21. 'The acquired nexus of psychic life which is encountered in the developed human being and includes equally the images, concepts, evaluations, ideals, firmly developed volitional orientations, and so forth, contains constant connections which recur uniformly with all human individuals, along with those which are peculiar to one of the sexes, a race, nation, social class and the like, and in the end to a single individual. As all men have the same external world, they all produce in themselves the same numerical system, the same grammatical and logical relations. As they live in the midst of relations between this external world and a common structural psychic nexus, there occur the same ways of preferring and choosing, the same relationships between goals and means, certain uniform relations of values, certain similarities regarding the ideal of life, where it appears' (Ibid. p. 106).
22. Heidegger, *History of the Concept of Time*, p. 18.
23. Wilhelm Dilthey, *The Essence of Philosophy*, trans. Stephen A. Emery and William T. Emery (1969). New York: AMS Press.
24. Cf. Ibid. pp. 61–2.
25. Ibid. p. 61.
26. Ibid. p. 64.

27. See Dilthey's letter to Husserl dated 29 June 1911 in 'The Dilthey-Husserl Correspondence', trans. Jeffner Allen in Edmund Husserl, *Husserl: Shorter Works*, ed. Peter McCormick and Frederick Elliston (1981). Notre Dame: University of Notre Dame Press, pp. 203–9.

28. Dilthey, *The Essence of Philosophy*, p. 64.

29. Ibid. p. 64.

30. Ibid. p. 65.

31. Ibid. p. 26.

32. Ibid. p. 66.

33. Ibid.

34. Ibid.

35. Ibid. translation modified.

36. Cf. Martin Heidegger, *Phenomenological Interpretation of Kant's Critique of Pure Reason*, trans. Parvis Emad and Kenneth Maly (1997). Bloomington: Indiana University Press, p. 15.

37. Heidegger, 'Wilhelm Dilthey's research and the struggle for a historical world-view', p. 159.

38. Heidegger, *Being and Time*, p. 72.

39. Heidegger, *History of the Concept of Time*, p. 18.

40. Heidegger, *Towards the Definition of Philosophy*, p. 7. See also Martin Heidegger, *The Basic Problems of Phenomenology*, trans. Albert Hofstadter (1982). Bloomington: Indiana University Press, pp. 6–8.

41. Heidegger, Towards the Definition of Philosophy, p. 188.

Chapter 5

1. 'The term "lived experience" is today so faded and worn thin that, if it were not so fitting, it would be best to leave it aside' (Heidegger, *Towards the Definition of Philosophy*, p. 55).

2. Heidegger, *Towards the Definition of Philosophy*, pp. 55–7.

3. For recent analyses of Heidegger's understanding of transcendence see Daniel Dahlstrom, 'Heidegger's transcendentalism', *Research in Phenomenology* 35 (2005), pp. 29–54 and David Carr, 'Heidegger on Kant on transcendence', in *Transcendental Heidegger*, ed. Steven Crowell and Jeff Malpas (2007). Stanford: Stanford University Press, pp. 28–42.

4. Heidegger, *Towards the Definition of Philosophy*, p. 57.

5. Ibid. p. 57.

6. Ibid. p. 57.

7. Ibid. p. 96.

8. Ibid. p. 57.

9. Aristotle, *Physics*, trans. R. P. Hardie and R. K. Gaye, in *The Basic Works of Aristotle*, ed. Richard McKeon (1941). New York: Random House, 187a 8–9.

10. Heidegger, *The Basic Problems of Phenomenology*, p. 17.

11. Heidegger, *Towards the Definition of Philosophy*, p. 56.

12. Ibid. pp. 56–7.

13. Husserl, *Ideas I*, p. 106, translation modified.

14. Cf. Edmund Husserl, *Cartesian Meditations: An Introduction to Phenomenology*, trans. Dorion Cairns (1969). The Hague: Martinus Nijhoff, p. 26. For recent approaches to the issue of world in both Husserl and Heidegger, see Dermot Moran's account in his 'Heidegger's transcendental phenomenology in the light of Husserl's project of first philosophy', in *Transcendental Heidegger*, pp. 135–50; Søren Overgaard, *Husserl and Heidegger On Being in the World* (2004). Dordrecht: Kluwer; and Lilian Alweiss, *The World Unclaimed: A Challenge to Heidegger's Critique of Husserl* (2003). Athens: Ohio University Press.

15. Heidegger, *Being and Time*, p. 93.

16. Of course this claim must be supplemented by Husserl's discussion of the relation between the personal environing world and the intersubjective 'common environing world' in *Ideas II*, although this certainly does not invalidate this claim.

17. Heidegger, *Towards the Definition of Philosophy*, p. 75.

18. Ibid. p. 73.

19. Husserl, *Ideas II*, p. 199.

20. Cf. Heidegger, *Being and Time*, pp. 86, 99.

21. Ibid. p. 93.

22. Cf. Fred Dallmayr, 'Ontology of freedom: Heidegger and political philosophy', *Political Theory* 12 (1984), 204–34.

23. Heidegger, *Towards the Definition of Philosophy*, pp. 60–61.

24. Cf. for instance, *Being and Time*, p. 177.

25. Heidegger, *Towards the Definition of Philosophy*, p. 61.

26. Heidegger, *Being and Time*, pp. 96–7.

27. Ibid. pp. 104–5.

28. Ibid. p. 176.

29. Ibid. p. 177.

30. Ibid. p. 178.

31. Kisiel, *The Genesis of Being and Time*, p. 24.

32. Ibid. pp. 24–5.

33. Heidegger, *Phenomenological Interpretations of Aristotle*, p. 65.

34. Ibid.

35. Ibid. p. 63.

36. Ibid.

37. Heidegger, *Being and Time*, p. 25, translation modified.

38. Aristotle, *Metaphysics*, trans. W. D. Ross, in *The Basic Works of Aristotle*, ed. Richard McKeon (1941). New York: Random House.

39. This includes all of the 'neo-pragmatists', e.g. Hubert Dreyfus, *Being-in-the-World: A Commentary on Heidegger's Being and Time, Division I*; Richard Rorty, 'Overcoming the tradition: Heidegger and Dewey', in *Consequences of Pragmatism* (1982). Minneapolis: University of Minnesota Press, pp. 37–59; Richard Rorty, *Essays on Heidegger and others: Philosophical Papers*, Vol. 2 (1991). Cambridge: Cambridge University

Press, pp. 1–82; Charles Taylor, 'Engaged agency and background in Heidegger', in *The Cambridge Companion to Heidegger*, ed. Charles Guignon (1993). Cambridge: Cambridge University Press, pp. 317–36; Robert Brandom, 'Heidegger's categories in *Being and Time*', *Monist* 60 (1983), 387–409; Mark Okrent, *Heidegger's Pragmatism*; John Haugeland, 'Heidegger on being a person', *Nous* 16 (1982), 15–26; and Cristina Lafont, 'Hermeneutics', in *A Companion to Heidegger*, ed. Hubert L. Dreyfus and Mark A. Wrathall (2005). Oxford: Blackwell, pp. 265–84. However, it is also influential for Habermas and Apel's interpretations of Heidegger. See, for instance, Karl-Otto Apel, 'Wittgenstein and Heidegger: language games and life forms', in *Critical Heidegger*, ed. Christopher Macann (1996). London: Routledge, pp. 241–74; Jürgen Habermas, 'Hermeneutic and analytic philosophy. Two complementary versions of the linguistic turn?' in *German Philosophy Since Kant*, ed. Anthony O'Hear (1999). Cambridge: Cambridge University Press, pp. 413–41; and Jürgen Habermas, *The Philosophical Discourse of Modernity: Twelve Lectures*, trans. Frederick G. Lawrence (1987). Cambridge, Mass.: The MIT Press, Chapter VI. Recently Blattner has put forward the view that Heidegger must afford primacy either to the objective, theoretical attitude or to the practical attitude, and that in fact he vacillates between the two. See William Blattner, 'Ontology, the *a priori*, and the primacy of practice: An aporia in Heidegger's early philosophy', in *Transcendental Heidegger*, pp. 10–27.

40. As we made note of in Chapter 3, Natorp maintains that scientific objectifications 'fulfill in a more developed and durable way the same tasks which language fulfills sufficiently for the immediate purposes of practical life' (Natorp, 'On the objective and subjective grounding of knowledge', p. 263).

41. Heidegger, *Being and Time*, p. 29.

42. As we saw in Chapter 2, this represents Husserl's insight into the 'law of motivation' that governs life. He says, for example, 'In each case, we have here an '*undergoing of something*' [*von etwas leiden*], a being *passively* determined by something, and an *active reaction to it*, a transition into action' (Husserl, *Ideas II*, p. 229).

43. Heidegger, *Phenomenological Interpretation of Kant's Critique of Pure Reason*, p. 17.

44. Ibid. p. 25.

45. Ibid. p. 15.

46. Ibid.

47. Ibid. p. 18. Cf. Husserl, *Ideas II*, pp. 28–9.

48. Aristotle, *Metaphysics*, IX.8, 105a 23. He goes on to say, 'And while in some cases the exercise is the ultimate thing (e.g. in sight the ultimate thing is seeing, and no other product besides this results from sight), but from some things a product follows (e.g. from the art of building there results a house as well as the act of building) . . .'

49. Ibid. 980a22.

50. Heidegger, *Phenomenological Interpretation of Kant's Critique of Pure Reason*, p. 13.

51. Ibid. p. 18.

52. Ibid. p. 19.

53. Husserl, *Ideas I*, p. 191.

54. Ibid.

55. Similarly, the technical comportments of the *Geisteswissenschaften* would produce facts, but of a quite different kind than those of the natural sciences, e.g. source criticism in history yields *historical* facts.

56. Heidegger, *Phenomenological Interpretation of Kant's Critique of Pure Reason*, p. 22.

57. Ibid. p. 20. Cf. Heidegger, *Being and Time*, pp. 29–30.

58. '... it is only on the basis of the elucidation of the ontological constitution that the being so determined can be set over against a knowing inquiry [*erkennenden Fragen*] *as* the being that it is and become an encompassable and determinable object or domain of objects and thus become thematic' (Ibid. p. 22).

59. Pragmatic interpretations of Heidegger, on the other hand, attempt to reduce this fundamentally new comportment toward beings to the level of a technical comportment, but in such technical comportments there are no objects as such.

60. This is in part Heidegger's answer to the question that he poses to Husserl: 'How is it at all possible that this sphere of absolute position, of absolute consciousness, which is supposed to be separated from every transcendence by an absolute gulf, is at the same time united with reality in the unity of a real human being, who himself occurs as a real object in the world?' (Heidegger, *History of the Concept of Time*, p. 101).

61. It is interesting to compare this account of science from the late 1920s with Heidegger's earlier account from 1919 where there is little talk of struggle and where the pre-scientific and scientific comportments toward beings is characterized not by struggle but by 'dedication' to the subject matter, 'serene' in the former case and 'absolute' or 'pure' in the latter case. (See Heidegger, *Towards the Definition of Philosophy*, pp. 179–80.) This is especially noteworthy in regard to Heidegger's eventual thematization of the essence of modern technological thinking, in e.g. 'The question concerning technology', in Martin Heidegger, *The Question Concerning Technology and Other Essays*, trans. William Lovitt (1977). New York: Harper & Row.

62. Cf. Heidegger, *Being and Time*, pp. 29–30 and Heidegger, *Phenomenological Interpretation of Kant's Critique of Pure Reason*, p. 24.

63. Heidegger, *Phenomenological Interpretation of Kant's Critique of Pure Reason*, p. 25.

64. Ibid. p. 25.

65. Ibid. p. 25.

66. Heidegger, *Being and Time*, p. 32.

67. Thus, although interpreters are certainly right to point out that there are 'pragmatic' elements in Heidegger's notion of ontology, e.g. that from the perspective of ontological inquiry he understands propositional attitudes as technical and practical comportments, it is untrue that he believes that all human activity is pragmatically oriented. The science of ontology, just as the ontic sciences, is a *praxis* of Dasein and not a tool that could be discarded if it did not fulfil its function or was not efficacious for our pragmatic purposes.

68. Heidegger would of course deny that this is the 'traditional' notion of ontology. It represents for him a complete misunderstanding even of Aristotle's ontological inquiries, which we will examine in Chapter 6.

69. Cf. Heidegger, *Being and Time*, p. 31; Martin Heidegger, *Kant and the Problem of Metaphysics*, trans. Richard Taft (1990). Bloomington: Indiana University Press; and Heidegger, *Phenomenological Interpretations of Kant's Critique of Pure Reason*. On this interpretation see David Carr, 'Heidegger on Kant on transcendence' and Daniel Dahlstrom, 'Heidegger's Kantian turn: Notes to his commentary on the *Kritik der Reinen Vernunft*', *Review of Metaphysics* 45 (December 1991), 329–61.

70. Heidegger, *Phenomenological Interpretation of Kant's Critique of Pure Reason*, p. 27.

71. Cf. Heidegger, *Being and Time*, pp. 41–9.

Chapter 6

1. Heidegger, *Being and Time*, p. 25.

2. Ibid. p. 56.

3. Ibid. ¶ 7, B.

4. Ibid. p. 56.

5. Aristotle, *Metaphysics*, 1003b 33–4.

6. Ibid. 1003b 2–9.

7. Martin Heidegger, 'Phenomenological Interpretations in Connection with Aristotle: An Indication of the Hermeneutical Situation', trans. John van Buren, in Heidegger, *Supplements: From the Earliest Essays to Being and Time and Beyond*, p. 127.

8. Ibid. p. 128.

9. Aristotle, *Posterior Analytics*, trans. G. R. G. Mure, in *The Basic Works of Aristotle*, ed. Richard McKeon (1941). New York: Random House, 100a 9–16.

10. Gadamer also makes use of this passage in Aristotle in his own analysis of how the world is encountered through language. Cf. Gadamer, *Truth and Method*, trans. Joel Weinsheimer and Donald Marshall (1989). New York: Continuum, pp. 542–6.

11. For example, Heidegger, *Ontology: The Hermeneutics of Facticity*, Chapter 2 and Heidegger, *Being and Time*, ¶ 6.

12. Ibid. 1023a 8–11.

13. Ibid. 1023a 11–13.

14. Aristotle, *Metaphysics*, 1022b 3–10.

15. Cf. Aristotle, *Categories*, trans. E. M. Edghill, in *The Basic Works of Aristotle*, ed. Richard McKeon (1941). New York: Random House, Chapter 4.

16. Aristotle, *Metaphysics*, 1048b 18–24.

17. Heidegger, 'Phenomenological interpretations in connection with Aristotle: An indication of the hermeneutical situation', p. 128.

18. Heidegger, *The Basic Problems of Phenomenology*, p. 126.

19. Ibid.

20. Gadamer, following Heidegger, makes this a central component of his hermeneutic philosophy. Cf. Gadamer, *Truth and Method*, pp. 438–56, 542–9.

21. Husserl, *Logical Investigations*, Investigation I, § I.

22. Husserl says, 'For signs in the sense of indications (notes, marks, etc.) do not express anything, unless they happen to fulfill a significant as well as an indicative function' (*Logical Investigations*, p. 183).

23. Husserl, *Logical Investigations*, p. 188.

24. Ibid. p. 192.

25. Heidegger, *Phenomenological Interpretations of Aristotle: Initiation into Phenomenological Research*, pp. 16–17.

26. Aristotle, *Posterior Analytics*, 90b 23–7.

27. Ibid. 94a 11.

28. Cf. Walter Brogan, 'The place of Aristotle in the development of Heidegger's phenomenology', in *Reading Heidegger From the Start: Essays in his Earliest Thought*, ed. Theodore Kisiel and John van Buren (1994). Albany: SUNY Press, pp. 213–27.

29. Aristotle, *Metaphysics*, 993b 26–31.

30. Heidegger, *Phenomenological Interpretations of Aristotle*, p. 26.

31. Heidegger, *Being and Time*, p. 454. Heidegger quotes Yorck here: 'If philosophy is conceived as a manifestation of life, and not as the coughing up of a baseless kind of thinking (and such thinking appears baseless because one's glance gets turned away from the basis of consciousness), then one's task is as meagre in its results as it is complicated and arduous in the obtaining of them. Freedom from prejudice is what it presupposes, and such freedom is hard to gain.'

32. Heidegger, *Phenomenological Interpretations of Aristotle*, p. 33.

33. Ibid. p. 36.

34. Cf. Ibid. part III.

35. Ibid. p. 64.

36. Ibid. p. 63.

37. Ibid. p. 65.

38. There is a foreshadowing of this in Husserl's own analysis of the distinction between 'I do' and 'I have', viz. between the acts of subjectivity and what is given to subjectivity through those acts. Cf. Husserl, *Ideas II*, pp. 329–30.

39. Heidegger, *Phenomenological Interpretations of Aristotle*, p. 65.

40. Ibid. p. 66.

41. Heidegger, *Being and Time*, p. 33.

42. Heidegger, *Phenomenological Interpretations of Aristotle*, p. 67.

43. Ibid. p. 68.

44. This is why, for example, Husserl's notion of pure consciousness as *absolute* being could never be situated in life itself, i.e. was de-vivifying.

45. Cf. Aristotle, *Metaphysics*, Book V, Chapter 22.

46. Heidegger, *Being and Time*, p. 243.

47. Heidegger, *Phenomenological Interpretations of Aristotle*, p. 68.

48. Ibid.

49. Ibid. p. 68.

50. Heidegger, *Ontology: The Hermeneutics of Facticity*, p. 78.

51. Cf. Heidegger, *Towards the Definition of Philosophy*, pp. 6–10; *The History of the Concept of Time*, pp. 1–9; and *The Basic Problems of Phenomenology*, pp. 1–15.

52. Heidegger, *Ontology: The Hermeneutics of Facticity*, pp. 28–33.

53. Heidegger, *Being and Time*, p. 29.

54. Aristotle, *Posterior Analytics*, 100b 13–15.

55. Ibid. 100b 7–10.

56. Martin Heidegger, *Plato's Sophist*, trans. Richard Rojcewicz and André Schuwer (1997). Bloomington: Indiana University Press, p. 41.

57. Heidegger, *Being and Time*, p. 25, translation modified.

58. This term was suggested to me by Fred Dallmayr.

59. See Franco Volpi, 'Being and Time: A translation of the Nicomachean Ethics?'; Jacques Taminiaux, 'Heidegger and *praxis*'; Jacques Taminiaux, *Heidegger and the Project of Fundamental Ontology*; Walter Brogan, 'The place of Aristotle in the development of Heidegger's phenomenology'; Walter Brogan, *Heidegger and Aristotle: The Twofoldness of Being*; and Robert Bernasconi, 'Heidegger's destruction of phronesis', *The Southern Journal of Philosophy*, Vol. 48 supplement (1989), 127–53.

60. Heidegger, *Towards the Definition of Philosophy*, p. 99.

61. Aristotle, *Metaphysics*, 982b 23–4.

62. Wilhelm Dilthey, 'Fragments for a poetics', trans. Rudolf A. Makkreel in Wilhelm Dilthey, *Poetry and Experience*, ed. Rudolf A. Makkreel and Frithjof Rodi (1985). Princeton: Princeton University Press, p. 230.

63. Cf. Martin Heidegger, *The Metaphysical Foundations of Logic*, trans. Michael Heim (1984). Bloomington: Indiana University Press. There he says, 'The finitude of philosophy consists not in the fact that it comes up against limits and cannot proceed further. It rather consists in this: in the singleness and simplicity of its central problematic, philosophy conceals a richness that again and again demands a renewed awakening' (p. 156).

64. Heidegger, *Being and Time*, pp. 49–50.

65. Heidegger, *Phenomenological Interpretations of Aristotle*, p. 29.

66. Heidegger, *Being and Time*, p. 263.

67. Heidegger, *Phenomenological Interpretations of Aristotle*, p. 50.

68. Ibid. p. 54.

69. Ibid. p. 56.

70. Ibid. p. 50.

71. Cf. Heidegger, *The Metaphysical Foundations of Logic*, p. 158. Heidegger remarks here that 'This art of existing is not the self-reflection that hunts around uninvolved, rummaging about for motives and complexes by which to obtain reassurance and a dispensation from action. It is rather only the clarity of action itself, a hunting for real possibilities.'

References

Alweiss, L. (2003) *The World Unclaimed: A Challenge to Heidegger's Critique of Husserl*. Athens: Ohio University Press.

Ameriks, K. (1977) 'Husserl's Realism', in *Philosophical Review* 86, 498–519.

—— (2003) *Interpreting Kant's Critiques*. New York: Oxford University Press.

Apel, K.-O. (1996) 'Wittgenstein and Heidegger: language games and life forms', in *Critical Heidegger*, ed. Christopher Macann. London: Routledge, pp. 241–74.

Aristotle, *Categories*, trans. E. M. Edghill, in *The Basic Works of Aristotle*, ed. Richard McKeon (1941). New York: Random House.

—— *De Anima*, trans. J. A. Smith in *The Basic Works of Aristotle*, ed. Richard McKeon (1941). New York: Random House.

—— *Metaphysics*, trans. W. D. Ross in *The Basic Works of Aristotle*, ed. Richard McKeon (1941). New York: Random House.

—— *Nicomachean Ethics*, trans. W. D. Ross in *The Basic Works of Aristotle*, ed. Richard McKeon (1941). New York: Random House.

—— *On Interpretation*, trans. E. M. Edghill in *The Basic Works of Aristotle*, ed. Richard McKeon (1941). New York: Random House.

—— *Physics*, trans. R. P. Hardie and R. K. Gaye in *The Basic Works of Aristotle*, ed. Richard McKeon (1941). New York: Random House.

—— *Posterior Analytics*, trans. G. R. G. Mure in *The Basic Works of Aristotle*, ed. Richard McKeon (1941). New York: Random House.

—— *Topics*, trans. W. A. Pickard-Cambridge in *The Basic Works of Aristotle*, ed. Richard McKeon (1941). New York: Random House.

Augustine, *The Confessions*, trans. John K. Ryan (1960). New York: Doubleday.

Babich, B. (ed.) (1995) *From Phenomenology to Thought, Errancy, and Desire: Essays in Honor of William Richardson*. Dordrecht: Kluwer.

Bambach, C. (1993) 'Phenomenological research as "destruction": The early Heidegger's reading of Dilthey', in *Philosophy Today* 37, 115–32.

—— (1995) *Heidegger, Dilthey, and the Crisis of Historicism*. Ithaca: Cornell University Press.

Barash, J. A. (2003) *Martin Heidegger and the Problem of Historical Meaning*. New York: Fordham University Press.

Bernasconi, R. (1989) 'Heidegger's destruction of phronesis', in *Southern Journal of Philosophy* 28, Supplement, 127–47.

Blattner, W. (1994) 'Is Heidegger a Kantian idealist?', in *Inquiry* 37, 185–201.

—— (1999) *Heidegger's Temporal Idealism*. New York: Cambridge University Press.

—— (2007) 'Ontology, the *a priori*, and the primacy of practice: An aporia in Heidegger's early philosophy', in *Transcendental Heidegger*, ed. Steven Crowell and Jeff Malpas. Stanford: Stanford University Press, pp. 10–27.

Brandom, R. (1983) 'Heidegger's categories in *Being and Time*', in *Monist* 60, 387–409.

Breazeale, D. (1995) 'Check or checkmate? On the finitude of the Fichtean self', in *The Modern Subject: Classical German Idealist Conceptions of the Self*, ed. Karl Ameriks and Dieter Sturma. Albany: SUNY Press.

Brogan, W. (1994) 'The place of Aristotle in the development of Heidegger's phenomenology', in *Reading Heidegger From the Start: Essays in His Early Thought*, ed. Theodore Kisiel and John van Buren. Albany: State University of New York Press, pp. 213–30.

—— (1995) 'Heidegger's Aristotelian reading of Plato: The discovery of the philosopher', in *Research in Phenomenology* 25, 274–82.

—— (2005) *Heidegger and Aristotle: The Twofoldness of Being*. Albany: SUNY Press.

Carr, D. (2007) 'Heidegger on Kant on transcendence', in *Transcendental Heidegger*, ed. Steven Crowell and Jeff Malpas. Stanford: Stanford University Press, pp. 28–47.

Copleston, F. (1963) *A History of Philosophy*, Vol. 7. New York: Doubleday.

Crowell, S. G. (1996) 'Emil Lask: Aletheiology as ontology', in *Kant-Studien* 87, 69–88.

—— (2001) *Husserl, Heidegger, and the Space of Meaning: Paths Toward Transcendental Phenomenology*. Evanston, Illinois: Northwestern University Press.

—— (2002a) 'The Cartesianism of Phenomenology', in *Continental Philosophy Review* 35, 433–54.

—— (2002b) 'Does the Husserl/Heidegger feud rest on a mistake? An essay on psychological and transcendental phenomenology', in *Husserl Studies* 18, 123–40.

Dahlstrom, D. (1991) 'Heidegger's Kantian turn: Notes to his commentary on the Kritik der reinen Vernunft', in *Review of Metaphysics* 45, 329–61.

—— (1994) 'Heidegger's method: Philosophical concepts as formal indications', in *Review of Metaphysics* 47, 775–95.

—— (2001) *Heidegger's Concept of Truth*. Cambridge: Cambridge University Press.

—— (2005) 'Heidegger's transcendentalism', in *Research in Phenomenology* 35, 29–54.

Dallmayr, F. (1984) 'Ontology of freedom: Heidegger and political philosophy', in *Political Theory* 12, 204–34.

—— (1991) *Between Freiburg and Frankfurt: Toward a Critical Ontology*. Amherst: University of Massachusetts Press.

—— (1993) *The Other Heidegger*. Ithaca: Cornell University Press.

Dilthey, W. (1969) *The Essence of Philosophy*, trans. Stephen A. Emery and William T. Emery. New York: AMS Press.

—— (1977a) 'Ideas concerning a descriptive and analytic psychology', trans. Richard M. Zaner, in Wilhelm Dilthey, *Descriptive Psychology and Historical Understanding*. The Hague, Netherlands: Martinus Nijhoff, pp. 24–120.

—— (1977b) 'Other persons and their expressions of life', trans. Kenneth L. Heiges, in Wilhelm Dilthey, *Descriptive Psychology and Historical Understanding*. The Hague, Netherlands: Martinus Nijhoff, pp. 123–44.

—— (1985) 'Fragments for a poetics', trans. Rudolf A. Makkreel, in Wilhelm Dilthey, *Poetry and Experience*, ed. Rudolf A. Makkreel and Frithjof Rodi. Princeton: Princeton University Press, pp. 223–31.

—— (2002) 'Studies toward the foundation of the human sciences', trans. Rudolf A. Makkreel and John Scanlon, in Wilhelm Dilthey, *The Formation of the Historical World in the Human Sciences*, ed. Rudolf A. Makkreel. Princeton: Princeton University Press, pp. 23–100.

Dreyfus, H. (1991) *Being-in-the-World: A commentary on Heidegger's Being and Time, Division I*. Cambridge, Mass.: The MIT Press.

Dreyfus, H. and Hall, H. (eds) (1992) *Heidegger: A Critical Reader*. Cambridge: Blackwell.

Embree, L. and Nenon, T. (eds) (1996) *Issues in Husserl's Ideas II*. Dordrecht: Kluwer.

Ermarth, M. (1978) *Wilhelm Dilthey: The Critique of Historical Reason*. Chicago: University of Chicago Press.

Farin, I. (1998) 'Heidegger's critique of value philosophy', in *Journal of the British Society for Phenomenology* 29, 268–80.

Fichte, J. G. (1982) *The Science of Knowledge*, trans. Peter Heath and John Lachs. Cambridge: Cambridge University Press.

Friedman, M. (2000) *A Parting of the Ways: Carnap, Cassirer, and Heidegger*. Chicago: Open Court Publishing Company.

—— (2002) 'Carnap, Cassirer, and Heidegger: The Davos disputation and twentieth-century philosophy', in *European Journal of Philosophy* 10, 263–74.

Gadamer, H.-G. (1976) *Philosophical Hermeneutics*, trans. David E. Linge. Berkeley: University of California Press.

—— (1981) *Reason in an Age of Science*, trans. Frederick G. Lawrence. Cambridge, Mass.: The MIT Press.

—— (1985) *Philosophical Apprenticeships*, trans. Robert R. Sullivan. Cambridge, Mass.: The MIT Press.

—— (1989) *Truth and Method*, trans. Joel Weinsheimer and Donald G. Marshall. New York: Continuum.

—— (1994) *Heidegger's Ways*, trans. John W. Stanley. Albany: State University of New York Press.

—— (2001) *Gadamer in Conversation*, trans. Richard E. Palmer. New Haven: Yale University Press.

Habermas, J. (1987) *The Philosophical Discourse of Modernity: Twelve Lectures*, trans. Frederick G. Lawrence. Cambridge, Mass.: The MIT Press.

—— (1990) *Moral Consciousness and Communicative Action*, trans. Christian Lenhardt and Sherry Weber Nicholsen. Cambridge, Mass.: The MIT Press.

—— (1999) 'Hermeneutic and analytic philosophy. Two complementary versions of the linguistic turn?' in *German Philosophy Since Kant*, ed. Anthony O'Hear. Cambridge: Cambridge University Press, pp. 413–41.

Haugeland, J. (1982) 'Heidegger on being a person', in *Nous* 16, 15–26.

Heidegger, M. (1962) *Being and Time*, trans. John Macquarrie and Edward Robinson. New York: Harper & Row.

—— (1977) 'The question concerning technology', in Martin Heidegger, *The Question Concerning Technology and Other Essays*, trans. William Lovitt. New York: Harper & Row.

—— (1982) *The Basic Problems of Phenomenology*, trans. Albert Hofstadter. Bloomington: Indiana University Press.

—— (1984) *The Metaphysical Foundations of Logic*, trans. Michael Heim. Bloomington: Indiana University Press.

—— (1985) *The History of the Concept of Time*, trans. Theodore Kisiel. Bloomington: Indiana University Press.

—— (1990) *Kant and the Problem of Metaphysics*, trans. Richard Taft. Bloomington: Indiana University Press.

—— (1992) *The Concept of Time*, trans. William McNeill. Oxford: Blackwell.

—— (1997a) *Plato's Sophist*, trans. Richard Rojcewicz and André Schuwer. Bloomington: Indiana University Press.

—— (1997b) *Phenomenological Interpretation of Kant's Critique of Pure Reason*, trans. Parvis Emad and Kenneth Maly. Bloomington: Indiana University Press.

—— (1999) *Ontology: The Hermeneutics of Facticity*, trans. John van Buren. Bloomington: Indiana University Press.

—— (2001) *Phenomenological Interpretations of Aristotle: Initiation into Phenomenological Research*, trans. Richard Rojcewicz. Bloomington: Indiana University Press.

—— (2002a) *Towards the Definition of Philosophy*, trans. and ed. Ted Sadler. London: Continuum.

—— (2002b) *Supplements: From the Earliest Essays to Being and Time and Beyond*, ed. John van Buren. Albany: State University of New York Press.

—— (2002c) 'The theory of categories and meaning in Duns Scotus', trans. Roderick M. Stewart and John Van Buren, in Martin Heidegger, *Supplements: From the Earliest Essays to Being and Time and Beyond*, ed. John van Buren. Albany: State University of New York Press, pp. 61–70.

—— (2002d) 'Phenomenological interpretations in connection with Aristotle: An indication of the hermeneutical situation', trans. John van Buren, in Martin Heidegger, *Supplements: From the Earliest Essays to Being and Time and Beyond*, ed. John van Buren. Albany: State University of New York Press, pp. 111–45.

—— (2002e) 'Wilhelm Dilthey's research and the struggle for a historical worldview', trans. Charles Bambach, in Martin Heidegger, *Supplements: From the Earliest Essays to Being and Time and Beyond*, ed. John van Buren. Albany: State University of New York Press, pp. 147–76.

—— (2002f) 'Comments on Karl Jasper's *Psychology of Worldviews*', trans. John van Buren, in Martin Heidegger, *Supplements: From the Earliest Essays to Being and Time and Beyond*, ed. John van Buren. Albany: State University of New York Press, pp. 71–103.

Hodges, H. (1949) *Wilhelm Dilthey: An Introduction*. London: Routledge & Kegan Paul.

—— (1952) *The Philosophy of Wilhelm Dilthey*. London: Routledge & Kegan Paul.

Holborn, H. (1950) 'Wilhelm Dilthey and the critique of historical reason', in *The Journal of the History of Ideas* 11, 93–118.

Hopkins, B. (1991) 'Phenomenological self-critique of its descriptive method', *Husserl Studies* 8, 129–150.

Husserl, E. (1965) 'Philosophy as rigorous science', trans. Quentin Lauer, in Edmund Husserl, *Phenomenology and the Crisis of Philosophy*. New York: Harper & Row.

—— (1969) *Cartesian Meditations: An Introduction to Phenomenology*, trans. Dorion Cairns. The Hague: Martinus Nijhoff.

—— (1970) *The Crisis of the European Sciences*, trans. David Carr. Evanston: Northwestern University Press.

—— (1973) *Experience and Judgment*, trans. James S. Churchill and Karl Ameriks. Evanston: Northwestern University Press.

Husserl, E. and Dilthey, W. (1981) 'The Dilthey–Husserl correspondence', ed. Walter Biemel and trans. Jeffner Allen, in Edmund Husserl, *Shorter Works*, ed. Peter McCormick and Frederick Elliston. Notre Dame: University of Notre Dame Press, pp. 203–9.

—— (1983) *Ideas Pertaining to a Pure Phenomenology and to a Phenomenological Philosophy, first book: General Introduction to a Pure Phenomenology*, trans. F. Kersten. The Hague: Martinus Nijhoff.

—— (1989) *Ideas Pertaining to a Pure Phenomenology and to a Phenomenological Philosophy, second book: Studies in the Phenomenology of Constitution*, trans. Richard Rojcewicz and André Schuwer. Dordrecht: Kluwer Academic Publishers.

—— (1999) *The Idea of Phenomenology*, trans. Lee Hardy. Dordrecht: Kluwer Academic Publishers.

—— (2001) *Logical Investigations*, trans. J. N. Findlay. London: Routledge.

Jalbert, J. (1988) 'Husserl's position between Dilthey and the Windelband-Rickert school of Neo-Kantianism', in *Journal of the History of Philosophy* 26, 279–96.

Kant, I. (1965) *Critique of Pure Reason*, trans. Norman Kemp Smith. New York: St Martin's Press.

Kern, I. (1964) *Husserl und Kant*. The Hague: Martinus Nijhoff.

Kisiel, T. (1993) *The Genesis of Heidegger's Being and Time*. Berkeley: University of California Press.

—— (1995) 'Why students of Heidegger will have to read Emil Lask', in *Man and World* 28, 197–240.

—— (1997) 'Husserl and Heidegger', in *Encyclopedia of Phenomenology*, ed. Lester Embree *et al.* Dordrecht: Kluwer.

—— (2002) *Heidegger's Way of Thought: Critical and Interpretive Signposts*, ed. Alfred Denker and Marion Heinz. New York: Continuum.

Kisiel, T. and van Buren, J. (eds) (1994) *Reading Heidegger From the Start: Essays in His Early Thought*. Albany: State University of New York Press.

Köhnke, K. C. (1991) *The Rise of Neo-Kantianism: German Academic Philosophy between Idealism and Positivism*. Cambridge: Cambridge University Press.

Kovacs, G. (1994) 'Philosophy as primordial science in Heidegger's courses of 1919', in *Reading Heidegger from the Start: Essays in His Earliest Thought*, ed. Theodore Kisiel and John van Buren. Albany: SUNY Press.

Lafont, C. (2005) 'Hermeneutics', in *A Companion to Heidegger*, ed. Hubert L. Dreyfus and Mark A. Wrathall. Oxford: Blackwell, pp. 265–84.

Landgrebe, L. (1981) 'Husserl's departure from Cartesianism', in *The Phenomenology of Edmund Husserl*, ed. Donn Welton. Ithaca: Cornell University Press.

Lask, E. (1911) *Die Logik der Philosophie und die Kategorienlehre; Eine Studie über den Herrschaftsbereich der logischen Form.* Tübingen: J. C. B. Mohr.

Luft, S. (2004)'A hermeneutic phenomenology of subjective and objective spirit: Husserl, Natorp, and Cassirer', in *The New Yearbook for Phenomenology and Phenomenological Philosophy IV*, pp. 209–48.

Makkreel, R. (1969) 'Wilhelm Dilthey and the Neo-Kantians: The distinction between the *Geisteswissenschaften* and the *Kulturwissenschaften*', in *Journal of the History of Philosophy* 4, 423–40.

—— (1982) 'Husserl, Dilthey, and the relation of the life-world to history', *Research in Phenomenology* 12, 39–58.

—— (1985) 'Dilthey and universal hermeneutics: The status of the human sciences', in *Journal of the British Society for Phenomenology* 16, 236–49.

—— (1992) *Dilthey: Philosopher of the Human Studies.* Princeton: Princeton University Press.

Makkreel, R. and Scanlon, J. (eds) (1987) *Dilthey and Phenomenology.* Lanham: University Press of America.

McDowell, J. (1996) *Mind and World.* Cambridge, Mass.: Harvard University Press.

Mohanty, J. N. (1976) *Edmund Husserl's Theory of Meaning.* The Hague: Martinus Nijhoff.

—— (ed.) (1977) *Readings on Edmund Husserl's Logical Investigations.* The Hague: Martinus Nijhoff.

—— (ed.) (1985) *Phenomenology and the Human Sciences.* Dordrecht: Martinus Nijhoff.

—— (1988) 'Heidegger on logic', *Journal of the History of Philosophy* 26, 107–35.

—— (1996) 'Kant and Husserl', *Husserl Studies* 13, 19–30.

—— (2000) 'Lask's theory of judgment', in *Phenomenology on Kant, German Idealism, Hermeneutics and Logic*, ed. O. K. Wiegand, R. J. Dostal, L. Embree, J. Kockelmans and J. N. Mohanty. Dordrecht: Kluwer Academic Publishers, pp. 171–88.

Moran, D. (2007) 'Heidegger's transcendental phenomenology in the light of Husserl's project of first philosophy', in *Transcendental Heidegger*, ed. Steven Crowell and Jeff Malpas. Stanford: Stanford University Press, pp. 135–50.

Motzkin, G. (1989) 'Emil Lask and the crisis of Neo-Kantianism: The rediscovery of the primordial world', *Revue de Métaphysique et de Morale* 94, 171–90.

Natorp, P. (1888) *Einleitung in die Psychologie nach kritischer Methode.* Freiburg i.B.

—— (1910) *Die Logischen Grundlagen Der Exakten Wissenschaften.* Leipzig: B.G. Teubner.

—— (1912) *Allgemeine Psychologie nach kritischer Methode.* Tübingen: Mohr.

—— 'On the question of logical method in relation to Edmund Husserl's *Prolegomena to Pure Logic*', trans. J. N. Mohanty, in *Readings on Edmund Husserl's Logical Investigations*, ed. J. N. Mohanty (1977). The Hague: Martinus Nijhoff, pp. 55–66.

—— 'On the objective and subjective grounding of knowledge', trans. Lois Phillips and David Kolb, *Journal of the British Society for Phenomenology* 12 (1981), 245–66.

—— *Plato's Theory of Ideas: An Introduction to Idealism*, trans. Vasilis Politis and John Connolly (2004). Sankt Augustin: Academia Verlag.

Nenon, T. (ed.) (1990) *Heidegger and Praxis*. Proceedings of the eighth annual Spindel Conference, *The Southern Journal of Philosophy* 28 Supplement.

Oakes, G. (1988) *Weber and Rickert: Concept Formation in the Cultural Sciences*. Cambridge, Mass.: The MIT Press.

Okrent, M. (1981) 'The truth of being and the history of philosophy', in *Monist* 64, 500–517.

—— (1984) 'Hermeneutics, transcendental philosophy and social science', in *Inquiry* 27, 23–50.

—— (1988) *Heidegger's Pragmatism: Understanding, Being, and the Critique of Metaphysics*. Ithaca: Cornell University Press.

—— (2002) 'Equipment, world, and language', in *Inquiry* 45, 195–204.

Overgaard, S. (2004) *Husserl and Heidegger On Being in the World*. Dordrecht: Kluwer.

Palmer, R. (1988) *Hermeneutics: Interpretation Theory in Schleiermacher, Dilthey, Heidegger, and Gadamer*. Evanston: Northwestern University Press.

Politis, V. (2001) 'Anti-Realist interpretations of Plato: Paul Natorp', in *International Journal of Philosophical Studies* 9, 47–61.

Reed-Downing, T. (1990) 'Husserl's presuppositionless philosophy', in *Research in Phenomenology* 20, 136–51.

Reinach, A. (1969) 'Concerning phenomenology', in *Personalist* 50, 194–221.

Richardson, W. (1967) *Heidegger: Through Phenomenology to Thought*. The Hague: Martinus Nijhoff.

Rickert, H. *The Limits of Concept Formation in Natural Science*, trans. and ed. by Guy Oakes (1986). Cambridge: Cambridge University Press.

—— (1962) *Science and History: A Critique of Positivist Epistemology*, trans. George Reisman. Princeton, New Jersey: D. Van Nostrand Company, Inc.

Rickman, H. P. (1979) *Wilhelm Dilthey: Pioneer of the Human Studies*. Berkeley: University of California Press.

Rorty, R. (1979) *Philosophy and the Mirror of Nature*. Princeton: Princeton University Press.

—— (1982) 'Overcoming the tradition: Heidegger and Dewey', in *Consequences of Pragmatism*. Minneapolis: University of Minnesota Press.

—— (1991) *Essays on Heidegger and Others*. Cambridge: Cambridge University Press.

Safranski, R. (1998) *Martin Heidegger: Between Good and Evil*, trans. Ewald Osers. Cambridge, Mass.: Harvard University Press.

Scanlon, J. (1989) 'Dilthey on psychology and epistemology', in *History of Philosophy Quarterly* 6, 347–55.

—— (2001) 'Is it or isn't it? Phenomenology as descriptive psychology in the Logical Investigations', in *Journal of Phenomenological Psychology* 32, 1–11.

Scharff, R. (1997) 'Heidegger's "appropriation" of Dilthey before "Being and Time"', in *Journal of the History of Philosophy* 35, 105–28.

Schnädelbach, H. (1984) *Philosophy in Germany, 1831–1933*, trans. Eric Matthews. Cambridge: Cambridge University Press.

Schuhmann, K. (1991) 'Neo-Kantianism and phenomenology: The case of Emil Lask and Johannes Daubert', *Kant Studien* 81, 303–18.

Schuhmann, K. and Smith, B. (1993) 'Two idealisms: Lask and Husserl' in *Kant-Studien* 83, 448–66.

Schürmann, R. (1987) *Heidegger on Being and Acting: From Principles to Anarchy*, trans. Christine-Marie Gros. Bloomington: Indiana University Press.

Sheehan, T. (1981) 'Heidegger's early years: Fragments for a philosophical biography', in *Heidegger: The Man and the Thinker*, ed. Thomas Sheehan. Chicago: Precedent, pp. 3–19.

—— (1988) 'Heidegger's *Lehrjahre*', in *The Collegium Phaenomenologicum: The First Ten Years*, ed. J. C. Sallis, G. Moneta and J. Taminiaux, *Phaenomenologica*, vol. 105. Dordrecht: Kluwer, pp. 77–137.

Spiegelberg, H. (1965) *The Phenomenological Movement: A Historical Introduction*. The Hague: Martinus Nijhoff.

Stapleton, T. (1977) 'Husserl and Neo-Kantianism', in *Auslegung* 4, 81–104.

Streeter, R. (2007) 'Heidegger's formal indication: A question of method in *Being and Time*', in *Man and World* 30, 413–30.

Taminiaux, J. (1987) 'Poeisis and praxis in fundamental ontology', in *Research in Phenomenology* 17, 137–69.

—— (1988) 'The interpretation of Greek philosophy in Heidegger's fundamental ontology', in *Journal of the British Society for Phenomenology* 19, 3–14.

—— (1991) *Heidegger and the Project of Fundamental Ontology*, trans. and ed. Michael Gendre. Albany: State University of New York Press.

—— (1992) 'Heidegger and *praxis*', in *The Heidegger Case: On Philosophy and Politics*, ed. Tom Rockmore and Joseph Margolis. Philadelphia: Temple University Press.

Taylor, C. (1993) 'Engaged agency and background in Heidegger', in *The Cambridge Companion to Heidegger*, ed. Charles Guignon. Cambridge: Cambridge University Press.

van Buren, J. (1994) *The Young Heidegger: Rumor of the Hidden King*. Bloomington: Indiana University Press.

Volpi, F. (1994) '*Being and Time*: A translation of the *Nicomachean Ethics*?' trans. John Protevi, in *Reading Heidegger From the Start: Essays in His Early Thought*, ed. Theodore Kisiel and John van Buren. Albany: State University of New York Press, pp. 195–212.

Watson, S. (1988) 'Heidegger, rationality, and the critique of judgment', in *Review of Metaphysics* 41, 461–99.

—— (1992) *Extensions: Essays on Interpretation, Rationality, and the Closure of Modernism*. Albany: State University of New York Press.

—— (1997) *Tradition(s): Refiguring Community and Virtue in Classical German Thought*. Bloomington: Indiana University Press.

—— (2001) *Tradition(s) II: Hermeneutics, Ethics, and the Dispensation of the Good*. Bloomington: Indiana University Press.

Welton, D. (2002) *The Other Husserl: The Horizons of Transcendental Phenomenology*. Bloomington: Indiana University Press.

Willey, T. E. (1978) *Back to Kant: The Revival of Kantianism in German Social and Historical Thought*. Detroit: Wayne State University Press.

Windelband, W. (1980) 'History and natural science', trans. Guy Oakes, in *History and Theory* 19, 165–85.

Zahavi, D. (2003) 'How to investigate subjectivity: Natorp and Heidegger on reflection', in *Continental Philosophy Review* 36, 155–76.

Index